Born in Luton in 1978, Kirk Wilson is a freelance advisor on international trade, and an adventurer. He's previously been an IT Professional, a Consultant with the United Nations, and Executive Director of Britain's trade support agency in China. He speaks fluent Chinese and some Spanish, and has lived and travelled extensively in Europe, Asia, and the Americas. His first motorcycle was a 1992 Suzuki RG125 Wolf, and he currently rides a Kawasaki Versys 650.

TWENTY THOUSAND MILES THROUGH SOUTH AMERICA

KIRK WILSON

Route Map

Contents

Prologue:
Caracas, Venezuela
13 June 2019

I'm nearing the end of my journey now, and I've travelled much further than planned. All being well I'll arrive back in Medellin Colombia where I started, in about two weeks, having covered more than twenty thousand miles and crossed ten countries, during the rainy season, and during a time of regional crisis. I had very little mechanical knowledge of motorbikes when I set off, and didn't bring any extra tools. There was no support vehicle, no on-hand experts or mechanics, no satellite phone, no pre-planned local contacts, and I didn't get health insurance. I did very little route or road conditions planning and continued on normal road tyres regardless of weather. I did however learn to speak some Spanish in Colombia before setting off, in the hope that everything I'd want or need on the route could be found locally. If you're thinking of doing a similar trip, I recommend you get health insurance, and install all-terrain tyres.

I bought the bike in Exposiciones, Medellin, a cool place if you like the smell of gasoline. Then just tied a rucksack to the back, and set off. This setup worked fine until I hit the Jesuit route in eastern Bolivia, the most remote and the bumpiest road in the world or so it felt at the time. It was there that the bungees snapped about ten minutes after I saw an absolutely massive black alligator sauntering along the road, although a friend of mine later told me that Bolivia only has Caiman, which are much smaller and definitely not black. But I can still see the reptile like it was yesterday, and I'm telling you that it was three metres long, fat as a cow, and black as night, just walking along enjoying the sunshine.

So much for the dramatic things I've seen along the way, here in Caracas I'm feeling slightly disappointed, but also relieved, that the place is nothing like the disaster zone portrayed on the BBC. I was half-expecting chaos, civil war, and people eating animals from the zoo, and now I feel ridiculous for having been taken in by the media. But then that's the point of travel isn't it, to discover, for yourself.

The two weeks back to Medellin are certainly going to be interesting, because yesterday someone told me that the Colombian border is closed to vehicles, including motorcycles. That's not what I was reading on the news, but to be honest after all that's happened, I'm not too disheartened. I've talked my way into and out of so many difficult situations on this journey that I don't think it's going to be a big problem. My bike is small enough that I've wheeled it over water onto a boat in Brazil across broken and misaligned planks of wood only 30cm wide, so I'm sure I can manage to wheel it across the border. And I'm sure that I can talk the guards into making a small exception, this is after all a unique journey, and I've come so far. Or maybe something else is making me confident, a slightly darker reality that after all that's happened, I'm going to do whatever it takes to complete what I set out to do. And serious though the problem is, I just can't process the possibility of being turned back after six months within a few days of the end.

I should probably explain why I decided to take this journey in the first place, and why now. It's not something you do every day just strap a bag to the back of a motorcycle, and set off on a journey across a continent, especially one so exotic, so alien and perhaps so dangerous, as South America. But I've dreamt of doing it for years and my curiosity finally got the better of me when I left my old job in Beijing, and found myself with the time, freedom, and cash to do something big. No. That explains why I did my first long distance motorcycle journey across Europe last Spring. Three months through seven countries ending at Santander in Spain, before taking a ferry home. But it doesn't explain this one. The reason that I put my life and my work on hold a second time, is because my inhibitions, and my fears about what might happen in South America, just disappeared one day. It was the day of my birthday, and I met in the same hotel as myself, a Dutch guy, with the same birthday.

When I told him that it was my birthday I was in the middle of complaining about the terrible weather in Portugal, and didn't think anything of it until his face went as white as a sheet, and he said 'It's my birthday too!' I thought that he was joking obviously, so I laughed and carried on complaining about my luck, when he pulled out his passport. I looked at the passport and there it was, different year, same day. I'd just met a guy with the same birthday as me, on my birthday. I remember at someone else's birthday party years ago that I met a girl with the same birthday as me and we laughed at the amazing coincidence. Of course it wasn't such a great coincidence, a 1 in 365 chance per person so it's more about whether you actually get into conversations with people about birth dates. And that's quite likely at a birthday party with a lot of guests, but this was quite different. A British guy on a long motorcycle tour of Europe, a Dutch guy travelling for a few weeks holiday from work. I couldn't think of any guiding factor like being at a birthday party with lots of people, that would bring us together. Why Portugal? Why Lisbon? Why that hotel? There were lots of other people there including two attractive Slovakian girls, so why did I talk to that guy. If you're a maths genius then please do work out the numbers and let me know on Instagram, thanks. Then please can you add in the probability that the first thing we see as we're walking out of the hotel to enjoy a joint Birthday Breakfast along with his girlfriend, was a statue commemorating a two-hundred-year old event that happened on that very day. Our birthdate was carved in bold, gold print right in front of our eyes, glistening in the now brilliant sunshine that had turned a rather depressing Lisbon wakeup, into a glorious summer morning.

Well I took it as a *Sign*. I'm not usually into *Signs* so I'm not quite sure what I even mean by that, but I knew that things had changed, and that all the inhibitions that were holding me back, had disappeared. I'm a bit of a stubborn guy though, so it took two more signs to give me the final push that I needed to act. They came in the form of a Book and a Bat, the animal not the sports equipment. The Book I found in a place called Sintra on the Portuguese coast near Lisbon which is where I went next with the Dutch guy and his girlfriend. It was called, The Act of Creation, and it was written in 1964 by a man called Arthur Koestler. He had the idea of a general theory of creativity that was the same across the arts, science and humour. It's not really the kind of thing you'd usually choose to take on a motorcycle journey. Novels are much better or maybe the odd autobiography, but it was the only English language book in the whole of Sintra. In fact, it wasn't even a whole book when I found it in a charity shop on a quiet backstreet. It was half a book sitting in a basket at the front of the store, and I had to hunt around to find the other half. The lady managing the shop helped me find it and tape the two halves back together, and I'm sure she felt guilty about charging me a couple of euros for it. But a book is not just a book to a traveller, I didn't explain to her, it's peace of mind, a thread that holds your days together, so yes I would definitely be buying this sixty-year-old, fallen to pieces book. Anyway having said that I only ever got to read five pages, because a few days later I gave it away, because of the Bat.

The Bat I found in Coimbra, about two hundred kilometres north of Sintra, and I only went there because it was half way to Geres in Northern Spain. Usually it wouldn't be a big deal to come across such a common animal, and I see twenty of them every night in my garden back home in the UK. But this bat was just sitting there on the floor in the middle of the main square in Coimbra, during a burning hot mid-afternoon. I only noticed it because I'd walked over to one corner of the square to look at the most beautiful rays of sunlight I've seen in my life. I'm talking cartoon style, wide yellow triangles extending directly out of a cloud, and bathing everything around me in a soft blanket of gold. And before you put this book down thinking that I'm going to exaggerate everything, hold on, because I know what I'm talking about. Some friends and I once jumped from an aeroplane 17,000ft above the Pyrenees at sunset, and opened our parachutes almost before we'd left the plane, just so that we could watch the sunlight dance over the mountains. But these rays of light in Coimbra were something different, the kind of thing that photographers from National Geographic take after six months living in a tent on top of a mountain.

Anyway the Bat was just sitting there because it was injured, and I was kneeling down checking on it when a lady walked over almost in tears for the poor injured animal. It turns out that she was a huge bat fanatic, bat websites, bat events, bat research, the works, and we went together to the university office on the square to let them know and to see if they could help. They did help, and as far as I know he's doing fine. Or maybe he got eaten by a fox, I'm not sure, but the point is that the lady and I spent the afternoon together and got chatting. And that's when she told me about struggling recently to find some happiness in life. When I asked her why, she said that her whole family were creatives, musicians or artists, but that she was an engineer, so didn't feel like she fitted in because she just didn't think or work in the same way. 'You do fit in,' I said 'because the act of creation is the same in every field, whether it's writing a book or solving an engineering problem.' I gave her the book, and she smiled for the first time since we met. If you believe in *Signs* like I did after the Birthday incident, then clearly the book was intended for her and not me. And clearly the Birthday incident only happened in order to introduce me to someone going to Sintra, and to give me a reason to follow them there to pick up the book. I'm not sure why the book had to be in two pieces, because it was a bit of a hassle to fix, but the real hero of the story is the unfortunate bat, who had to lay down, injured, in the mid-day sun, waiting for us both to arrive. And as should now be completely obvious, it was time to make the trip to South America.

Well it was obvious to me anyway, and these *Signs* came back to my mind often during the journey. Like when I ran out of petrol 200km from a petrol station in the Atacama Desert in Chile, or when I broke down in torrential rain in the middle of the Amazon jungle in Peru, or when my hands stopped working because of the extreme cold as I rode across a 5000m high mountain in Ecuador. If the Birthday, the Book and the Bat hadn't come along in the way that they did, I'm not sure that I'd have had the will to go through with it all. Anyway I'll continue writing later, because today I'm heading to Parque Carabobo in central Caracas to find Richard M. I need to give him a message from a talented musician called Clodio, who I met in Tacarigua de la Laguna. I'm not quite sure how I'm going to do this without an address or phone number, and given that the last time Clodio saw Richard was over 30 years ago, and that my only photo of him is also over 30 years old. But I promised, and he assured me that I can find him just by asking anyone over fifty sitting in a park in central Caracas, reading the *Ultimas Noticias* newspaper, or playing cards. So that narrows it down a bit.

1
In at the deep end: COLOMBIA

Colombia was formed along with Venezuela, Panama and Ecuador in the early 1800s after the breakup of the former Gran Colombia, which had itself only existed a short time, since independence from Spain. It's a sad history, because across the region despite economic and ethnic differences, the people are culturally similar. But while separated, they suffer from divide and conquer on everything from trade deals to elections. Colombia is also a dramatically unequal country and its Gini coefficient, a blunt but useful measure of income inequality, runs at 50.8, one of the highest in the world. For comparison Finland is 26.8, Britain is 34.1, China is 38.6, Iran is 38.8 and the USA is 41.5. The country is also blessed with immense natural beauty and is extremely bio-diverse, rich in natural resources, and one of the best locations in the world for a motorcycle tour.

I first arrived in Colombia in September 2018 after a long journey from the UK including a 24hr stopover in Mexico City. My flight touched down around 4am, so I slept on a seat in Jose Maria Cordova airport near

Medellin for a few hours, before getting a taxi to my hotel. A year later on my way back to the same airport from Medellin, I noticed the beautiful winding mountain road that leads there. But the first time, it was night, so I saw nothing, except when we got close to the city and could see the sparkling lights down in the valley, and rising up the hillsides. It was an enjoyable car trip though, because I got to try out my Spanish with the taxi driver and although I struggled, it was clear that a couple of months of using online apps and my one day in Mexico had given me at least a few usable words. Mexico City was fascinating, it was National Day, and sadly there had been three murders the previous night, so there were more police than I'd ever seen in one place before. Literally every single street in the centre was lined with police and military vehicles. Quite an intimidating sight, and it was the first time that I'd spoken with a real life *Latin American Cop*. But I found, as I have done hundreds of times since with few exceptions, that they're the friendliest, most helpful, and professional people you could meet.

National Day seemed to go well with endless music, street parties and speeches on the main square, but my mind was focused on getting to Colombia. I was relishing the opportunity to start integrating into a country which before now, I'd found to be amongst the most alien and intimidating you could imagine. I like to think of myself as open minded, but when all you ever hear about is Pablo Escobar and Narcos you do get a bit brainwashed. Why then would I choose Medellin as a place to learn Spanish and to start my journey of a lifetime you might ask? Well both Colombia and Venezuela have amongst the clearest and most well-structured spoken Spanish in the region, they're also packed full of natural beauty with amazon jungle,

Caribbean beaches, and Andean mountains all in one place. But Venezuela was going through a political crisis made worse by outside interference and sanctions, so on balance I thought Colombia was a safer bet, and I would take a decision on visiting Venezuela later. Once I saw the photos of Medellin though, any lingering doubts disappeared and I knew that it was the place for me, it's beautiful. So my first real life extended conversation in Spanish was with a young taxi driver on the way to Medellin city, from an airport that's actually closer to Rio Negro city. And would you believe, that he was driving at a reasonable and safe speed, another myth busted, this time about *South American Drivers*. Well maybe not totally busted, because later I found myself riding towards two huge trucks hogging both lanes of a highway in Peru, but I'll get on to that later.

Overall I spent four months in Medellin. I didn't intend to stay that long but after a few weeks I met Andrea, outside Exito supermarket in Laureles. Well that's not quite true we met online, but we *met* for the first time outside the supermarket. Andrea told me later that in real life I seemed a bit boring, a bit straight, with my slightly overgrown but still conservative British haircut, and my formal way of talking with her about the weather, the city, and the how was her day? I didn't have a great impression of her either, all bouncy Colombian gregariousness and batting eyelashes. Kissing my cheek and holding my arm like we'd known each other for years before we'd barely even said hello. But something got her attention because we met up again a few days later, and I realised that she was one of the nicest people I'd ever met. The bounciness and eyelashes grew on me.

Suddenly I was living in Colombia with a beautiful girlfriend and now looking around for some kind of work, while the motorcycle journey went on to the back-burner. It was a wonderful few months, and I met a fantastic and eccentric group of people that would become my friends. Like Jaime, a Colombian guy who'd lived in Taiwan and was learning Chinese, and who had the misfortune to get a British guy as a Chinese teacher. I met him at the Confucius centre near the University where I went occasionally to practice the language. He worked for an American manufacturing company but had enjoyed a couple of years in Taiwan, and wanted to go back sometime. There's not much of a Chinese community in Medellin, so when he heard me speaking fluently with one of the staff and realised that I was learning Spanish, he offered to meet up for language practice. I definitely got the best out of that deal, because I got to torture him with my horrific Espanol while at the same time practising my own Chinese the best way possible, by teaching. It was a lot of fun and Jaime, like Andrea, was one of the warmest people I'd ever met. When I think of Colombian people now I no longer think of media constructions like Pablo Escobar or even that famous actress from Modern Family, I think of Andrea and Jaime. And also Diego, even though he took me to a partly abandoned theatre in the middle of a dodgy part of Medellin at midnight on a Saturday night one time, just to video record him shaving his head in the bathroom. It's not as a scary as it sounds, Diego was an aspiring actor and I'd done some acting lessons back in the UK so we went to a few plays together, and I got to know the local performance scene. I'd actually heard that they were making international movies in Medellin and thought I'd be perfect for an extra part in *Hostel: Part IV Medellin Motorbike Massacre!,* but like a lot of things these days, the industry trend was mostly marketing. There was a period a few years ago when the Government paid out a lot of money in incentives to get a few movies made there, in the hope of building the Hollywood of the South, but it didn't go far, and once the incentives stopped so did the interest from film companies. I've seen the same process happen in different parts of China, it's a shame because the government is often genuine in its attempt to build some local industry, but the global companies are not honest about what it would actually take to secure a permanent base. As always the losers are the local taxpayers who lose a lot of money, and also don't get the new jobs promised, before the companies move on to the next city. I loved living in Medellin though, not only because it's an attractive city but because it was nothing like you'd expect from watching Narcos. The centre of town is packed full with nice cafes, restaurants, and shops, while the residential areas are quiet and low rise. The artist and sculptor Botero was born in Medellin and there's a plaza in the town centre, Plaza de las Esculturas, entirely dedicated to his work. It's a way for the public to appreciate some impressive pieces and it's right outside the Museum of

Antioquia, so it's ideal for a lazy, cultured afternoon. Although it's also a bit of a magnet for prostitution.

The people of Medellin are also warm and friendly, and the place has an interesting although troubled history, which you can explore on the *Pablo Escobar Tour,* although personally I chose not to do that and visited the excellent Memorial Museum instead. I never liked the over-promotion of the Escobar link, it definitely holds the city back in some ways, but then perhaps you've heard of Medellin whereas you've never heard of the nearby city of Rio Negro, so who knows. They've definitely overdone it a bit on the censorship now though, I just searched the Wikipedia entry for Medellin and it doesn't mention the man once, which is a bit odd as he's by far the most famous person from the city.

Medellin is located in the Andes Mountains and while most of Colombia is hot, this area has a temperate climate year round. There are two rainy seasons but the rain only lasts a few hours and even then most days come with blue sky and occasional clouds. Combine that with dramatic lightning storms and broody skies during the rain, and you have quite an exciting mix of weather that is always visible from almost the whole city because it's located in a valley and is mainly low rise. The mountains are beautiful, and I was lucky to appreciate them the best way possible by hiking and Paragliding, an excellent way to escape the main downside of living in Medellin, pollution. Having lived in Beijing for eight years, it's not like I'm new to the problem. But it's seems like a special kind of irony to be located high in the Andes mountains surrounded by a vast green jungle in the middle of Colombia, and be breathing in exhaust fumes. Just search Medellin in a mapping app and you'll see what I mean, you'll be looking at millions of square kilometres of countryside with just a few grey spots for the small cities. The irony continues when you realise that it's those same mountains that are trapping all the exhaust fumes in the city. So escaping at the weekend has become an obsession for many of the city's inhabitants.

They mostly leave by bicycle and that's a sight to see, because there's also an ongoing paranoia about safety that makes wealthy Colombian cyclists employ a huge 4x4 support vehicle to protect them both from the traffic and kidnappers. The less wealthy employ a delivery motorcyclist, and while that's fine for refilling on water and snacks, I'm sure it's actually more dangerous in terms of traffic. The motorcyclist is much wider than the cyclist so more likely to be clipped on the winding mountain roads at slow speed. And if they were hit by a car they'd lose almost no momentum as they collided into their unfortunate clients. Anyway my VO2 max, although strong from months of walking up and down the hills of Medellin, was probably not up to mountain cycling. So I chose Paragliding instead, probably because it reminded me of skydiving which I've done about a hundred and thirty times. It's not exactly a hobby now, but I've been dipping in and out of the sport since my Dad bought me a one week parachuting holiday in sunny Peterborough for my sixteenth birthday. What an experience, as if a week away from home on my own wasn't enough at such a young age, combine it with hanging out on a drop zone with skydivers, and throwing myself out of aeroplanes, dream come true. I've no idea how my Dad came to believe that this was a good idea. As far as I know he'd never done anything similar, and there's no one in our family who was an obvious role model. So I guess he just thought I was spending too much time with my nose buried in books and needed to get some fresh air, at 3000 feet above the ground. It wasn't long after that, that I bought my first motorbike, a Suzuki RG125U Wolf in racing red. An awesome machine that like my skydiving career, never really went anywhere. I bought it just before college exams took over my life then didn't use it again until after I graduated and moved to Cheltenham, but when I did finally get the thing on the road, I wasn't disappointed.

The feeling of freedom as I cruised through the gorgeous Cotswold countryside was wonderful, and I spent many happy weekends and evenings enjoying *The Wolf*. I have to say though, it was a ridiculous name for a 125cc bike that needed 10,000rpm just to get the maximum 22 horsepower. A more appropriate name would have been *Parakeet*, but I suppose that doesn't appeal so much to teenage boys.

Anyway I guess I'm rambling on about my skydiving and motorcycling memories because to me they're very similar, and have always been connected. Skydiving is the only other thing I've found that's comparable to adventure motorcycling, and although I was always without doubt rubbish at the sport, I have had some awesome experiences. There's nothing quite like somersaulting from the side-door of a tiny Cessna 182, or back-flipping from the rear of an SC7 Skyvan cargo plane, or jumping, carefully, from the side of a helicopter. Even the rubbish days are actually good days skydiving, and one of my best memories from University was opening the plane door at 13000ft in minus fifty degrees Celsius, only to be blinded by snow as the air moisture in the cabin froze.

Despite all these experiences though, I've never felt able to properly communicate the feeling of either motorcycling or skydiving, to someone who hasn't already done them. The best thing that I ever came up with, and it applies to both motorcycling and skydiving equally, was when someone asked me once what is was like to do a skydive. I said, 'imagine going through one of the most intense few minutes of your life, a near death experience or seeing or hearing something that just completely throws you off balance so your body has no idea if it's fight time or flight time, eyes wide open, neurons firing at 10x speed. And just at that moment of intense focus, being presented with some of the most glorious sights you could imagine, floating between thick layers of white clouds in heaven, or watching the world spin around below, or soaring above Swiss mountains.'

A motorcycle adventure is to me like a months-long skydive, replacing one controlled near-death experience with a steady stream of far less-controlled near death experiences, as you navigate pot holes, and dodge mentally deficient car drivers. And replacing one, expected, vision of heaven, with a thousand surprise visions that you weren't expecting. Like riding a mountain road above the clouds, or looking down the length of a canyon, or watching sun-rays turn an already beautiful village golden.

It was the owner of the Paragliding school in Medellin, Ruben, who reminded me that I needed to get back on track with planning the motorcycle journey and choosing a bike. Ruben was a bike fanatic, and an experienced mechanic and tinkerer who owned several 1960s Nortons. He told me some fascinating stories about bringing dead engines that he'd found around Colombia and Venezuela back to life, and the satisfaction of cruising on the rejuvenated machines among the hills outside Medellin. He also told me that he taught Pablo Escobar how to Paraglide, which is probably true.

I told Ruben that I was going to do a motorcycle journey down to Buenos Aires and he said 'That's great, what bike?' I hadn't even thought about it, but in my mind I assumed the journey would be on something similar to my Versys at home. An adventure bike developed for endurance and definitely not a low-riding classic like a Norton. It's not that I can't see the appeal and romance of riding that kind of bike with all the connotations built up from a thousand motorcycle movies, but it's not very practical. And I'm definitely no mechanic, I do my own chain, oil and filters, but it takes me half a day, and even that's only possible because I have the owner's manual with me. Anything more complex and I'd be lost, so taking a rare old classic was just not an option.

I sold my first bike, *The Wolf,* when I went to live in America, then a few years later I bought my second one, a naked blue Suzuki SV650 with V-Twin engine, a huge step up from the one-two-five. The V-Twin meant power all over the range and the popularity of the bike meant a low price and easy maintenance. Again I fell in love with the SV but not because it was a famous or exotic bike, it wasn't. Actually I think it was mostly marketed at female riders and my 188cm height was a bit cramped on top, but I loved it because it gave me everything that I wanted from motorcycling, didn't cost the earth, and never let me down. I used that bike to ride back and forth to RAF Weston on the Green for skydiving. And the journey from where I was living in Tring along a well-known biking route through the Oxfordshire countryside was an important part of my weekends for a long time. I used to finish off a perfect Sunday morning by reading a book in Chinese with a coffee and lunch in the Costa on Tring high street, and relating my morning's exploits to the girl who worked behind the counter. Unfortunately, she had a boyfriend, so yet another non-starter on the romance front.

My third bike was a black Kawasaki Versys 650 KLE which I still own. I bought the bike shortly after returning from a period working in China, and it was fate that brought us together. I did a lot of research before buying it, unlike the previous two times, and knew that I wanted something big with a good seat height, upright adventure style, and if not a V-Twin then at least a parallel twin 650. I didn't care what colour it was, so long as it was black, probably because Street Hawk repeats were on TV around the same time.

Although I'm usually quite a decent negotiator, and even used to work for a negotiation consultancy, the purchase of the Kawasaki was never going to be done for a good price. I walked into the showroom on the A41 near Bicester, helmet in hand, having been driven there by my brother and nephew, and was determined to leave with a bike, which I did, eventually. They had an amazing range, Ducatis, Harleys, Suzukis, Hondas, from barely-passed-the-MOT run-arounds, to brand new 1000cc racers. But they didn't have a Versys, nor anything adventure style in black at a reasonable price. I had almost given up, and was about to leave when the salesman remembered that they had a second list of bikes that hadn't yet been prepared for the showroom. He went down the list and almost screamed 'Yes! I knew we had a Versys' and told me about a bike that had literally arrived the day before. It was still filthy, but had been checked over and was in good condition. He wheeled the bike out to the front and that was that. Three hours later, after a clean and service and after I'd arranged insurance and tax over the dealership phone, I was on the road, minus a few thousand pounds, with zero discount obviously. It was on the Kawasaki that I completed my first extended motorcycle tour around Europe last Spring. Three months, seven countries, from England to Spain. Perhaps in future I'll write something based on my journal from that trip too but to be honest, it was a very different experience. If anything that trip was even more true to the ethos of this book, *a journey that anyone could do,* because I used the same bike that I was riding every day in England. My insurance covered Europe, my mobile phone worked across Europe, my VISA card worked everywhere, the roads looked the same, and the rules were the same.

Although we like to complain about European car drivers in the UK, in reality they're fine and obey the road rules pretty much the same way we do. The only major difference is driving on the right, and although I've heard that other people sometimes find it difficult, I didn't even notice as we came off the ferry on the other side. The roads all across Europe are so well planned that you get nudges and hints constantly about where you should be on the road, and how junctions will work, which is not true for many parts of South America. I called that first trip my *Brexit Goodbye Tour,* because it was probably the last chance to do such a journey with so little hassle before Britain exits from the European Union.

So it was my fourth bike, a bike absolutely nothing like the others, a bike with 25% less power than even The Wolf/Parakeet, an Indian made bike that they don't even sell in the UK, that I chose to take me across the dangerous and unpredictable continent of South America. Perhaps it's worth explaining in some detail how exactly I made that decision.

After I left Ruben to his idyllic life paragliding and motorcycling in the glorious Colombian countryside, I really started to give some thought to the *Hows* and the

Whys of this journey. The Europe trip was done on a 650 parallel-twin engined bike and I couldn't imagine using anything less. So I started looking into similar bikes, but perhaps with more off-road capability. All terrain tyres, high clearance, uprated suspension, luggage frames, a proper Adventure Motorcycle. First I looked at Suzukis. My first two bikes were Suzuki and their range includes some of the best bikes in the world. The V-Strom is world famous as a touring machine and the DR650 is the go-to bike for many adventurers, but they also make an excellent series of smaller all terrain motorcycles. If you sat down and made a list of all the attributes you wanted in a bike to handle desert, mountain, and jungle, but didn't need the sheer power of a 650. Which nobody does unless they're intending to tow a Mini Cooper. Then you'd probably come up with the X300 as it's known in Colombia, or the similar DR-Z400S. Talking of power requirements, if you're wondering why the BMW RS1250/1200GS are not on this list it's not only because I can't afford one, it's also because they're way too heavy. The extra power is more than cancelled out by the aggravation of having to drag a 300kg machine around on anything other than flat tarmac, although to be fair I can see the appeal for comfortable two-up highway cruising. Why people use them for adventure motorcycling is beyond me, because as soon as you go properly off-road, weight becomes a major issue, and they're also a devil to get fixed. The giants are really much more suited to cruising to the supermarket, or making films about adventure motorcycling, than actual adventure motorcycling. Next I looked at Kawasakis and considered getting another of my beloved Versys', but the price-tag in Colombia was eye watering. There were similar, very capable smaller capacity off-road bikes, like the KLX250, but at that point I was still thinking anything less than 400cc was a waste of time. Royal Enfield also had some excellent machines and I looked at the Himalayan. It's a nice looking 410cc dedicated adventure bike that looks like it's been half way around Africa before it leaves the showroom, with luggage frames and AT Tyres as standard. But after looking at hundreds of bikes in the dozens of dealers in Exposiciones, I still couldn't make up my mind, so I went for lunch.

If you're into motorcycles and visit Colombia, don't miss Exposiciones, it's motorcycle nirvana and even as you leave the subway station you can smell the gasolina, and hear the engines. There are about thirty main dealers and hundreds of smaller mechanics, along with insurance sales, independent outlets, and retailers selling everything from full replacement frames to tiny British Union Jack stickers. And as I was sitting eating a delicious cazuela and lulo juice, I started watching the motorbikes whizzing by.

In Medellin you can both love and hate motorbikes, because the streets are absolutely full of them, but as I watched them go by I noticed something that I hadn't really registered before. Absolutely no-one, was riding big bikes. The most common ones I saw were small Hondas, Bajaj and AKTs, all under 200cc, and all going like a bat-out-of-hell, over pot holes, up kerbs, and between cars. The next thing I noticed was that half of them were carrying three people, while others had a huge deliveryman-style top box, that seemed to be weighing the bike down at the rear. And that's when it occurred to me. Here I was looking at expensive, relatively rare and difficult to repair, heavy engined bikes, just so that I could ride over a bit of mud or some pebbles, and carry a bit of kit. While the whole world was racing 150cc Bajaj workhorses up and down 20cm high pavements.

They were weaving between fast moving trucks over oil slicked half completed lanes, and carrying 100kg of wood and metal around like it was nothing. I decided then that I would do this trip local style, on a bike that anyone could afford, that could be repaired by any local mechanic, and that generally didn't need any special treatment. All of the well-known manufacturers had dealerships in Exposiciones, Bajaj, Honda, AKT, Suzuki and Kawasaki, so I spent the rest of the day looking around. But after hours of looking through the showrooms and seeing some awesome bikes, I still couldn't decide, so I went to meet Andrea for dinner, and tried to think about something other than motorcycles.

Of course I couldn't think about anything else, and when I started talking about the bikes, I could tell Andrea was getting tense. When we first met, I'd told her straight up that I planned to travel around South America but naturally, as we got closer, I'd wavered. So when she saw that I was re-energised about the journey, she wasn't happy, and I wasn't sure what to do. During dinner I suddenly had the idea to ask if she'd like to do the first week together, and half expected her to storm out, but she said yes.

After a couple of days, I went back to Exposiciones to make a final decision, and spent another half day retracing my route through the Bajaj, Honda, Suzuki and AKT showrooms. Only this time I walked a bit further up the road, and came to another dealer for a brand that hadn't even made it onto my list, TVS.

Unless you live in India where the brand is apparently very popular, you're probably wondering who on Earth are TVS? And I was thinking the same thing, but in the absence of finding the right bike in the other places, I thought I'd give it a go. I walked in and spoke with the sales guy who immediately recommended the TVS Apache RTR160. Of course I didn't just take his word for it and proceeded to ask questions about all the other bikes on display. I also left the showroom after an hour or so, and spent another half day going round the other dealers again. But to cut a long and very boring story short, he was right, and I bought the bike a few days later, in red and black.

The TVS Apache RTR 160 is a single cylinder 15hp urban style motorbike with no special modifications for off road riding. It's quite an attractive bike with modern half fairings, stylish lines, and red/black colouring. But what really sold me was that it came with crash bungs, a front disc brake, and good component quality at least as far as I could tell from looking and sitting on the bike. It cost me only five million Colombian pesos which is about 1300 GBP, quite a lot of money in itself, but a good price for a motorbike in South America, and it was fairly common on the roads. The fifteen horsepower was just enough to drag my 88kg self and 20kg of kit up the Andes mountains, and the front disc break was the minimum needed to slow me down again as I descended.

Reliability wasn't a major concern because I'd already decided that I wanted something that could be repaired anywhere, but I was happy that I found a bike that felt decent for the price. After watching the urban bikes cut through sand piles, oil slicks, mounting pavements and weave in traffic, I decided against all-terrain tyres, or any other off road modifications. Except for looking into the different styles of luggage mounts that would be needed, for kit and spares.

After buying the bike, I confidently rode out into the afternoon traffic, then suddenly realised the time, 5:30pm, rush hour. Well I might as well jump in at the deep end I thought, as I barged my way in front of a bus and ran a red light within a minute of getting on the bike. I found a petrol station on the next block, filled the tank, and spent the next couple of hours mixing it with the other fifty million motorcyclists of Medellin. It was a huge step down from the power of a 650cc engine, but I got used to it pretty quickly and the agility was fantastic, I was soon weaving through the traffic like the best of them.

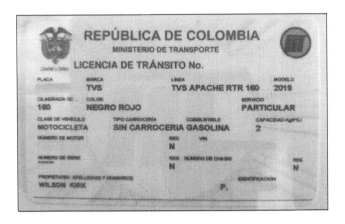

There was just one little problem, or actually a pretty huge problem, when the gear lever fell off just as I was slowing down for a major roundabout. I was in third gear and couldn't shift down, so just tried to minimize the speed changes as I made my way back to the showroom. Luckily I'd made a circuit of Medellin and I was only two blocks away but it was still unnerving. I rode the bike straight back into the showroom, and literally right up to the salesman's desk, then pointed at the gear shifter. It turned out that the shifter wasn't broken but had just worked its way loose and they fixed it immediately, but my faith in Indian manufacturing had taken a knock and I was having a bit of buyer's remorse. In hindsight though, after all the punishment I've put the

Apache through since, and seeing it prove itself a thousand times over, I look back on the shifter issue as a positive. Because I got to have a mechanic take a good look over the bike, right before I set off.

Now that I'd made my decision on the bike, I really got on-board with the idea of a journey that anyone could do, and my next task was to compile a minimal kit list. I've written out the full kit list for the journey and attached it at the end along with a picture, so if you're thinking of doing a similar journey then this is a good place to start, to see what my own experience actually looked like. I don't believe that you'd need anything more than the things on the list, sparse though it is, because I never felt that I needed anything that wasn't there. And if you're wondering about the machete, it was for cutting the grass and tree roots when camping, and path clearing when jungle hiking. Although I must admit, it was also nice to know that it was there, when the dogs and the snakes were lurking around. It did cause me a bit of a headache when I was stopped by an over-zealous policeman on a remote road in central Venezuela. But I simply couldn't have camped in some places without it, so it was worth the extra weight. Some highlights from the list are:

Highlander Nevis 66 bag: I chose the bag back in 1996 when I moved to Scotland to study at Edinburgh University, and went hiking in the highlands with my friend Russell from Fort William. He was an experienced hiker and complimented me on my fine bag, so I've thought highly of it ever since. I haven't used it all that time though, and left it at home when I lived in China for eight years. I used an even smaller bag, a Eurohike Aqua 35, for my European tour, but I thought that a 35 litre was pushing it a bit this time. Also the separate outer waterproof cover was fine for downward falling rain, but perhaps not quite up to the Amazon jungle, so I called the Highlander back into service. It's made of super strong canvas, has a solid pole frame, and the waterproofing is inbuilt. Although as a double precaution, I also lined it with a rubble sack as I always do when travelling.

Waterproof jacket, trousers, and boots: I actually started the journey wearing trainers and the free plastic poncho and trousers that the bike dealer had given me. But after a couple of absolute drenchings, I decided to upgrade the footwear, and paid a visit to a workwear store in Bogota. I've still got the boots that I bought, and apart from a few scratches on the front, they look like new, a bargain at just twenty dollars. I wore them every day of the journey, not just for riding, but also hiking. They've been filled with sewage water, I've got them stuck under the bike, caught on loose nails, walked on tar, everything you could image, but they keep on going, and have always been super comfortable.

Sandals: Essential travel wear to let your feet breathe after riding and hiking in boots all day, and rubber flip flops are super easy to maintain, comfortable, and light, so that's what I used. But you could also consider something with ankle bindings, because I almost got swept down a river when my sandals dragged in the water one time and broke.

Helmet with sun visor: From the previous European tour I knew that it was absolutely essential to have an integrated sun visor in the helmet. You can do it with sunglasses of course but they're fiddly and you might have to stop to take them off if you go through a tunnel, whereas an inbuilt visor can be flicked up and down in a second, with one hand.

Formal White Shirt: Because you never know when the Queen will invite you to tea!

Tough Denim Jacket: In the UK I use an armoured jacket and my recommendation is just to get the best protective gear that you can afford, because you will definitely fall off. Having said that, I chose to stick with denim mainly because of the comfort and because I was aiming to use the same kind of gear everyone else on the road had, but it's definitely not the best option.

Tent: For camping I later picked up a Kelty two-man tent, second-hand. This wasn't in the bag when I set off, but was given to me later by another biker, Dustin, who I met near Popayan in Colombia. And finally, the last item on this highlights list is, the Bike Lock, and I'm highlighting it not because it's essential kit, but because I never used it. Bike locks are heavy and awkward to carry, and no substitute for good judgement on where to leave the bike. And ironically, the lock was the only thing that I had stolen on the journey.

Once I'd worked out a detailed kit list, the next problem was how to stow it all. Originally although I was trying to do a journey that, anyone could do without any special kit, I did still think that I'd need a luggage frame and panniers. But after gathering all the kit together, I realised that it would fit into a single bag, with lots of space to spare for adding a tent and sleeping bag. During the earlier Euro tour and with a much smaller and lighter bag, I'd used some stow netting with hooks to fix the bag to the frame at the rear. That was a much larger and heavier 650cc engined bike though, and I didn't even notice the smaller bag while riding. This time was a bit different, because the bike-to-bag ratio was much worse and also because there weren't any convenient places to hook on the netting. In the end I went with an even simpler solution, wrapping two bungee cords around the entire bag and the rear wheel arch, sorted.

With my bike and bag all finalised it was time for the fun part, visas, insurance, licensing, and general administration, but actually this turned out to be completely painless. I'd bought the bike new from a dealer so already had the owners license document and Colombian vehicle insurance, which was valid for use all over South America. There was a couple of weeks left on the health insurance that I'd bought for studying in Colombia and as far as I could see it didn't exclude motorcycles, so that was fine for a while. And visas were even less of a problem because UK Citizens don't need one for any of the countries visited, or rather the *visa* is given at the point of entry. Information online about vehicle insurance outside Colombia was patchy, but I assumed that could be dealt with at the border where there would be more accurate information. Vaccinations I'd done already for Colombia and there wasn't anything new required, so all that was left to do, was to end the rental contract on my apartment, and set off. Suddenly I found myself packed and ready to go before I'd even run−in *The Apache* as I now called the little bike that would get me into, and out of, a lot of trouble for the next few months. Andrea had managed to get some time off work, so off we went.

Originally my plan had been to take an easy ride out to Rionegro, sticking to the big highways, as a way to gently run in the bike. Not too challenging, safe, comfortable and definitely nothing risky. Which is exactly how it started as we coasted out of Medellin enjoying the lush green hillsides all around us. The towns that we visited along the way like San Rafael and San Carlos were gorgeous. But the best part was a riverside swimming area in the countryside where we met up with Andrea's family, who were having a BBQ and enjoying the sunshine. I got to taste some delicious Colombian home cooking that included pig's feet, something that I hadn't had since I lived in China, and which is delicious although not exactly the first part of the pig we'd choose in the UK. Then we all went for a walk across the fields where Andrea's cousin dared me to jump off a high bridge into the river. I obliged and so the pride of Britain was upheld for another year in this particular area of the Andes mountains.

Not too challenging, safe, and comfortable is unfortunately not how I'd describe the route that we took home a few days later. I did something that has come to be a bit of a bad habit, and relied completely on the mapping app to calculate a route to Medellin. It found a route alright, and it looked fine on the tiny smartphone screen, but when the asphalt turned into rocks I knew we, especially Andrea on the back, were in for a painful afternoon. Not only that but we'd worked out the timing to be back in Medellin before nightfall by riding highways, and now we were doing 20kmph over huge stones. To her credit Andrea took it well, she hung on tight and went with the flow for about an hour before she got tired of it and told me to stop. There was a local farmer standing further up the road so while I rested my arms for a few minutes, she went and asked him the way.

Colombian women generally don't do quiet and disappointed which delays a confrontation, they do loud and angry which unloads a confrontation, and is arguably much healthier. So when Andrea got back on the bike and said quietly with a disappointed look 'OK I know the way let's go' I knew that I would get the loud and angry part at some point later. I guided my brand new Apache over the rocks as fast as we safely could for the next two hours, and the poor thing was carrying the weight of two people and a rucksack, with a combined weight more than the bike. What a way to run in a new motorcycle. Then when we got to the end of the rocky road and again found some flat asphalt, I pulled over and we took a rest. It was an ideal spot with a couple of cows munching away at the grass on top of a mountain, and I used the opportunity to pre-empt an ear-bashing from Andrea. I told her she was amazing, which she is, and I told her that she was more beautiful than the mountain, which she is, and that I was very very sorry that we took the awful road. She laughed and thank goodness it didn't come up again, except to tease me.

We had actually made relatively good time given the circumstances, and arrived back in Medellin just as it was getting dark. I stayed for only a few more days. Then we said goodbye. It was wonderful riding with Andrea, but now that I was on my own, the feeling of freedom as I rode out of Medellin was intoxicating. I could have been at any point on Earth, it was just me, my motorcycle, and a bag full of kit. I retraced the same road east, quickly passing some of the places that we'd visited, and continuing on to the first stop of my journey, Puerto Berrio.

If you want to get off the tourist trail and see something of the real Colombia, then head to Puerto Berrio. It's a town that's been swept along by the political and economic headwinds that have buffeted the country over the last hundred years, and is currently looking for the next boost. The town looks a little tired if I'm honest, but the people were friendly, as always in Colombia, and when I asked in the police station about hotels, they were not annoyed at being asked tourist questions. The officer gave me detailed information and helped me on my way, and I easily found a hotel by the square. Once I'd settled in, I went to ask about something to eat and Erica, who I met in the lobby and was related to the owner, told me about an excellent place for fish soup. She wasn't wrong, and it was great to find some more quality Colombian food, after the disappointment of Bandeja Paisa. Bandeja is famous in Medellin, but not really my thing. It's like a poorly balanced English fry up, but twice the size, with more meat, and a large helping of tough pork scratchings. That probably sounds amazing to you, but I was happy with my fish soup. Could never argue with the portions though, they were always huge.

I spent the next few days visiting some more traditional tourist destinations like Giron, Barichara and Villa de Leyva, listening to traditional Colombian folk music, and drastically improving my Spanish, before I turned South and headed to Bogota. In Villa de Leyva I spoke to some local people about the region near the border with Venezuela, and considered extending the loop to include Merida. But their advice was to skip it because it was too dangerous, and as I was less than a week into my journey, I took the advice.

In Bogota I met up with my friend Esteban, another amazingly warm Colombian who knew absolutely everything about the city and promised to take me on a tour of the real Bogota. Things got a little bit too real when we put on our red scarfs to watch a football match, and got abused by some local hooligans on a bridge, but other than that it was brilliant. The match was awesome, which reminds me, I forgot to write about a game that I went to in Medellin. That one was the match of the year, the local derby between Independiente and Nacional. I have literally never been to a football match or any other event, with an atmosphere quite like it. Green and red smoke filled the stadium, the drums and singing did not skip a beat the entire match, and people looked like they'd lost a relative whenever the opposition scored. Before the match we'd gone for a burger and outside the cafe there was a bus with way, way too many people hanging off the side, and off the roof. They all had their shirts off, Aguardiente alcohol in hand, and proceeded to fall, not climb, off the bus all at the same time, before heading into the stadium.

The game in Bogota was similar, but not quite so intense, it had the smoke and the drums, but the actual match wasn't quite so important. After the game I explored Colombian food a bit further when Esteban took me to the Calorie Palace Cafe outside the stadium. Eight different parts of a cow or pig, fried and offered in a bowl with a can of beer, it was actually rather nice. Later we went for a cycle ride around the city and visited the fruit market where I loaded up on anything that I didn't recognise from Britain or China, which was quite a few things.

Bogota is another city located high up in the mountains, but even colder than Medellin. I was beginning to freeze in my sports fleece and trainers, which were also probably not the best protection in case of a crash, so we went to the industrial district to find some new clothes. First I bought the rugged twenty dollar boots that I mentioned in the kit-list, and then found a tough denim jacket. I bought it for an amazing price but got a level of service more suited to Savile Row when the lady proceeded to trim and cut the button holes, and burn off excess material with a lighter. She must have spent thirty minutes preparing it for me to wear and it was excellent quality. I know that because it saved my skin a few times later on in my journey, as I slid along various roads across the continent.

After our trip to the shops, Esteban and I went to a cafe and I was reminded of another surprising thing about Colombia, the poor quality of the coffee. After trying a few bland Tinto coffees in various cafes in Medellin I had asked a friend about this, and they confirmed that yes indeed Colombia exports all the good stuff. Unlike the Chileans or the Chinese or the French, who export the rubbish and keep all the best stuff for themselves, Colombians seem happy to take their caffeine in a much less pretentious way. Esteban wasn't happy with this summary though, so he took me to a proper coffee place that called itself a laboratory and that served the coffee out of a series of glass tubes, and I have to say it was delicious.

My next stop after Bogota was Girardot which is not a common tourist stop, but a pleasant little industrial town with quite an impressive Ferrocarril railway, and well placed on the route between Bogota and the Coffee region in western Colombia. I later learned more about the history of the ferrocarril as I saw more of them across the continent, and whereas Europe has really embraced train travel over recent years, South America along with the USA has pretty much abandoned it. This has left some quite impressive sights like the train graveyard near Uyuni in Bolivia, and hundreds of ferrocarril museums across the region. It was also in Girardot that I started to miss home for the first time since I set off a couple of weeks before, because the nephew of the owner of the hotel was about the same age as my own nephew, Ollie. We chatted for a while in the hotel lobby, me practising my Spanish, and him practising his English, before I made a call home and caught up with all the news.

I'm aiming to make this a complete journal, and include all the details, no matter what, but I'm seriously considering just skipping over Filandia and the entire coffee region of Colombia. Or I could just write a few lines like, 'oh it was lovely, the coffee was lovely, and the sunsets were lovely'. You'd never know any different, and I wouldn't be lying. But that wouldn't be the whole truth, because it was in Filandia that I had one of the most embarrassing experiences of my life. Basically I got really sick, and soiled my pants in a supermarket. For four months I'd been drinking the tap water in Medellin with no problems, and I assumed that the water in the agricultural coffee region would be like a mountain spring. I even asked the lady who gave me the cup of water if it was potable, or drinkable, and she said yes, but it wasn't. It hit me a couple of hours later, extreme diarrhoea, the kind that hollows you out and is made worse by drinking more water. What I should have done was add salt and a little sugar to the mineral water that I was now drinking, to make a rehydration solution, but I wasn't thinking straight. By the time I decided to get up out of bed, and go to the supermarket for more water, I was delirious. In hindsight I remember people looking at me strangely in the street so I obviously looked unwell, but I didn't realise how bad it was, and even took a detour to the main square to take a photo of the sunset. But by the time I picked up my two litre bottle of water in the supermarket I was already half keeled over, and the last thing I heard as I collapsed onto the checkout was the commotion of people rushing towards me.

When I woke up I was surrounded by people mainly helping me and calling for more help, but also some onlookers. The entire floor of the supermarket around where I was sitting was covered in my own diarrhoea. I kept insisting that I was fine and just needed to get back to my hotel, but it didn't take much for them to stop me standing up and help me wait for the car that screeched to a halt outside the supermarket a few moments later. I was whisked to a local clinic and within a short time was washed, lying in bed, and hooked up to a rehydration

I.V. The rest of the evening was uneventful, good doctors, good equipment, good care and I recovered enough to have a bite to eat before slowly walking back to my hotel, and collapsing into bed. One slight complication was that by this time my health insurance had expired and I'd decided not to renew, but the total cost was less than 40USD which was probably less than an excess payment anyway. Other than that, Filandia really was lovely, the coffee was lovely, and the sunsets were lovely. In fact, the sunset the very next day was one of the best I've ever seen and made for one of my favourite pictures from the trip, it's posted on my Instagram along with some other outstanding shots from the journey.

From Filandia I headed to Solento which was more of the same, that is glorious sunsets and beautiful countryside including the famous Cocara Valley which has the tallest palm trees in the world. And from Solento I headed South towards Ecuador, but before that I passed Cali, I say passed because I didn't actually go to Cali. If you like Salsa dancing you shouldn't miss it, but I have two left feet and even a few weeks of salsa lessons in Medellin didn't sort me out. I never really understood the formality of it, surely dancing is just about feeling the music and moving your own way, but I'm not going to argue with half a billion South Americans so I'll just accept that it's brilliant and I'm just rubbish at it. Instead of Cali I made a stop at a roadside motel near Palmaseca, and I'm glad that I did, not only because the motel had a clean outdoor swimming pool, but because it was there that I met Dustin.

Dustin is a proper biker. Not like me who just bought a bike, strapped on a bag, and set off. Dustin is a Classic Car mechanic by day and adventure biker by, other days. He had the correct large adventure bike for the terrain, and the right tools to fix the bike under any conditions. He'd ridden down from Colorado where he lived, all the way through the whole of Central America including a boat trip over the Darien Gap between Panama and Colombia, and he was heading all the way down to Ushuaia in Argentina. When I met him in Colombia he was travelling with Guy, another experienced biker from Canada doing a similar journey. And like many times later in my trip, I had a conversation with proper adventure bikers about the, no-frills, journey that I was attempting on the tiny Apache. I think they were slightly sceptical of my chances, after all there are roads in South America called The Worst in the World and it was the middle of the rainy season. But they wished me well anyway and we shared some beer and crisps, which they reminded me are called chips. We also swapped contact details and keep in touch throughout the trip. The next day as they roared off down the highway on their 650cc bikes, I felt a little bit envious and would have liked a couple of hours' blast on a big bike. But as I settled into my regular pace on The Apache I was soon enjoying the more relaxed cruising style. I got another reminder of the huge difference in bike size when I met Dustin again later in Argentina, and we took a photo of the bikes together, little David and big Goliath.

While Filandia and Solento are cool and mountainous, which is why they're perfect regions for growing coffee, the area south of Cali is hot, very hot, and flat. It's also here that you notice the stark racial segregation in Colombia. Almost everyone that I met in Medellin and Filandia were light skinned, here almost everyone was dark skinned. The economic inequality is stark too and there have been frequent street protests. I was lucky and my route to the border was clear, but the Panamericana highway was closed a few weeks later for more than a month due to huge local protests against inequality and poor economic opportunities. The Government of President Duterte is not a Government of national unity, and the targeted killing of social leaders, tearing up of the peace process, and lack of resources to help former guerrilla fighters has taken its toll. Protests in Colombia are not the same as in the UK though. In the UK the protest is held at the discretion of the police who may move in to break up the gathering if it becomes disruptive. But here in Colombia the protestors can be supported by guerrilla fighters, so the police act cautiously. This doesn't stop police violence of course and paramilitaries on the Government's side are also keen to stake their claim for relevance, so the whole thing can escalate quickly. And talking of outlaws, I became a criminal myself a few days later as I crossed the border illegally into Ecuador, without getting my entry visa. I didn't mean to do it, and I was fully expecting someone to stop me and ask for my documents until about an hour past the actual frontier. Then I realised that I was half way through the first border province of Ecuador, and it was getting dark, so I decided to just head to the nearest town and go back the next morning to sort out the administration.

Although South America is not a Union in the same way as the EU, there are few border checks and the border between Colombia and Ecuador is a completely open road bridge, or at least it was on the rainy Sunday that I went through. The police do occasionally stop vehicles for checks, but it's no different to the thousands of regular road checkpoints around the region. As no one stopped me at the busy junction that I later realised was the frontier, I didn't think to stop. The next morning, I crossed back over the border again into Colombia, and presented myself for customs. The process was smooth but there was a long wait as hundreds of people who had emigrated from Venezuela, waited to cross. You've probably read about the three million people that have left Venezuela over the last few years to find work in other countries. But you may not know that Venezuela itself had a huge influx of people over the last thirty years, as the economy boomed. Most of the people that I talked to in the queue were not Venezuelan by birth, but only by residency, and they or their parents had gone there to work. They're part of a huge flow of migrants not only between countries, but also internally within countries, in South America that makes migration in Europe look tame. Colombia alone has over nine million people internally displaced, forced to move from their homes by powerful groups on either side of the fifty years long armed conflict. And 17% of all land has either been stolen or taken under coercion. Despite the natural beauty, in some places this is a difficult place to live. After five months in Colombia, I was sad to be leaving and as my plan at this point was just to make it to Buenos Aires in Argentina, I wasn't sure if I'd ever go back. I was already missing my life in Medellin, but now my casual ride around the country had turned into a proper international motorcycle journey, as I rode along the highway through the border province of Carchi in Ecuador.

2
Open borders:
ECUADOR

Ecuador like Colombia is one of the most biodiverse countries on the planet. Habitats range from rich rainforests in the east, to cold mountainous central regions, to dry coastal areas on the Pacific Ocean. And it also includes the marine reserve region of Galapagos, famous for blue footed boobies, giant marine iguanas and some of the richest underwater habitats in the world. It's a tiny country, which makes the level of biodiversity all the more amazing, and it has a GDP of just 100Bn USD, or 11,000 USD per person. Although not as extreme as its former Gran Colombia partners of Colombia and Panama, inequality in Ecuador runs at a high Gini 45.4. And if you're wondering why you've heard of Ecuador in the news recently, it's probably because the founder of WikiLeaks, journalist Julian Assange, was given refuge in their London embassy to escape extradition to the US on charges of espionage. They've since thrown him out again, and I'm sure the story will run for years, but one thing is certain. Ecuador may be a small country, but they know how to make themselves stand out.

Technically this is the story of my second visit to Ecuador, given that I spent one night as a fugitive when I forgot to stamp my documents the previous day. But once I made it through the long queue at the border the process was easy and I was on my way quickly. This time I headed to Lluman, a small village near Ovatulo which I had heard was a peaceful traditional town and a good place to get to know the culture of the border region between Colombia and Ecuador. As with most of the border regions in South America, it's a complex place.

Country border lines that were put in place centuries ago matter very little to the local populations whose culture, families, friends and work span the frontier. Often the local population have much more in common with neighbours and even cities a few miles over the border, than with far away elites in their country's capital. This is the main reason why the borders are open, because local people traverse the frontier frequently without needing border checks. Travellers from other parts are of course supposed to take responsibility for their own border administration, which will then be checked the next time they come across a police checkpoint. And I'm very glad that I did sort everything out quickly, because it didn't take long for me to meet a checkpoint, and they did indeed ask for the border documents. It went fine though, as did all the checkpoints in Colombia.

In Lluman I found a small office that was advertising a place to stay and asked about a room. As it turned out, the accommodation itself was in another location outside of town that had no internet, which was bliss. So for the next couple of nights I stayed on a lovely farm with two dogs, four cows, a flock of chickens and about a hundred guinea pigs. In case you're wondering why a farm would have a hundred guinea pigs, it's because they're considered a delicacy in that part of Ecuador, and they were being raised to be eaten. It didn't bother me though, and I've never been shy about eating exotic meats. I believe every animal has as much right to life as any other and although, ideally, we wouldn't eat any of them, if you're going to murder and eat a cow, it's a bit rich to judge someone else for eating a guinea pig, or a dog, just because they're cute. I didn't get a chance to try the guinea pigs though, because I cooked fish that night, and had eggs for breakfast. Having said that, I'll probably continue to be cautious about eating dogs, not because they're cute, but because on the farm I saw one of them happily munching on a freshly minted turd as it was coming out of a cow's arse. When I think of all the times I've let dogs lick my hands and thought it was adorable, all the time they were just cleaning their tongues.

Another thing I had already learned as I moved across Colombia, and that was confirmed on the farm, was that parking would rarely be a problem. Here they had a covered carport on site that kept my bike dry, and elsewhere I've found that even in hotels people are always willing to find a space to fit a small motorbike. I'm not sure that this would have been so easy with a giant BMW 1200, but my little Apache was welcome everywhere and rarely spent the evening on the street, although I'd often leave it parked on the street during the day. I slept like a log on the farm, which was fortunate because the next day I started the long slog to Coca about 600km to the East, across the mountains of Cayambe national park and down into the Amazon jungle. I didn't realise it from the map, but tomorrow would be one of the hardest riding days of the trip so far.

It wasn't the first time that I'd crossed the Andes mountains, and I'd lived in the mountains in Medellin for months then crossed them again a few times as I made my way across Colombia. But this was different, the mountains of Cayambe national park are high, they are remote, and on this particular day they were intensely cold, around zero not including wind chill, despite being located exactly on the equator. When the weather closed in I found myself in low visibility, soaking wet and shivering violently from the cold. My tyres were gradually releasing their tight grip on the asphalt as they stiffened and as the roads became slightly icy. High up on the mountain as I crossed into the Natural Reserve area, the police checkpoint guard, who was also visibly freezing, told me to 'cuidado' (take care) because the roads higher up were slippery. *Cuidado* was something that I would hear a lot more as I made my way down to Argentina, from police, military guards or ordinary people that I met who couldn't quite believe what I was doing.

Anyway I certainly did *cuidado* and slowed right down as I began to slide, more than ride, along the roads and my hands stopped moving because of the cold. But eventually after around four hours the mist cleared, the rain stopped and I descended to about half the altitude, where it was much warmer. From here to the jungle was fantastic, I could actually see the mountains now, and as the terrain changed you could see and feel the ecosystem adjusting. New different kinds of trees, different kinds of grasses, more delicate and more active birds and mammals, and a mountain that was grey on one side and a lush verdant green on the other. If on the mountain top I had serious doubts about the wisdom of the trip, the winding road down into the jungle reminded why I wanted to do it in the first place. Six hundred kilometres is no small distance though, and it was another seven hours before I reached Coca.

Although technically Coca is in the middle of the Amazon jungle, and I passed some amazing places on the way, it's not quite what I'd call paradise. It's Oil Country, and another reason that Ecuador has been in the news recently was the failure of an effort by the previous President Rafael Correa, to stop oil drilling in the area. He vowed not to drill in the Yasuni national park, if the world agreed to compensate Ecuador for the lost revenue. They asked for a low amount, only about half of the government share of profits from the projected reserves at the time, or about 3.6Bn dollars and they even made it returnable if they did eventually drill there. But while Ecuador got pledges for around 1.6Bn USD, they received only about 13 million. For all our talk about saving the environment, no other country came up with a significant contribution and the US ignored the plan completely.

The result was that Ecuador took the difficult decision to extend drilling in Yasuni, and damage one of its most beautiful areas in order to use the estimated 1Bn barrels of oil buried beneath. The upside of course is the economic benefit to millions from the income and, I have to say, a very nice highway leading straight into Coca. The downside is that tourism has collapsed. The nice new highway quickly gives way to local mud roads carved to pieces by the huge oil trucks, which are the most regular traffic now. And tourism infrastructure has disappeared and been replaced by Oil Camps for oil industry employees. It was fascinating though and I always intended this journey to be as much about discovering reality as enjoying beauty, so east Ecuador was the perfect place to see these two worlds collide.

I left Coca early the next morning and headed further into the Amazon region without any particular plan but hoping to find a bit more of the beauty. As I was riding along one of the carved to pieces dirt roads, I saw a huge but faded sign pointing tourists to Lake Taracoa. Surely there can't be a major tourist point so close to all this oil infrastructure I thought, and decided to take a look.

The surprise on the guards face when he saw me pull up next to the entrance on my motorbike was clear. He initially thought I was there on some kind of work assignment, and when I said 'No I'm just riding around and fancied a trip out on the lake', he laughed. The visitor book showed there had be no other visitor for three months before, and no other foreign visitor in the last two years. We talked for a while about the changes and overall I felt that he was cautiously optimistic, lots of regret for the damage, but ultimately happy that economic development was happening to his home region.

This balance of feelings is something that I've thought about a lot over the years, and I remember when I first went to Beijing in China one of the contradictions I saw was both the presence, and the destruction, of ancient single story Hutong neighbourhoods. Initially I joined the tide of sympathy from foreigner visitors to the city who crave more of *Old China* and I stood against the development. But then one day someone asked me 'what was there before your own house was built in England?' To which I replied honestly that I had no idea, and immediately understood the hypocrisy. I actually went and researched what was there before my house was built, and found that it was not a bare dusty unused plot of land as I'd hoped. It was a brick factory, employing hundreds of people as part of a thriving industry in my home town, and in its way, it was beautiful. The buildings were demolished when the industry collapsed and that was that, I've no idea what happened to the employees of the factory, but I suspect there were few happy endings.

The guard at Lake Taracoa was a friendly old guy and he suggested I take a boat out onto the lake, and he'd get someone to come and do the rowing, for just five dollars. I said the five dollars is fine, but I'd prefer to take the boat out myself, and he was delighted. The lake is actually quite large and it was a blisteringly hot day, I had my trusty cap with neck cover and plenty of water but it was still tough. I rowed for about two kilometres before finding a silent inlet where I could park up the boat and sit and listen to nature, if there was any left.

After ten minutes of waiting, nothing, except one fly that had been bothering me since I set off. Then after twenty minutes a small caiman slipped into the water from behind a bush. After twenty five minutes a flock of huge birds settled in the trees above me, and I could hear monkeys in the row of trees behind. Then after thirty minutes all hell broke loose and the place came alive, screeching, howling, barking, growling, I saw glimpses of all kinds of animals and the trees rustled with larger mammals moving through, but only the birds sat in the nearest trees watching me back. It was a lovely experience and I was really glad to find that despite the development, the animals were thriving, of course it's only my anecdotal experience.

As I turned to row back out of the small inlet, something much larger than the small caiman that I'd seen slipping into the water, started moving too. It caused a wake in the water not much smaller than my own boat, so I rowed a bit quicker back out into the open water. After I said goodbye to the guard I headed further East, deeper into the Amazon, but actually heading towards a small town called Shushufindi to find somewhere to sleep.

When you see those programmes on National Geographic about the Amazon Jungle, they're filmed in specific locations where people know that the target flora or fauna exist. The reality is that most of the Amazon Jungle is populated with small towns, roads and industry. Even where it wasn't convenient to build roads, there are cities that use the rivers as transportation highways, so you actually have to look quite hard to find the idealised pristine environment. Shushufindi is definitely not a pristine environment, but it's pleasant enough, a fairly clean town with one major advantage in my opinion, a Chinese restaurant. Not that the food was totally authentic, but it was OK and I got to practice my language skills again with the owner, a Chinese man who had lived there in the Amazon jungle for more than ten years. He joined an oil company back in China when he was young, and was later posted to Ecuador to work on drilling projects near Coca when they opened up. He'd seen the whole development as it grew and also lamented the extension of drilling into Yasuni National Park. But he really liked living in the area and so when his job posting ended, he decided to stay and opened the restaurant.

Being located right here next to the Yasuni ecological reserve it was tempting to put the motorcycle journey on hold, and go on one of the extended week-long treks into the jungle. I'd definitely recommend it, but for me I decided to stick with the biking as there would be better opportunities to explore the amazon later on in Peru and Bolivia. I set off at 6am hoping to blast all the way back through the jungle and mountains and make it all the way to Mindo in west Ecuador by evening. And that's exactly what I did, as I said, Ecuador is a tiny country. On the way I stopped in a hugely wet and lush jungle valley to have lunch and decided to try the Trout fish that I'd seen advertised everywhere throughout this part of the Amazon, it was delicious.

If you haven't heard of Mindo then you must have been living under a rock for years, or perhaps you're just not part of the global birdwatching community, either way you're losing out. Mindo is arguably the number one global destination for birdwatching and I headed there with lofty expectations of seeing vast flocks of bright red parrots on my hotel roof, and being attacked by giant toucans as I tried to eat my breakfast. No such luck, and the usual mist and rain that had been the background scene to my rainy season motorcycle journey through South America played its part, making the first day a washout.

The second day I saw a sign that said '*Guide 60 Dollars*' and thought '60 dollars! I have eyes, I'm sure I can see the birds myself, what do I need a guide for?' and off I went. I have to say the walk was lovely along a quiet jungle road, but I saw nothing, except the usual raucous green parakeets which I could have seen from the balcony of my hostel anyway. One interesting thing did happen though, when I passed the gate of a jungle lodge and the huge resident Rottweiler seemed to take an unhealthy interest in me. He stared at me as I walked passed and then bolted off somewhere inside the compound. I didn't think much more of it until he reappeared fifty metres in front of me in the lane and started running at full speed in my direction. He looked like Cerberus guarding the gates of hell as he came running powerfully towards me, but instead of tearing me to pieces, he proceeded to jump up and get my clothes filthy from his paws then give me a tongue mauling. Far from being a dangerous dog, he was adorable, and slightly cowardly, and we walked together for the next few hours. Him guiding the way, and me protecting him from the tiny yapping terriers and confident stray dogs that terrorised him at every opportunity. Later in the evening I found two German travellers interested to do some birdwatching, and we split the cost of the guide which is what I should have done the first day.

What a difference, the expert tracker not only had professional quality binoculars but also sound recordings to attract the birds we were interested in, and we saw everything. Toucans, eagles, cuckoos, parrots and hundreds of humming birds, it was so good that I later bought a small pair of binoculars for spotting wildlife along the road.

There's only one negative thing to say about Mindo, and it's really not about Mindo itself but about travelling in the jungle generally, you absolutely cannot wear short trousers. I did, and as I sat dangling my pasty naked legs off of a decking platform watching the humming birds during the guided hike, the mosquitoes were busy enjoying a seven course meal of my calves. I didn't even realise until later that day when my leg began to throb and I spent the evening desperately trying not to scratch over a hundred red blotches. Seriously, wear trousers, I was lucky and the only result was itching, but mosquitoes can bring you much worse news.

As I left Mindo I did something that has now become a feature of my travelling style, I got lost. Now you might think that this is impossible with GPS, but I wasn't using the audio directions, and kept the phone in my pocket. Partly because they're annoying, but also partly because they took away from the adventurous spirit of my journey. So although I did have GPS on my phone, I checked it only occasionally and was happy to just move roughly in the right direction, and choose places to stay as I went. Anyway this time I got seriously lost and went for more than an hour heading north, when I should have been heading South. When I realised the error I thought, well there's no way I'm just turning back and spending an hour retracing my steps, so I looked at the map for somewhere nearby to stay, and I found Mashpi.

Mashpi is a nature reserve deep in the cloud forest north of Mindo, and not the easiest place to get to. I had to cover about twenty kilometres of rocky tracks along a river to get there, and by the time I arrived I was committed, come what may, to staying there the night. This was unfortunate because the only person that I met on the road had said that there were no hostels around, and in the tiny town of about seven buildings including a closed school and church, no one was interested in having me crash on their floor. Luckily one lady told me about a man who lives in a school down the road, who speaks English and may be able to help me out.

The school turned out to be an ecology education lodge that took groups of schoolkids from Quito into the forest to learn about nature. And when I pulled in on my motorcycle the guy thought I was delivering something that he hadn't ordered, and gave me a puzzled look. It turns out that he did indeed speak some English, because he lived and studied in the UK for a while about ten years before, and he said that I could stay in one of the bunk rooms as they didn't have any groups in that week. He also said that I was the first person who'd just walked in off the road in the ten years that he'd been running the lodge, and also, that he didn't have any internet.

The place was incredible, proper thick lush green rainforest, cloud forest actually but it was raining more than in the Amazon, and chock full of wildlife from frogs, insects and birds, to monkeys, and puma apparently. The owner introduced me to his family who also lived with him in another building nearby, and we sat down together for a delicious, completely organic and locally sourced dinner. Then for dessert we had sweet bananas, covered in an even more delicious bitter chocolate sauce that they made themselves with cocoa from the next farm. What an experience, and all from getting lost. Later back home in the UK there was a programme on TV called Amazing Hotels: Life Beyond the Lobby, and one of the episodes was all about a luxury lodge that had been built by the former mayor of Quito, out in the middle of nowhere. It was Mashpi, just a few kilometres from where I'd stayed, and I'd ridden there on my little motorcycle, incredible.

One of the best things about motorcycle travel is how directly you feel the change of ecosystems, and as I rode from Mashpi to my next stop, the mountain lake of Quilotoa, I felt the air get cooler, and my breathing get harder as I ascended through the mountains outside Quito. I was nursing a bruised arm and leg because after taking a wrong turn down a wet and muddy lane, I'd dropped the bike trying to do a U-turn a bit too fast, and the Apache got covered in mud including the chain. But luckily it got a clean a short while later, when I had to cross a deep and flowing mountain stream and as usual the bullet proof bike went through the water engine deep without any complaint.

The constant mist and rain on the mountain was tough though and it was again very cold, so I decided to take one more overnight stop before visiting Quilotoa itself. I stayed in Zumbahua, a small town about twenty minutes away from Quilotoa and I can't describe the bliss that I felt when I found the place had a burning hot stove where I could warm my frozen feet. The owner of the hostel meanwhile served me coffee with cheese in it, a surprisingly tasty combination, and complained about vagrant Venezuelans who were invading the country to take their jobs, steal money and generally cause trouble. After another good night's sleep I set off early the next morning to Quilotoa.

Sometimes you visit a place and rather than try to come up with some flowery language to describe it, it's better to just say it how it is, and Quilotoa is one of those places. It's simply a clear lake on top of a mountain, that formed when rainwater filled a crater left by a meteor impact. I sat on the edge of the crater and just looked at it for two hours straight without moving. I guarantee that no matter how much filtering and Photoshop has been done on the pictures online, none of them will be anything like the real thing.

After Quilotoa I headed further West to the coast, and although Ecuador has some of the most beautiful maritime regions in the world around The Galapagos Islands, to be honest the mainland coast is just average. The beaches are OK, and the towns are fine but I wouldn't make a big journey here just to visit. My first stop on the coast was Puerto Lopez, and I was greeted by a city wide water shortage where water had to be delivered in trucks once per day and was never enough to meet demand. Not a comfortable couple of days given the extreme heat, but on the other hand I did get to visit the Isla de la Plata, *The Poor Man's Galapagos.* There I saw blue footed boobies and sea turtles, so I didn't feel too bad about missing out on *The Rich Man's Galapagos,* in Galapagos. For me the Galapagos Islands go on a short list of high profile, slightly touristy, and expensive places that I didn't intend to form part of this tour. The kind of place like Torres del Paine in Chile, or the Caribbean island beaches of Venezuela, Colombia or Barbados, that would be better to see on some romantic future trip with a partner rather than toughing it through the continent on a motorcycle. The risk is that once I'm settled back into life somewhere else, that I don't bother to make the return trip, but I hope I do and so I've left myself some special reasons come back.

Also as you've probably gathered from the water shortage, this part of coastal Ecuador is incredibly dry and as I rode further down the coast on an arid semi-desert highway, I was beginning to get a bit light headed from the dryness and heat. But I was brought right back to my senses when a huge desert horsefly bit me right on my throat. I know it's only a fly, but it really was massive and it was super painful. He bit me while I was riding at high speed and I almost dropped the bike. I pulled over and while I was having a coughing fit, looked in the side mirror. The fly had left a huge black spike sticking in my throat, and I had to carefully pinch it out with my nails. I've never been a fan of flies, and much prefer spiders which take care of all the other biting insects in the house. I love lizards too because they eat just about anything insect-sized including mosquitoes.

My next planned destination was Guayaquil, the biggest city in Ecuador, and apparently one of the most dangerous and crime ridden in South America. There I was going to meet my friend Luis for dinner but on the way I stopped in Salinas which is the Ecuadorean equivalent of Brighton, the nearest beach to the city, and absolutely packed with tourists. I arrived on a Sunday afternoon and couldn't see a grain of sand because it was entirely covered in umbrellas keeping the scorching sun away from impressively large family groups blasting salsa music from portable radios. When I woke up the next day, a Monday, it was deserted. The entire crowd had been from Guayaquil and on a work day the place is tranquil, and rather pleasant. The hostel was nice too with a large balcony overlooking the beach, so I stayed a couple of days enjoying the peace and quiet and swimming in the sea, before heading to the city.

Luis and I met when we studied together for an MBA at Cambridge University, and he's since gone on to have a successful career in banking and consultancy back in Ecuador. He also thinks that I'm planning a socialist revolution in South America because I was riding a motorbike like his hero Che Guevara, or it might have been his anti-hero, I can't quite remember. We met up for dinner in a fancy mall near the centre of the city and talked about old times, and about how to overthrow the imperialists and their capitalist lackeys. We also drank Coconut lemonade which is one of the most delicious drinks you can imagine. It's just the right amount of sweet and refreshing, and I drank three, so I didn't get a good night's sleep.

Sitting chatting with Luis in the middle of dangerous Guayaquil reminded me of something else that I've noticed on this trip, the fact that the information online about crime and security in all of South America is quite different from the reality. I've lost count of the number of supposedly dangerous cities that I've wandered around for hours, and the number of times I've left the Apache sitting unlocked on the street all day, without issues. I know it's anecdotal and in reality crime is happening all the time everywhere, even in the UK, but I have noticed that the way people talk about crime and security is exactly the same whether you're in London, Bogota or Sao Paulo. People with some assets to protect get paranoid, talk up crime and build walls, while people with almost no assets suffer the real crime. Travellers meanwhile, often exaggerate crime to sex-up travel stories, and I've only met a couple who've told me ones that I believed. Then again my own experience has been unusual, and although I've travelled to more than fifty countries, I've only been the victim of crime twice. One time was the theft of a bicycle, and the other time was a backpack containing everything that I owned. They happened in Cambridge in England, and Lund in Sweden, two of the safest places on the planet, according to statistics. But even in high crime areas you're still unlikely to be a victim of crime on any given day, so for me the important thing is, as my Mum always says before I leave, and as the policemen and military guards have been saying to me all the way along the journey, just to 'take care'. My simple approach to this journey also helps of course, and you might not want to copy me and leave your bike on the street all the time without a padlock if it's worth 20,000 dollars and covered in

GoPros. When I park the Apache in the middle of a line of other similar local bikes it disappears, and although the Colombian registration is not exactly commonplace in Ecuador, it certainly draws less attention than a US plate on a giant KTM. In fact, not standing out is something that I would thoroughly recommend to anyone considering a motorcycle journey, or any kind of adventure travel. It's not just that you can engage with local places and communities in a much richer, and more natural way, but you can also minimise the residual impact from the infrastructure needed to get you there.

I stopped over in Cuenca on the way from Guayaquil to the border with Peru, and while Cuenca is famous for being a beautiful town full of narrow cobbled streets, to be honest I found it a bit disappointing. The traffic is absolutely horrendous, and you're not allowed to park the bike up next to cafes and restaurants as I usually do, because they're mainly inside buildings facing narrow pavements. The fact that it was pouring with rain probably didn't help, and I only stayed one night. The next day I stopped in Arenillas, a pleasant town near the border which, unlike Cuenca, is not famous for being beautiful, but I liked it. Partly because there's an attractive plaza with palm trees, a small bridge and good lighting that was pleasant to wander around, but mainly because I was able to park my bike wherever I liked on the street without problems.

Also it was local election time in Arenillas, and in the evening as I was looking for a place to eat, I walked right into an election campaign motorcade. Twenty 4x4 trucks and cars, another twenty or so motorbikes, and each one packed so full that people were hanging out the windows. Loud party music was blaring from the stereos and they were trying, presumably, but failing completely, to keep in rhythm with each other. The motorcade was promoting a candidate for local elections with the same party style that I'd seen in Colombia and I think it's a great approach that does seem to get people engaged. But it's ironic to think that a party is the right forum for engaging people in decisions that can lead to such dramatic and serious outcomes. The continent has experienced some extreme right–left–right swings during the last decade and the stakes keep getting higher. Politics generally, in the US, Europe and in other countries is getting more polarised, and countries, states, and regions are being pushed to take sides.

It might seem a stretch to link this small local election to global politics, but when international organisations are being constructed, then deconstructed, based on the temporary whims of national governments, and national governments depend on the make–up of local elections, then things start to look serious. For example, the countries of South America have long dreamed of being able to work together like the European Union to reduce the costs of trade internally, but more importantly to make better trade deals globally. They went so far as to form such a union in 2004 covering 410million people called UNASUR, but in the last couple of years as several of the largest countries elected more right leaning governments they decided they didn't want to be part of the Union which was formed during a period when most counties had left wing leaders, and so suspended their membership.

And if you're thinking, well yes that's because right wing leaders are more free–market and don't like Unions and restrictions, well you'd be wrong. In 2019 the leavers started their own right–wing Union called PROSUR and the net result may be that both attempts at collaboration fail. South America will continue to be fragmented, and Europe, China, and the US will continue to get lucrative trade deals by picking off the countries individually. Brilliant for me as a British citizen of the EU, for now at least, but terrible for the individual populations. I sat down to eat in a cafe where I could watch the procession and asked a guy at my table what he thought 'They're all terrible, they're all corrupt' he said 'what we need is someone who will sort them out.'

3
The worst place in the world to breakdown: PERU

'Do you also have an American passport?' asked the border guard looking at me suspiciously as I stood waiting to get my documents stamped at the Ecuador/Peru frontier. 'No, I don't' I replied in as neutral tone as possible, trying not to sound suspicious, or angry, or sad, or too happy, or too excited, or anything else that would cause the guard to take an interest. I wasn't in a huge hurry, but I'd still rather avoid him rifling through my bag, or performing a long-winded read through of all my documents. 'Wait here' he replied. This was not a good sign. The question itself is odd and when a border guard walks away with your passport, then you know there's potential for some serious problems and delays. But he returned just a few minutes later and stamped me through. Once I had the stamp I relaxed a bit and asked why the question about the American passport? 'There's an Interpol Red Notice out for someone with your name so we just needed to make sure' he said. So it could have been worse, and I spent the rest of the day imagining who on Earth was this other Kirk Wilson who managed to get an international arrest warrant issued in my not particularly common name.

Peru, home of Paddington Bear and the Shining Path Maoist–terrorist group is, like Colombia and Ecuador, massively bio–diverse and if anything the changing habitats are even more distinct here. If you enter from the North you'll ride straight into a desert that goes on for hundreds of kilometres, but there are also mountains over 7000m high. In fact, there are an awful lot of mountains, and one of them has an ancient Inca city on the top. Then there's another major region of the Amazon Jungle, and last but not least, one of the highest lakes in the world, near the south eastern border with Bolivia. Peru gained its independence from Spain in the 1800s only to fall straight into a regional war with its neighbour Chile, and suffer extended periods of conflict for most of the next century. The mid 1900s were more stable but the 1980s saw the rise of the Sendero Luminoso, or Shining Path terrorist group. The group was formed by Abimael Guzman who like most terrifying guerrilla generals started his career as a University Philosophy Professor, in Ayacucho. After repeated and failed efforts to win equality under a military government, many working class people had lost hope. They began to support armed groups instead, and the resulting guerrilla war became world famous for its brutality on all sides. The population of Peru is over 32 million, and it has one of the highest ratios of native peoples. So one odd thing that I learned while I was there, is that it keeps getting foreign sounding Presidents. Like Fujimori from Japan, or Kuczynski from Poland, and I've never quite understood why?

My first stop in Peru was, like most backpackers, Mancora, a coastal party town with a nice beach and some decent hostels. Other than the mosquitoes

Mancora was a pleasant place to stay, and I managed to find a relatively laid back hostel near the beach away from the crowds. Well I thought it was laid back until the softly spoken Peruvian guy staying in the same dormitory room came home at 4am stuffed full of cocaine and started talking loudly to himself, and playing with himself on his bunk. The three other girls in the room didn't make a sound so I thought they must be asleep, and I went over to shine my phone light on his face, and ask him to be quiet. To be fair he did for a couple of hours, until he started again, so I went over to speak to him again, and then he slept through to morning. He was gone when I woke up and at breakfast the girls told me that he'd been asked to leave, that they were all wide awake and terrified the whole time, and that they were massively grateful that I dealt with it, so I was a hero for a day.

I've heard other travellers talk about odd goings-on in hostels but that's by far the weirdest experience I've had. And the weirdness continued as I rode my motorcycle for hours through the desert to Chiclayo when I saw, miles from anywhere, a well-built middle aged guy covered in tattoos walking along the road, completely naked. He wasn't asking for help so I didn't stop, but I can't imagine where he thought he was going to, or where he came from. After the hostel experience I had no doubt that what I was looking at was a guy who'd taken a bit too much strong Peruvian cocaine, and had walked all the way from Mancora. Or maybe his wife threw him out of the car after an argument right in the middle of the desert, while they were naked for some reason. Who knows, but I remember thinking, 'Wow! Peru, what a country.'

After Chiclayo I rode on to Barranca and it was during this stretch that I realised my fuel gauge was broken. Most likely because some over-zealous fuel attendants had overfilled the tank right to the brim a few times, putting pressure on the sender. After filling up at the next station, I started to do calculations on fuel, which I continued all the way to the end of my journey despite the fact that the gauge started working again after a few days.

From first refuel at 6966km on the odometer to 7195 was 229km, the tank took 1.794gal at second refill which gives 128kmpg or 28km per litre. The price worked out at around £3 British pounds per 100km at a steady 90km per hour through the desert, and a bit less for uphill off-roading I guess. This confirmed that my bike would go 541km on one tank of fuel, including about 100km on reserve. Then I realised that I'd been looking at US Gallons, and redid the litres calculation, it was actually even better at 33.8km per litre or 97miles per gallon in British English with Imperial Gallons, I think. I'm not sure how fuel quality affects these calculations, and to that point I'd been using a variety of fuels from 98 octane when I was still trying to take care of my new Apache like a new-born baby, down to just 84 octane when there was no other choice on remote stretches in Peru. The engine was coping fine though, except perhaps slightly lumpier with the low quality mix. Anyway whatever the figure, if it was even close to that, I'd been worrying way too much about refuelling and decided to call 400km the safe amount to ride before thinking about petrol, or 300km in remote places.

Remember earlier when I said that I'd busted a myth about South American drivers when my taxi driver from Medellin airport was the calmest and most professional driver you could wish for? And how I said that impression lasted until Peru, well the road to Barranca was where I came across the two trucks. It wasn't the first time that I came across insane driving, and even in Medellin itself I realised that my first impression from the taxi wasn't quite right, when the swarms of motorcycles started weaving across the whole road. Bogota and Quito had been pretty bad too, but it was on the road to Barranca that I found myself staring directly at two huge trucks driving parallel to each other, at full speed. They were coming round a blind corner, and neither one made any indication of slowing down. I couldn't even get off the road because of the thick bushes and trees. I slowed down as much as I safely could, and just prayed as I flicked up my visor and looked the overtaking driver directly in the eyes.

Luckily he realised that he was about to kill me, and also braked sharply letting his opponent win the race, he stopped about ten metres short of my front tyre. He smiled in that way that you could find quite offensive unless you know that it's to hide embarrassment, at having done something terrible. I drove around him to the left and headed on my way. As for Barranca, it was nice, a fun little beachside town full of fairgrounds and junk food, and they have something similar to the Jesus statue in Rio de Janeiro (Cristo Redentor) that was quite impressive during sunset.

At this point I was basically following the famous Panamericana road for the long desert stretches through Peru and Chile. And you might think that it's impossible to get lost when you're riding on such a famous and straight road, but apparently not. I managed it, and ended up on a quiet dirt track on some guy's farm on the edge of a small town. He was cutting loose foliage from some trees on the side of the track when he looked up and saw me on his property. He was reasonable about it though, he just laughed and said 'Panamericana?' I said yes and he pointed me back to another dirt track after a right turn at the edge of his farm, the track led directly back to a kind of half constructed T-junction with the highway. Next stop Lima.

Lima has the most chaotic driving conditions in the entire world, I'm certain of it. Chaos. CHAOS. CHAOS!!!!! ...no it still doesn't quite express it well enough. Imagine absolutely no concept of road lanes and zero use of rear view mirrors. Imagine black smoke blinding you from cars using, at best 84 octane fuel, and at worst an unholy concoction of sugarcane, other alcohols and presumably air pumped directly from hell, plus all the dust from constant roadworks. Imagine no regard for the direction of traffic, and I don't mean a cheeky Mini using the other lane for a quick ten second hop back to a junction, I mean trucks blatantly going the wrong way at speed and not giving a damn who has a problem with it. Imagine no road signs or worse, signs that are blatantly wrong. Imagine major highways ending in a single lane dirt track that splits into four dirt tracks, again with no signs. Imagine pot holes a metre deep and three metres across. Imagine suicidal pedestrians with no idea when would be a good time to walk slowly across a four lane highway, or what would be a four lane highway, if there were any lane markings. And no it's not a mysterious working system that I just don't understand, like those videos you see of rickshaws working through traffic in Delhi. There were wrecks of cars everywhere and I saw tons of car-on-car and car-on-pedestrian accidents, it's a death-trap. Fair enough I didn't die though, or actually have an accident, so I won't go on about it, but even now after I've been through just about every driving condition you could imagine in South America, Lima stands out in my mind.

The city centre was pleasant enough though with a calm and tranquil Embassy quarter where I found a surprisingly cheap hostel, but outside that area it's a tough city to navigate. I didn't have plans to stay in Lima but I ended up staying a couple of days partly because it really was quite pleasant, but also partly because I needed time to brace myself for trying to get out again.

When I did finally venture out into the traffic I got lost, and ended up spending two hours navigating steep side streets through the outskirts. Eventually I did manage to escape though, and made my way back over to the coast. There I found a place that was pretty much the opposite of what I'd experienced for the last few days in the Capital. It was the calmest, most laid back place with the least cars in the whole of Peru, and it was called Paracas. The reason that I was passing through Paracas was because it's the jumping off point for, *The Other Poor Man's Galapagos,* the Islas Ballestas, where you can see more blue footed boobies, penguins, in fact just about any kind of seabird you can imagine, and also the islands main attraction, Sea lions. But before I took the boat out to the islands, I decided to stay in Paracas for a few days to enjoy the laid back vibe, and that's when I bumped into a German girl called Linda.

Linda was backpacking through South America minus her boyfriend, who she left back in Germany, and she was beautiful. I fell in love immediately, despite the fact that she made it clear that she was not interested in any kind of holiday fling. Linda shared my interest in healthy eating, to balance out all the chocolate and cakes that I eat, so we made smoothies and cooked together, then checked out the beach and went for a sunset motorcycle ride. It was wonderful having a gorgeous girl riding pillion again, holding on tight as we cruised along the coast without helmets, and got stopped by the police. But it did also remind me that I was doing the trip alone, so it was bittersweet. The police let us off with a warning.

These kind of moments can only happen on a motorcycle journey. Sure we could have met and cooked and walked and talked, but there's something about being there with your own motorcycle, a complete feeling of freedom that just doesn't come with buses and taxis, or even renting a bike locally. You're completely in control of your own journey, and you can take it slow and cruise, or you can race. You can meander through a national park stopping whenever you want, wherever you want, then watch as the bucket–list backpackers all stop at the same place, fight each other to get a photo, then storm off again on freezing cold coaches. If you do find yourself getting bored or if you come across a particularly inviting stretch of winding mountain road, then you can ramp up the speed, and have some fun guiding the bike fast through the curves. I guess you could, theoretically, also race against other bikes and cars. But that would be irresponsible on a public road, so I wouldn't dream of doing that. Then you have those days when you've taken off your heavy riding kit, put down the luggage, have no far away destination that you need to get to, and can just cruise around town admiring the view. And that's exactly what Linda and I did in Paracas.

Naturally even during that short evening ride, I managed yet again to completely cock up the navigation, but like so many times before, I was rewarded for it. We ended up at a surfer's beach just as the sun was setting, and just as a huge flock of birds had settled a bit further along the sand. As we approached, the whole flock of two or three thousand birds rose up as if to fly away, but instead of flying away each one of them found their own place on a warm breeze that was coming in from the sea, and just hung there in the sky. They were barely moving their wings, and making very little sound, as if they were just admiring the sunset, like we were, it was a special moment. Then we carried on down the coast a little and found ourselves, to our great surprise, back in Paracas where we'd started.

I'd managed to mess up the navigation in a very convenient way, ending up 180 degrees from the direction that I thought we were heading, and we arrived back at the hostel just in time for dinner. Yes, I know, the sea was right there, the sun always sets in the west, don't ask me how I managed to get lost next to a beach, but neither of us noticed, so you'll just have to go there for yourself to see how's it's possible. After dinner we joined a few other people from the hostel for a beer on the beach, and I took a night-swim out to the boats in the harbour. Linda was definitely an adventurer, but was a bit paranoid about sharks so didn't join me, then the next day we set off for the Islas Ballestas.

It wasn't long before we started seeing the wildlife that makes the islands so famous, and every kind of seabird was flying overhead almost as soon as we left the dock. Sea lions were our constant companions along the way, bobbing along chasing shoals of fish and generally enjoying themselves, and it was the first time that I'd seen them up close. They're very impressive and although they don't have quite the same reputation in human society as Land lions, I'm sure that within fish society they're considered the most noble and fearful of predators. We continued on to the Islands themselves and my initial feeling of privilege and gratitude at having seen glimpses of these creatures gliding through the waves, quickly gave way to a sense of being overwhelmed.

My eyes were filled to bursting point with the largest group of mammals I've ever seen. I haven't been to

Kenya or Tanzania so I'm sure the wildebeest and giraffes are more impressive, but it was still incredible to see thousands of huge sea lions slipping and falling over the rocks like an unstable herd of Jabba the Huts. The noise is hard to describe but it sounded a bit like one of the more graphic scenes from Doom, the computer game. I was a fan of gaming when I was younger and DOOM was one of my favourites, a first-person-shooter and one of the original titles to really perfect the 3D perspective. It was full of monsters and ghouls all straining at the leash to devour the human special forces heroes coming to kill them. The sound of the sea lions was exactly like one of the scarier zombie monsters in Doom, a deep yet penetrating, mournful howl that makes you feel like you've stepped into a dragon's lair. Thousands of sea lions all going at it on the rocks was definitely something new for my ears.

But it wasn't all bloated aggressive howling, and among the giants there were plenty of the cutest little teddy-bear baby sea lions being protected by their mothers. Also the herd wasn't confined to the rocks, and the sea surrounding our boat was filled with the far more graceful sight of groups of sea lions working together to corral fish. They surfaced occasionally to take a breath and, I'm sure, check out the weird bony mammals sitting in the wooden shell floating above. 'Those bony mammals would definitely sink in the water, so what on earth are they even doing here in that shell?' one of them might say 'I wonder if I could get one in my mouth?' his friend might reply. Unfortunately, the experience was slightly tarnished by seeing one of the sea lions struggling in a fisherman's net on the way back. The poor thing was wailing and frightened to death and the fish must have been having a good old laugh at his expense.

The next morning, I woke up early and after chatting with Linda for a while, and saying another sad goodbye, checked the map. Machu Picchu, the Lost City of the Incas and one of the highlights of any journey to South America, was around 800km to the East. But Cusco, the famous city that serves as the usual jumping off point to reach Machu Picchu by train was much further away, to the south. 'Why waste time following the highway down there when I can just cut directly across!' I said to myself confidently 'after all I'm here to see the real Peru, and the direct route across the mountains to Machu Picchu looks much shorter, although maybe a bit bendier...'.

Five days later, after one of the most challenging, and fascinating motorcycle rides you could imagine, I arrived in Santa Teresa from where I could reach Machu Picchu itself by foot. Of course I knew before setting off that it would be demanding, and although my navigation skills are undeniably terrible I did at least realise that it would involve one or two overnight stops. But I still didn't realise quite how challenging it would be.

As I sat in my hotel in Paracas looking again at the map, I tried to find a place that would serve as a target for the first days riding, and found Ayacucho. This was the town that I'd read about as the home of the Shining Path armed rebel group so it definitely sounded like an interesting place to explore, and the route there looked quite straightforward. Of course it was rainy season so nothing is really straightforward, and I came across the usual water overflows and small landslides, as well as sections of road that had recently been torn apart by the relentless rain, temperature changes and debris from the jungle hills above. But overall the route to Ayacucho was mostly a fast wide highway so I made good progress, and arrived on schedule. Later that evening I went for dinner in a busy local restaurant and asked some people about the dreaded Senderoso Luminoso or Shining Path. I had thought that this was an historical group that had long since disappeared, but to my surprise they told me that, far from being historical, the Shining Path was still active today and there had been guerrilla attacks carried out within the last two years. They also said that despite the violence, the group still has a lot of support and that many believe they are the only ones who can do anything about the ongoing inequality in Peru. A worrying thought, but it's no different from the UK where support for violent extremist groups has been growing again since the Brexit vote. As I rode out of Ayacucho the next morning, I realised within about ten minutes that this day was not going to be anything like the day before. The road literally disintegrated before my eyes, and after a mile or so I was basically riding off-road.

An asphalt highway looks, when it's new, like an impenetrable, solid, unnatural and formidable band of ecosystem killing permanence that will be there in a thousand years. And when I was younger, and before I'd done much travelling, I used to think of the frequent protests we have in the UK anytime someone wants to build a new bypass or motorway, as a kind of battle for the future. A battle between people who loved nature, and those who wanted to destroy it to save a few minutes of journey time. But the idea that an asphalt highway, or indeed anything that has ever been constructed by human beings, could permanently alter Earth's ecosystem is just bizarre to me now. Don't get me wrong, nuclear weapons, pollution and rapid climate change could, and perhaps will, kill off swathes of humanity and should be controlled. But I've learnt that life on Earth is far more powerful, remorseless.

Here in the Amazon jungle of Peru, roads that were built less than ten years ago are barely visible. The rain soaks the road, the heat and cold cause it to crack, the tree roots push from below, the wind blows from above. Then once the road is uneven and cracked, the real damage starts. Water begins to accumulate in the spaces and the hot and cold expansion and retraction go into overdrive, tearing the road apart in months. Once gullies form, the water now flows through the road itself and unlike the much gentler, pure rain, the new flows bring with them hard debris which bites at what is left of the defenceless tarmac. They don't stand a chance, and the only thing keeping it all together is the near constant roadworks that you'll see as you try to make your way across the country. I read somewhere that even radioactive waste and gold mines through solid rock would be undetectable within a million years, and if we stopped maintaining everything, there would eventually be nothing left to show for our ever having existed. I'm not sure if that's true, what about diamonds, or Dinosaur fossils? But after seeing what happens to the roads here in Peru, the idea has definitely become much more real for me.

As I slowly pushed on through the rain and the mist, which reduced visibility to less than ten meters at times, I also had to navigate a ton of police checkpoints. At each checkpoint I had to get off my bike, in the rain, and try to shield the paperwork as the guard read my documents in the torrent. It was no better for them of course, and I did have some sympathy. It may be a beautiful place, but in the freezing cold, and when there's so much mist that you can't see anything anyway, it can't be the most enjoyable job. Not to mention the fact that this was Peruvian cocaine country and there were armed groups, including well-funded and well-armed splinter groups of the Shining Path, who probably wouldn't take too kindly to a random vehicle check. So I never complained about police stops no matter how long they took, those guys do a dangerous job under difficult conditions.

Although most of the roads were terrible, there were occasional stretches that the jungle had decided to save, to be eaten another day, and so overall my average speed was a respectable 38 kmph. Just enough to keep me from going insane, but not enough to get me to Santa Teresa. I checked my map in the mid-morning and decided to head for Kiteni, then I checked it again in the afternoon as the sun went down and realising that there was no way I'd make it even that far, settled for a place about half way there, San Francisco, would you believe.

San Francisco was exactly like the other San Francisco, hilly, but it was much colder as I was already high up in the mountains by now, and the people were much nicer. I went to a fruit market in the evening after I'd put my clothes up to dry and when I realised that my wallet was still in the wet clothes, they gave me the fruit for free. This is partly explained by the fact that I always buy fruit as ripe as possible, because that's when it's at its most flavourful in my opinion and great for smoothies. But it's also because the ladies in the market were just decent human beings, like 99% of all the other people that I've met on my journey. The idea that we are all selfish creatures hell bent on beating each other into submission is a lie, something made up by people who just want to see society that way. Yes, we all compete, but the overriding impulse is to cooperate, work together, to be social. I was a recipient of kindness daily on this journey, and I tried to return the favour by helping other people whenever possible.

In fact, a few hours earlier, just before I reached San Francisco, I had the opportunity to do just that, when I saw a small hatchback car stuck in one of the many pools of water, lagoons more like, that had covered a half destroyed road. It got stuck because the exit from the pool was slightly uphill, and there was zero grip on the soft mud under the water. I pulled up behind the guy just as he had given up and was making a call, but I got off my bike and signalled to him to push together. It wasn't so difficult actually, there was a solid rock to push from and it was only a small car, my riding gloves gave me an excellent grip on the rear bumper. Then as I leaned down to get in position, I noticed that the man's son, who looked around ten years old, was guiding the steering wheel as we pushed, he did a good job though. Once the car was back on the so-called road, I followed them through the water. And of course my lightweight, bulletproof, and apparently completely waterproof Apache, passed the obstacle easily, like it was a puddle on the M25.

The tough weather conditions continued the next day, but I soon found that the road conditions were much worse. The rain carried on like before, falling in torrents on my helmet and reverberating around my skull, but I was using my trusty earplugs, which helped a lot. The police checkpoints continued as well, only more frequently. The big change was that, perhaps just because another days' worth of rain had fallen on the roads, the water was much deeper, more frequent, and flowing faster than it had been further back down the route. If I'd have continued to slow down and cautiously assess every deep water stream across my path, I'd never have made it to the next town. So I raced through them like a jet ski spraying water high up into the air, and getting absolutely soaked. Not that I could have gotten much more soaked than I already was, after sitting in torrential rain for hours. And whereas yesterday I was doing calculations about how far I'd have to backtrack to avoid fast moving water, today I was calculating which rock I'd grab if my bike was pushed over the cliff by the flow. The cold temperature didn't improve either, and I saw a giant, yellow black and silver, frozen waterfall, that had formed on the side of a mountain, showing where another powerful force of nature had overcome even the might of the flowing water.

After another couple of hours bumping along on the rocky single-lane dirt road just praying that I wouldn't find it blocked, I found it blocked. By a pool that went on for about fifty meters. Judging by the slope of the ground either side, I guessed that the water would be almost knee deep on the motorcycle, which meant that there was no way I could race through. The engine would get completed immersed above the air intake and although to be honest, I actually had no idea what immersing an engine in water would do to it, I knew that it couldn't be good. Ignition is after all an explosion, and explosions need dry conditions for the reactions to occur. But then again motorcycles are made to be used outside in all weathers, so they must be to some extent waterproof?

I didn't push on, I stopped, got off the bike and thought about it, luckily there was a break in the rain so I took off my helmet and looked at the water. I guess I could have carefully walked through to properly test the depth at every point, but instead I suddenly just thought 'to hell with it, what's the worst that could happen?' I didn't bring tools on this journey for the simple reason that I didn't want to ride like an aloof and self-sufficient adventure motorcyclist, I wanted to just ride the bike normally and deal with problems like everyone else. That is, by talking with people, and putting some cash into the local economy by hiring a mechanic. The actual worst that could happen if I went through deep water would be that I fell off, and the water penetrated every single part of the bike. Not ideal but not the end of the world, and then I'd just have to sit and wait until some kind soul gave me a lift to the next town to find a mechanic. I was confident by now that there are lots of kind souls in Peru, so I put my helmet back on and revved up the engine to 6000RPM based on the not particularly scientific theory that if the engine is racing, then the water wouldn't be able to get in. Then I let out the clutch and moved slowly forward into the water.

It was as deep as it looked, and the bike was submerged up to just below my knees. After a few metres the engine started complaining, and when I was half-way through it sounded like it was about to drown. But it didn't, and after a few more seconds I was heading up the slope on the other side. As I rode out and the water fell away, I kept up the engine speed, slipping and sliding on the mud bank for a few seconds before finally, I dropped the bike hard on the ground. My bruise was only just healing after the last time I dropped it so it hurt, a lot, and I got absolutely covered in mud, but the bike was fine. I picked it up, pressed the starter button, and it wouldn't start, then I waited five minutes and tried a few more times, and finally it did. The road actually improved after that, and I continued at quite a respectable pace for another couple of hours, until I got properly blocked by workmen felling trees next to a road to clean up after a landslide. I spoke to the guy who looked to be in charge and he said the road was just mud now, but would be rideable once the trees were gone and that would take an hour. I parked up the bike, took off my boots, emptied them of water and put them in the sunshine to dry off while I ate sandwiches for lunch.

As I was eating my jam and cheese sandwiches (don't judge, just try it), I had a bit of time to think about all this off-road riding. And when I say off-road, what I mean is something other than an asphalt or hard mud road. I don't mean cutting across fields, although I did plenty of that too when it was drier, I just mean roads that are not really fit to be called roads. That could be because it was covered in rocks and mud, underwater, obliterated by weather and the jungle, or undergoing maintenance. One of the good/bad things about South America is that you can keep riding on the roads even when they're undergoing major roadworks, something that I'd regret later on in Eastern Bolivia. But riding on these surfaces is hard, really hard. Motorcycling always requires concentration, but on rocks and mud you can't take your eyes off the road in front of your tyre for a second without hitting something at the wrong angle, and dropping the bike. Whereas on asphalt you're moving fast and the tyres are always flexing and gripping hard with the surface, here there was almost no grip and it felt more like a constant balancing act. It's also not a straight line because you're constantly trying to avoid the slightly bigger rocks or deeper mud stretches. For the first few hours it's a lot of fun, but after that it's just hard.

Bumps and vibration become an issue too, and I found myself controlling my breathing because the bumps would constantly knock the wind out of me, sometimes every two or three seconds, for hours. So you're timing your exhaling to coincide with what you think you're looking at in the road, while your body gets shaken to pieces. Speed is obviously an issue and you can't push it more than a quarter of normal road speed. The tyre direction as you inevitably do hit things is important too, get it wrong and you'll be thrown off. So sometimes you're making a judgement about letting the bike take a full-on direct impact and damaging the suspension, or hitting a rock at an angle and doing even more damage to the bike and yourself. Then other times you're putting your foot down and straining hard on the handlebars just to keep the bike upright. Hours of gripping motorcycle handlebars can cause your hands to ache at the best of times. But when they're constantly under vibration, constantly changing gear, and really straining to hold the bike up, you're just asking for an injury.

Anyway I did eventually make it, but not to Santa Teresa, I stopped much earlier along the route at Kiteni. The next day I had an early morning start in similar conditions but without so much rain, and it wasn't long before I went through another deep stream. Then I took a thirty-minute detour/slide down a hillside farm track because of a small landslide and it was a couple of hours before the road finally improved. After such a beating, it was a wonderful feeling when I saw, around a hundred metres in front of me, the bland, grey, flat, splendidly uninteresting form of a paved road, glistening wet in the sunshine. The rain started up again as it always does, but the rest of the route to Santa Teresa was on smooth roads so passed quickly and by evening I was within seven hours hike of the Lost City of the Incas.

Machu Picchu is a small city, or citadel, that was built on top of a 2400-metre-high mountain by the Incas as a home for their emperor in the 1400s, and abandoned about a century later as the Spanish advanced into Inca territory. Along with the Great Wall of China and the Taj Mahal it's one of the Seven Wonders of the World and should not be missed by anyone visiting Peru. It's a majestic sight, and I was lucky enough to enjoy perfect weather on the day that I visited despite being right in the middle of the rainy season. The whole two weeks before and after were totally washed out, and too misty to see anything. There were virtually no tourists of course, because of the weather, but I did meet one Chinese couple who were visiting from Shanghai and we chatted for a while comparing the place with the Great Wall.

When I lived in Beijing I used to visit a small hostel in the countryside within an hour's walk of a very remote, and beautiful, part of the Wall, and I would often go for long hikes along the top. I'm ashamed to say that I got quite blase about it, and didn't really think of the wall as being one of the Seven Wonders of the World. This time because I'd fought hard for five days then hiked for seven hours just to get to Machu Picchu, and because I'd read a lot of the history, I was able to fully appreciate the experience. Like the mountain top lake in Quilotoa, Ecuador, I sat there on a slope overlooking Machu Picchu for hours just looking at the city before taking a walk around the ruins. The question is constantly in your mind as to how on Earth they built this thing, out of solid stone, on top of a mountain. The Peruvians have maintained the site well too, not too touristy and no tackiness whatsoever, just the minimum high quality infrastructure needed to get people there to enjoy walking the grounds. I spoke to some other people who had come the regular route from Cusco including some who took the luxurious, purpose built Orient Express style train, and it sounded amazing.

Perhaps I'll come back at some point when I do the luxury version of my South America tour, and perhaps I'll also learn a bit of Quechua language before I come. I'd been hearing Quechua spoken since the mountains of Ecuador and it's common outside the cities in Peru. The ancient Inca language is the same, or a close relation to that which would have been spoken in the streets and homes of Machu Picchu. And far from being on the brink of extinction it's still popular, and even undergoing something of a renaissance. A court in northern Peru recently gave the first official judgement, entirely in Quechua.

From Machu picchu I headed directly to Cusco where I bought some winter gloves, thermal underwear, and a pair of binoculars to see more of all these incredible places that I was visiting. The winter clothes really should have been bought a few days earlier as I headed up into the mountains, but it was still great to finally have them as I walked around the chilly streets of Cusco, at an elevation of 3400 metres. After a couple of days' rest in the Old Town of the city I decided to head back into the Amazon Jungle once more, and set off for Manu. And it was in Manu that I really got to test out my theory that it was not necessary to travel with expensive kit or a special motorbike, nor have a lot of mechanical knowledge. The theory that it really doesn't need to cost much, and it's not nearly as difficult nor as dangerous as people think, to complete a long distance motorcycle adventure. Because on my way from Cusco back into the jungle at Manu, I broke down, six hours from the city and three hours from any village, in the pouring rain, on a narrow mountainside track. I distinctly remember thinking, less than ten minutes before it happened, 'Wow this would be the worst place in the world to break down, six hours into the Amazon jungle, what on earth would I do?' Then ten minutes later, as my body was being shaken to pieces for the third straight day, on the rocky mountainside road that led deep into the Manu Reserve, I got to find out.

It happened just as I came out of a dark tunnel, through a corner of the mountain. And right after I'd felt some rocks fall onto my helmet from the steep mountainside above, a good sign that it isn't stable, and there may be a landslide. The drive chain jumped right off the sprocket, my engine stopped dead, and I turned the air blue for a few minutes as I quickly went through the denial and anger phases. I got off the bike and pushed it as close to the five hundred metre sheer drop by the side of the road as I dared, so that it wouldn't block the unsighted single lane coming out of the tunnel. Then I stood on the other side of the lane, and just stared at my useless vehicle as we got soaked by the now torrential rain. I was frantically thinking of how I could perhaps just flick the chain back on, or turn the wheel or something. But it was useless, the chain had jumped completely off both ends and was stuck somewhere inside the engine, so that only a mechanic could fix it. As I moved to the acceptance phase, I would have taken off my helmet and calmly assessed the situation, but it was raining so hard that I kept it on. Which was probably for the best, because more small rocks were starting to fall around me from the mountainside above.

By now it was already 3pm in the afternoon, and I hadn't seen another vehicle for a few hours since I left the last village. I knew that it was another three hours by motorcycle to Pilcopata where I was heading, so I started to think about my options. But there weren't any. It would have taken me seven or eight hours to walk forward or back along the road until I found at least a small dwelling where I could ask about getting to the next village, and it would be dark in only four hours. In any case I definitely didn't fancy knocking on someone's door in the dead of night, they'd probably shoot me as a robber rather than offer me a lift. The only option was to wait. True I hadn't seen another vehicle for a few hours, but there were rainforest lodges in the area and I felt certain that some kind of vehicle would come along, at some point. My concern was that it was already mid-afternoon, and travellers would usually arrive at a lodge much earlier, so it could be the next morning before a vehicle came.

At that point I still didn't have a tent, and even if I did there was nowhere safe to pitch it without being directly in the road. So staying the night would actually have meant sitting, or probably standing to avoid the snakes, next to my bike, for ten hours, in the rain. Add to that, the fact that this was right in the middle of Peruvian Cocaine country and that this road was known to be used at night for shipping product, and you really have the worst possible place to breakdown.

Had I really been forced to stand next to my bike overnight, then I probably would have ended the journey right there and caught a bus back to Cusco, but reality was much kinder. Within an hour of breaking down, the most beautiful little colectivo mini-bus that I ever saw, came bobbing and weaving along the road. I threw my hands up in the air and starting waving frantically, as it continued right past me and didn't look like stopping. But it did stop, and I ran over to speak with the driver. I asked him if he'd give me a lift to the next village, and I was expecting him to smile and say 'of course my friend!' and welcome me on board, but he didn't. He had a frown on his face and started shaking his head, then he spoke with someone sitting in the front row of seats. There was no way that I was not getting on that bus, and I already had one foot on the step. But my bag was still strapped to the bike so I was getting a bit nervous when finally, he said OK. It turned out that the reason he was hesitating, was because he thought I wanted to take the Apache with me on the bus. Once he realised that I was happy to leave the bike here and come back for it later, he waved me on-board and I sat down in the first row.

The look on the faces of the Swedish tourists who had hired the mini-bus to take them to a remote jungle lodge a few hours away, was priceless. I took a GPS reading so I'd know where to come back for the bike, and we set off. Meeting this particular bus was extra lucky, because the guy sitting in the front row was a local guide and after an hour or so on the road, he asked the driver to stop. Playing in the trees right next to the road, not that I or any of the other tourists on the bus would have noticed, was a troop of Woolly Monkeys and we pulled over to take some videos and enjoy the spectacle. The guide said it was the season for males to try their best to show off to the females, and that's why when we got closer, they didn't leave. Instead they seemed to dare each other to get closer and closer to us, and it was a great experience. I said goodbye to my new Swedish friends when we reached the next town of Patria, where I saw that there was a mechanic, a hostel, and a small shop, but not much else.

If I thought I was lucky to meet that particular bus and guide, I was even luckier to meet this particular mechanic. His name is Josue, in case you find yourself in Patria with a broken down motorcycle, and he's excellent. I asked Josue if he could help me find someone with a pickup truck or 4x4 to help me get the bike, and he asked me what kind of bike it was. I told him it was a TVS Apache and he said they don't have that in Peru, but then I told him that it's similar to a Bajaj, which they do, and he said no problem and went off to talk with someone across the street. Getting anything done in South America really does always seem to be a bit complicated. And Josue spent the next hour, between fixing various problems on various bikes that pulled up off the street, talking and negotiating with various people about collecting the bike. In the meantime, I checked into the hostel, and had some dinner. Eventually a woman came over and said that she could do it for sixty dollars and I said fine. Then a man pulled up in a small Toyota who was the person that I'd actually contracted with, and said 'Let's go!' I was wondering why we needed to drive a car, just to go and collect the 4x4 or pickup truck that we'd be using to transport the bike, when it dawned on me that he was planning to use the Toyota.

'You can't fit a motorbike in there!' I said in my now decent Spanish.

'No problem!' he said, 'I've done it many times'. He sounded confident, and I trusted Josue who seemed fine with the idea, so I got in and we headed off back into the jungle.

By now it was almost 6pm, and beginning to get dark. We raced along the road that I'd just come down on the bus, at breakneck speed sliding into corners near the edge of the mountainside much faster than I'd have dared on the bike. Even when we passed by a truck that had fallen off the side of the mountain, and my driver said that he'd been involved in the rescue and the driver was in quite a bad way, we still didn't slow down. We made it back to the GPS point that I'd tracked at about 8pm, and sure enough there was the bike, sitting just where I'd left it by the side of the road. We moved a few things inside the boot and took down the rear seats of the car, then with an almighty effort and several minutes of twisting and turning, we loaded the bike straight into the back. Try doing that with a BMW R1250GS.

We took the drive back to Patria at a slightly more reasonable pace, listening to Tarzan Boy which was appropriate as we were in the jungle, and a variety of other 80s hits. It took us a while to get back, partly because of the slower speed, but also because we passed a new police checkpoint that was set up most evenings apparently, to prevent cocaine shipments crossing the area. After another short delay to stop and turn off the Apache's fuel tap, which he'd forgotten to close and was making the car smell like a petrol station, we arrived back in Patria around 11pm.

To my amazement, Josue was still there working on another bike, and as soon as we pulled in he walked over to help. We carefully unloaded the bike and I spent the next hour watching Josue work. He saw what was wrong right away, and opened up the casings to replace the chain. Then he gave the bike a free service by cleaning out the filters and giving me an oil change. He charged me a reasonable amount for all this out-of-hours work including the new chain and oil, and even let me store the bike in his garage until morning, he is a superstar.

And in case you were wondering, yes the breakdown was my own fault. You need to pay attention to drive chain maintenance on a motorbike, and this usually means an occasional adjustment and regular lubrication. The tough rocky mountain conditions in Peru were constantly jerking the chain and loosening it much more quickly than usual. And the never ending rain, muddy water, and small stones from the road were removing any trace of lubrication within hours. So by the time I got to the bumpy road in Manu having done no maintenance for a few days, I was riding on borrowed time and the drive-chain was just waiting to fall off. My maintenance schedule wasn't always rigid after that, but it was much better and I didn't have the same problem again.

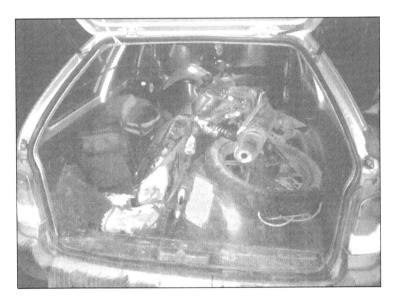

The next day I continued on to Pilcopata where I found a fantastic little jungle lodge and stayed for a few days. Then early in the morning on the second day I took the bike out minus the helmet, gloves, rain gear and rucksack, for a relaxing ride and hike along a jungle path. The place was packed full of wildlife and I kept the engine on low speed to try and stay as quiet as possible. I saw just about every famous species of bird in this part of the Amazon including Scarlet Macaws, Casiques, and Howitzson, and also huge rodents called Agouti. I couldn't continue all the way to the small river port I was aiming for because of yet another landslide that had blocked the road, but it was still a wonderful morning. Then just before lunch I had an idea and did something that I wish I'd done for all the other beautiful places I'd been before. I went up onto the balcony of the lodge which had a jungle view, poured myself a coffee, and found an online National Geographic programme about Manu, the place I was visiting. Then with the Manu jungle itself as a backdrop, I watched the programme while eating a late breakfast and identifying all the amazing birds and animals that I'd seen earlier. It was the perfect morning.

With my bike now in tip-top condition, the next day I decided to take advantage of the dry weather and ride all the way back out of the jungle to the highway, then continue all the way down to the Bolivian border. I set off early around 6am and the jungle road was a completely different experience in the dry. I was able to move much more quickly and didn't worry about falling off the edge of the mountain as the visibility was now fine. I saw dozens of green toucans along the way and made it back to the highway in about four hours, then turned south. The highway didn't last long though, and after an hour it turned into a much narrower road as the route made its way around a mountain. Then I came to a bridge, and it made the already narrow road look like an eight lane super highway. The so-called bridge, was about fifty centimetres wide at the widest point and looked to be constructed from loose branches held together by a mix of mud and rock dust. It had a big rock at either end that helped to close the distance down to the road, but it would still need a lot of momentum to get up onto the span. I'm usually a big fan of momentum, but not when you're trying to cross a narrow bridge across white–water rapids over fifty metres high. So I parked up and walked onto the bridge to check it out.

It actually felt pretty solid and under the loose branches there must have been quite a bit of timber and rock, so I went back and got on the bike. In any case my only other option would have been to retrace my route back to the highway, then find a much longer way round, wasting a day, so I was always going to give it a go. I rolled about twenty metres back down the road, and turned on the engine. Then I looked at the rapids for a few seconds trying not to think about what would happen if I got this wrong, and went for it. I didn't get it wrong, but also not quite right, and hit one of the smaller rocks near the start of the span sending my front wheel flying into the air, and making my life flash before my eyes. But somehow the wheel came back down again in the right place and I was up onto the bridge and down the other side in a flash, with a huge sigh of relief. The road on the other side of the bridge was actually pretty decent, and I made good progress for another hour or so. But then, to my horror, I was stopped in my tracks by yet another landslide. This time half the mountain had moved down to completely cover the road, and there was no way that I could cross. Not to say that it would have been impossible, because although the landslide was recent and rocks were continuing to fall, I watched as two local guys on a tiny bike with no helmets took a suicide run. They crossed over from the other side dodging the rocks and picking their way through the rubble for about a hundred metres, as they carried their bike together over a makeshift path.

I considered asking them to help me give it a go, but then had a change of heart. The worst case would have been to come across yet another landslide later down the road and then I'd be proper stuck. On my own, on a cold mountainside, with no forward or return route. Or thinking about it I suppose the real worst case would be that we slipped on the loose rocks, and ended up at the bottom of the mountain. Instead I sucked it up and turned around for a four-hour detour including a second run over the makeshift bridge, I was gutted. After being turned around by the landslide I was also in no mood to fail again, and after flying back over the bridge at almost full speed I continued on for one of the longest riding days of the journey. Thirteen hours in total from Pilcopata with no stop for lunch, until I arrived mid-evening in Urcos. A tough day, and it's incredible how brave local riders are to meet and overcome these kind of challenges every day, just to get to work.

In Urcos I quickly found a hotel and put down my things in the room, before going back outside to park my bike at the rear of the building. I'd walked out without my helmet but it was only a thirty second ride, and in any case this was Peru and I'd seen people ride without helmets all the time. But with impeccable timing, about ten seconds after getting on the bike I heard a loud whistle and I was being pulled over by a traffic cop. As I later realised, the main square was full of police and they were having a kind of focus event on traffic violations. But I hadn't noticed in my rush to get settled down and have some dinner. The policeman was officious and I fully expected the situation to get complicated, but perhaps he could see that I was in a rough state, so he just told me to leave the bike there and get my helmet. I saw him again in a police car ten minutes later as I rode by with my helmet on, and he gave me a thumbs up. I was completely exhausted, but by pushing hard to get to Urcos I'd made excellent progress and put myself within striking distance of Puno, next to Lake Titicaca on the border with Bolivia, which is where I rode to the next day.

Lake Titicaca is the highest and largest lake in South America, and it's stunning. It's over three hundred metres deep in places and has a jagged shoreline with thousands of inlets, islands, and communities which on the Peruvian side have almost no tourist infrastructure. I took a ride along the lakeshore early the next morning, and after an hour or so found a peninsula to explore. It had several beaches, a selection of route options, and winding roads up and down hills that offered excellent views over the lake. There is tourism in the area, but it's mostly centred around a small number of restaurants that cater to boat trips making their way along the shore. Inland there are only working communities of farmers, and as I rode around the area, I realised that it was all looking very familiar. The reason was that the small farms on this fertile, well-watered peninsula and in particular the stone walls that separated the fields, looked just like a typical village in rural England. Kind of like Emmerdale, but without the high murder rate.

After riding along the small country lanes for a while, reminiscing about home and whistling the theme tune to Postman Pat, I made my way down to a place called Karina. It was a small hamlet, just a few buildings along the shoreline, next to a quiet sandy beach. There I spent a couple of hours just sitting on a stone pier, gazing at the completely clear waters, and watching a farmer and his wife chasing two cows along the shore. Lake Titicaca actually spans the border with Bolivia, so the frontier was now just a short ride away and there are two border posts to choose from. I went for the slightly closer one to the north, which took me into the small town of Copacabana in Bolivia, the main starting-point for tours to the Isla Del Sol.

4
Heaven on Earth:
BOLIVIA

The Plurinational State of Bolivia, as it's formally named, is an incredibly proud and independent country to the north of Chile and Argentina. It's currently landlocked as a result of historical wars with its neighbours, and has one of the lowest GDP per capita in the region at 3,823 USD. Bolivia is one of the most challenging, and dangerous places in South America for motorcycling because of the extremely remote desert roads, but overall it's safe, with an unusually low rate of violent crime. It's also the location of the single most beautiful place that I saw on this journey, and possibly in my whole life, The Salar de Uyuni. A vast salt desert that at certain times of the year, after a little rain, and when there's no wind, turns into an infinite mirror. On a day with just a few white clouds in the sky, the spectacular double landscape looks just like an image of Heaven. And for Bolivians, this comparison is even more true when you learn that underneath the salt, there are natural resources that will power their economy for decades, if not centuries.

The Isla Del Sol on Lake Titicaca, my first stop in Bolivia, is another one of the jewels in Bolivia's crown. I already mentioned the crystal clear waters and rugged coastline, and add to that a warm breeze and blue sky overhead, and you'll get a picture of what I mean. The weather's probably not like that every single day, but it was perfect the day that I visited, so I went for a long hike. The island is hilly, so you get amazing wide open views of the lake from the top of the hills, and then you can visit the tiny villages nestled between them. But perhaps the most interesting thing about this particular island, is that there is a dark side.

The island is split into distinct communities in the North, and the South, and while one side of the island is open and welcomes tourists, the other is closed and withdrawn, preferring to protect their traditional way of life. The restriction is so serious that, according to one local I spoke to, a tourist had once been killed for straying into the wrong area. Well as I walked around the island it wasn't easy to work out which part you were in, as there are no visible markings, so unfortunately I did stray into the wrong part, and was indeed told to leave. But curiously, I was later told that the person who told me to leave, was actually from the open side of the island. He lived right on the dividing line and had been telling people not to go into the other side for years.

Apparently, according to my source, the problems all started when the closed side of the island, which is even more beautiful than the open side, started to open up and build tourist facilities. The open side didn't like the idea of all the tourists suddenly choosing to go elsewhere, after they'd spent so much money building restaurants and hotels, so started making a commotion and telling tourists not to go there. Whatever the truth of the story, I hope the two sides manage to make peace, because the whole place is stunning. There are restaurants on the hills overlooking the lake, with what must be some of the best dining views in the world.

My next stop was La Paz, which I always thought was the capital of Bolivia but apparently not. The capital is actually Sucre, even though the main government and financial centres are in La Paz and the largest city is Santa Cruz. Some people really love La Paz and it's a quintessentially chaotic, colourful, dusty South America city. Some people hate it for the same reasons, and on balance I'm probably in the latter group, but only because I was traumatised by riding my motorcycle for several days through Lima in Peru. I'm now paranoid about having a highly undignified death by falling into a pot hole, or getting crushed between two trucks going in the wrong direction. It's a cool place though and there are some amazing markets, but I didn't stay long. I'd heard about a special place in Bolivia that's been described as Heaven on Earth and I was keen to get moving South. So for the next two days, I spent most of my time on the road.

It's about 550km from La Paz to Uyuni going through the town of Oruro, and most of the route is a long, straight, highway. The most interesting things that happened were that I saw a llama running along the road with a pack of ten dogs, and I found a massive free cake in the *comida libre* section of a fridge in my hostel. Actually one other interesting thing did happen, I crossed the 10,000km mark on my journey. But otherwise, it was so boring that I started doing fuel calculations in my head, because Bolivia has a split system of charges for fuel, Domestic and Foreign, and I was keen to better understand the costs. The domestic price was 3.74 BOB per litre, while the foreigner price was 8.68 BOB, and from the first refill at 10200km to the second refill at 10468km was 268km. The tank took 6.92litres of fuel for 60 BOB, and the capacity of the Apache's fuel tank is 4.23 US Gallons according to the owner manual. Which would mean a total range of 620km including 100km on reserve. So either the bike was getting even more fuel efficient as it aged, or that road from La Paz was even more straight and boring than I had thought. There's also not an awful lot to report about my one night stay in Oruro except the fact that I arrived, the day after, a huge music festival. So I spent the afternoon listening to all the fascinating night–before stories being told by a group of exhausted French musicians recovering in the lounge of my hotel. The festival sounded incredible so if you do happen to visit, try to time it better than I did. I finally arrived in Uyuni the following day.

At an elevation of over 3600 metres and covering more than 10,000 square kilometres, The Salar de Uyuni is the world's highest, and largest, Salt Flat. It's so flat that satellites calibrate their equipment by focusing on it, and so large that the water underneath the salt contains more than half the world's Lithium. In case you're wondering why you should care about some random chemicals under a salt flat, it's because Lithium is a key ingredient used for making lithium batteries, and lithium batteries power everything from consumer electronic devices to electric cars. Bolivia, being Bolivia, is experimenting with excluding the big US energy companies, and is working with global experts to build domestic expertise in Lithium extraction and even battery production. The aim is that longer term, more of the benefits from this valuable resource will stay in the country. And the reason for their determination to make this successful, is probably because of lessons learned the last time Bolivia had a natural resource boom in the 17th

Century. Back then, huge amounts of Silver were found at Potosi, but local people saw little of the benefit. The big winners were Spanish settlers, who used the resource to take over the area and grow the African slave trade. Good for Bolivia, and I hope they're successful. They probably will be because the Lithium being exported from Chile, the other big producer in South America, is running out.

As I rode the final thirty kilometres along the highway to the town of Uyuni I saw a huge sign for the Salar, and couldn't wait. I turned straight onto the dirt road next to the sign, and had my bones shaken for another few kilometres before finally reaching the edge of the salt flat. The weather was ideal, so from there I rode straight out onto the salt and it was even more impressive than I'd imagined. Like many exquisite things in nature there's nothing particularly complicated to it, just a vast white floor, and a vast blue sky. But the perspective is so new and challenging to your senses, that it becomes captivating. Great mountains on the horizon become tiny dark ridges where God forgot to colour in the blue of the sky. And the actual expanse itself is so massive and so flat, that there is no perspective between near and far distances. During the dry season you can use this unique phenomenon to create amazing photographs, and one tourist favourite is to put small toys on the salt close to the camera, then stand as far away as possible, to make the items look huge. It all looks like great fun, but this was rainy season thank goodness, so I got to see something quite different.

The Salar de Uyuni is usually baked-hard by the sun and so flat, that when it does finally rain, there's nowhere for the water to go. As it can't flow anywhere, nor be absorbed by the hard ground, the rain just sits there on top of the salt, until it evaporates. Ten thousand square kilometres of water just a few centimetres deep, or to put it another way, the world's largest mirror. I did ride the Apache out onto the salt, but only a few hundred metres. Any further would have been risky because although the water is mostly shallow, there are some deeper pockets. You've no idea where the deep parts are because it all just looks flat, and remember this is water mixed with salt, so getting an engine full would not have been good. After taking a few pictures and videos, and spending a couple of hours enjoying the view, I rode back off the salt and continued on to Uyuni, to find a place to stay.

The next day I joined a 4x4 expedition that went much further out onto the Salar, but before that, in the morning, I visited the Train Cemetery that I mentioned earlier in the chapter on Colombia, when I was talking about the Ferrocarril railways. There was a huge investment in train infrastructure in South America during the 1800s and most places have extensive networks. The effort was not totally successful though, and Peru even went bankrupt at one point from the cost of overbuilding tracks, and getting into debt with foreign entrepreneurs. Bolivia had a different problem, wars. When Bolivia did finally start building railways after extensive delays due to regional conflicts, the country's land area was much larger than it is now. So they built rail networks all the way to the coast. But after another fierce conflict with its neighbour Chile, they lost a huge amount of land and became landlocked. Relations between the two countries didn't improve for a long time and so without trade to the coast, there was little point in a railway. The line fell into disuse, and the last major station before the border was at Uyuni, so that's where the trains stayed, left to rust in the desert just outside town. They've been left exactly where they were, and now form an excellent living, or decaying, museum that graphically illustrates the history of the region.

Later that day, I joined a group of around ten tourists in two 4x4s, and we went out onto the salt. At first I was a bit disappointed, because we were driving through places where the water was being kicked up by a light wind, and the wake from our vehicles made it feel like just driving on the surface of a lake. Actually that does sound quite cool, but it wasn't. Don't bother inventing a 4x4 that can drive on the surface of the water, because it feels just like taking a boat, no-one will pay to do that. Also the driver seemed completely lost and kept calling his friend to ask where he was heading. But after a short time we found a spot where we were completely alone and surrounded by flat, calm water with absolutely no movement. We were all wearing Wellington boots provided by the tour guide, and so we gently stepped out of the car onto the water. I watched one person getting out of the car after me, and as his left foot touched the ground, the sole of the right foot of his reflected twin who was stepping out of his own reflected car at the same time, reached up to the same place. Then I turned around and watched a bird flying in perfect parallel formation with his reflected mate, it was surreal. There wasn't even the tiniest movement on the water, except near the car where people were moving around, and the day was completely quiet and still.

What would you do if you found yourself standing on the World's Largest Mirror? Throw shapes obviously, so after giving us a ten-minute rehearsal, the tour guide drove the 4x4 around in circles filming us doing a short routine. The video is definitely the best one from my trip and I'm sure it's completely unique, and never been done before, and that this tour guide just thought of the idea on the day, and never repeated it again. Well anyway I don't care if ten thousand other people have exactly the same video, mine's got me in it, and I love it.

After all the mirror dancing and a couple of hours taking thousands of pictures and videos, we settled down to watch a majestic double sunset. We watched the reflected sun rise to meet the real sun at the horizon, then watched the stars come out, beneath our feet. Although they weren't as clear as in some other places in the Atacama Desert, it was still an incredible experience. And if you do decide to visit the Salar, I thoroughly recommend the *Sunset and Stars* tour. There are lots of other options, but this is the only one where you get to see the sunset, and the stars. It's a bit cold there at night though, so take gloves.

The Salar de Uyuni is located in south-west Bolivia and many people who visit combine the experience with an extended, and slightly dangerous, 4x4 journey even further down into the deep south west. The route crosses hundreds of kilometres of empty desert and a chain of lagoons that are a breeding ground for thousands of flamingos, before reaching a remote border post with Chile. Definitely not the kind of thing that you'd want to do alone, on a little motorbike. Then again, according to my previous calculations the Apache was a dream for fuel consumption, and could theoretically go for up to six hundred kilometres on a single tank of petrol, including reserve. Fuel consumption is not always consistent though, and it's affected by all sorts of factors like the road surface, speed, gear changes, weight, even tyre pressure. When travelling through a populated area, I'd be comfortable to push the bike all the way, but I didn't fancy doing it in the middle of a desert where the temperatures dropped below zero at night. There was just no infrastructure in the area, no petrol stations, and no mechanics.

But it's not often you get the chance to visit one of the remotest regions in the world, and see huge flocks of flamingos, so a challenge presented itself and I took the bait. I calculated that to get down through the lakes and into Chile at the farthest border post would not be possible without extra fuel cans. And in any case I'd heard that the route after the lakes was just too rocky even for the Apache, only large 4x4s with good ground clearance take the route. On the other hand, it should be possible to get down into the lakes, see most of them and then travel back up to another slightly closer frontier at Ollague, in under five hundred kilometres. That way the roads should be fairly good and probably even asphalt all the way, as they had been from La Paz, because this was a continuation of the same route. And even if they weren't, I could always turn back, but I'd need to do the whole thing in one day before the border post closed at 4:30pm. Otherwise, I'd be out in the middle of the desert without camping equipment, as the temperature dropped below freezing point. One other slight concern was that if I had an accident in such a remote place, I'd be stuffed, because although I had a mobile phone with GPS, I didn't bother with cellular coverage. There was no traffic on these roads though, and my bike was in good condition. So as long as I rode cautiously, having an accident really shouldn't be a problem. I bought enough food and water for two days just in case, and set off at 6am the next morning.

You might be thinking at this point that it's madness not to carry a mobile with cellular coverage on this kind of trip. And you're probably right, but I found early on in Colombia that in many places, although my GPS signal always worked perfectly, cellular signal did not. I wasn't interested in investing in a satellite phone just for the odd difficult day, and in any case that wouldn't be in the spirit of the journey. So I decided to do without, and for communications I relied on WIFI which I managed to find almost every day. Besides, this wasn't a hiking trip on some mountain path that might not see another walker for a week, this was a motorcycle adventure on public roads and, theoretically, even the remotest routes through the desert should see at least one car every day.

In fact, even if I had a phone, and even if the signal actually worked which it probably wouldn't out here, and even if the phone survived an accident and I was able to use it, who would get to me first? An ambulance from God knows where, or a Llama herder doing his daily rounds? Much better to have it fixed in your mind that there is no phone, and there will be no ambulance, so take care.

After setting off just after 6am, by 7am I'd already covered 80km and there was no sign of any town or village. The next hundred kilometres went by in much the same way, and the monotony of driving along vast stretches of unending yellow and blue was broken only by the occasional llama herd. They were usually grazing on the plains next to the road, but sometimes one or two of them would be sitting right in the middle of the tarmac, and I'd have to slow down and sound the horn. I passed three or four herds in the same way, but by the fifth herd I barely slowed down, confident that they always seemed to jump up and scamper off to the side in plenty of time. It was a big mistake, because when I sounded the horn to move the one llama that was blocking my way, the whole herd panicked. They started running in all directions all over the road, and I had to skid to avoid hitting them. I missed some of them by literally inches. Then as soon as I'd come to a stop and it was silent again, they went and sat back down in the road, right in front of me, odd animals.

I carried on for another hour, slowing right down for the llamas, until I came to the place where I was supposed to turn south and head toward the lagoons, but there was bad news. This was where the highway ended, and what looked on the map like a road heading south, turned out to be a vast sand trap, impossible to cross without full Mud Terrain Tyres. It suddenly occurred to me, and I'm not sure why it didn't before, that the four or five vehicles that I'd seen in the hours since I left Uyuni had been huge 4x4s. And I don't mean urban Range Rovers with basic all terrain tyres, I mean vehicles with big blocked Mud Terrain tyres that wear out in months on the highway, but are essential to drive over sand or pull yourself through large wet rocks.

I could have cut my losses and continued on the highway to Ollague, reached the border post early and enjoyed an extra day in Chile, that would have been the sensible option. After all, there would be lots of other scenic places on my journey so this wasn't a make or break decision. And I'd just visited the Salar de Uyuni, Heaven on Earth, what difference would it make to miss a couple of lagoons and some pink birds. But I wasn't here on a two-week holiday to see the sights, I was challenging myself to see what I was capable of, and this just didn't feel like the day that I'd be beaten. So I pushed the Apache into the sand, and we cruised slowly over the top for a couple of hundred metres as my confidence returned. Then the sand got deeper, and I started to use my feet to balance as the front wheel lost traction, but I continued on. And then, finally, the sand got so deep that as I accelerated, my rear wheel began to spin impotently, and I dropped the bike, I was stuck. Again I turned the air blue with completely pointless rage as I started sinking into a pile of fine grained sand that would have looked just great on a Caribbean beach. And the people of Manu Cloud Forest in Peru where I got stuck the first time probably heard my cries as they bounced off the heavens and back down to Earth. But in this remote place there was no one nearby to hear me, so after a few seconds of shouting, I just stood there for a while, surrounded by silence. I stared at the Apache lying in the sand for a few minutes, then I picked it up, and started to push.

First I tried to push forwards, but it wouldn't move. Then I tried to push backwards and it still wouldn't move. So then I tried turning the engine on and adding a bit of gas as I pushed, and it moved a little bit, before the wheels started spinning again, and it sank back down. I felt completely disheartened, but I wasn't concerned for my safety, it was still only lunchtime and I was certain, or fairly certain, that at least one 4x4 would come past on the highway which was only a few hundred metres away. I just couldn't believe that I'd been so stupid to think I could cross a sand trap, what on earth was I thinking, and all just to see some flamingos.

I carried on tinkering with the position of the bike, pushing it here and there, a bit of gas, no gas. Until eventually, the rear tyre caught a tiny piece of grass that was growing near my feet. I got enough momentum to push the bike up the little sand bank next to the sand path I was on, and let it roll back down, this time facing the other direction. Better. At least now I was facing the right way and I just needed to get back to where I was riding earlier. This time I didn't bother with the gas and just pushed, hard, with everything I had, to try and roll the bike forward even if it took hours. It did roll, eventually, and slowly I felt the sand getting shallower. Then once I was back in the shallows, I jumped on and started the engine. Then I turned it off again, and took out my phone. The map was showing me a route directly through the sand trap and I was right on it, but there was definitely no road, how could that be?

At that moment I saw a 4x4 Toyota driving slowly along the highway coming from the other direction, and to my amazement it turned South about five hundred metres in front of me. It looked like it had driven into the sand, but it also hadn't slowed down. I headed back towards the highway and continued on a small service road heading in the same direction to where I thought the 4x4 crossed. Sure enough, there was a path, also covered with sand but this time also occasional small rocks, and that was enough to give my tyres some traction to pass through. After riding slowly along this path for another five hundred metres or so, I reached the hill behind the sand trap and the small rocks that had helped me pass the sandy path, turned into big rocks. Not big enough to completely stop my progress, but big enough to mean that hitting one would be a very bad idea. So I spent the next couple of hours gingerly traversing from side to side as I made my way up, then down, then up, then down, then up, then down again along the rocky road that led over five or so hills on the other side, until I found myself at the first lagoon, Laguna Pastos Grandes.

The road conditions had seriously eaten into my time and by now it was mid–afternoon. I had to recalculate for the much slower route back to the highway, so 4:30pm was looking tight. But the lake was truly amazing, and I took a moment to just lie down by the shore and enjoy the sunshine. While I was lying there a group of European tourists came over and looked at me with amazement. They had been in the 4x4 that I saw turn off the highway and even commented to the tour guide that it was amazing how some local people would dare come here on motos. When they realised that I was British and on a motorcycle journey, they couldn't believe what they were hearing. We laughed about it and they wished me luck and said 'take care', before they went off for lunch. While they were eating I joined the tour guides to get a bit more information about the route. Again they were completely amazed and if I'm honest, I was enjoying it, I knew that I'd achieved something special as vehicle journeys go. They warned me about the route and said it really was only for 4x4s, but that as I was already here, I couldn't miss the second lagoon which was far more impressive. Time was moving on but all going well, I still had time to make it to the second lagoon and back to the border post before it closed.

The route continued on as before, rocky bone shaking stretches followed by deep sandy stretches that demanded complete concentration. Unfortunately, I clearly wasn't able to give complete concentration by this point, because I dropped the bike again, this time breaking the indicator. But I made it to the second lagoon, Laguna Capina, and they were right, what a beauty, deep blue water and hundreds of pink flamingos, all framed by a mountain ridge. I would have loved to stay longer but by now I was feeling rushed. I asked another guide if he could help me fix the bike, and he had exactly the right glue and tape to do the job, for five dollars. A bit steep for two minutes' work, but who's complaining in the middle of the desert.

There were no more surprises on the way back to the highway, and the road to Ollague was thankfully decent. It still had a lot of sandy stretches were I needed to slow down, but overall my progress was fine and I made it to the frontier by 4pm. I passed through Bolivian customs in minutes, moved through to Chile, parked the bike, and took my documents into the Chilean customs office praying that I'd make it before they closed. I needn't have bothered, the whole area on the Chilean side was experiencing a power-cut. They said they'd try to complete the process if the power came back on before they went home, but had no idea when that would be. What more could I do, I took out my book and sat down to read.

5
A bitter cold morning:
CHILE

Chile is the long narrow country to the west of Argentina, plus the World Heritage site of Rapa Nui (Easter Island) which sits in the middle of the Pacific Ocean half way to New Zealand. The current borders were settled after Chile beat Peru and Bolivia in the War of the Pacific, extending their territory in the Atacama Desert and cutting off Bolivia from the coast, leaving its trains to rust at Uyuni. In the 1970s the US waged an economic war on Chile to remove their democratically elected leader, President Allende, in favour of a military dictatorship led by General Augusto Pinochet. It lasted for 16 years and like the other military dictatorships implemented by the USA as part of Operation Condor, led to a great deal of bloodshed. The Chileans managed to get rid of Pinochet in the 1990s though, and since then the country has been relatively stable, and leads South America on just about every social and economic measure.

It was definitely a surprise to be met with a power−cut at the Ollague frontier post, given all that I'd heard about Chile being the most developed and the most prosperous country in the region, but these things happen. In 2004 I lived in New York and still remember having to walk home from Manhattan to Queens over the Queensborough bridge when half the Northeastern USA went dark, so you can forgive a few hours' power outage in the middle of the desert. I sat down to read my book, and before I knew it an hour had passed and the power came back on. I was first in the queue so I was stamped and through within minutes, after I'd completed a reassuringly thorough bag and bike search of course. Luckily I'd ditched my coca back in Uyuni, but the guard still managed to find a contraband onion to take home for his dinner.

To say that Ollague is a remote border post is a bit of an understatement, there are just a few buildings, and one hostel thank goodness, but no petrol station. Which was a bit of a shock, having just travelled five hundred kilometres across the desert. Naturally though, I thought there must be a petrol station after a few more kilometres down the highway into Chile, so I didn't think it was a huge problem. Then the next morning as I was riding down the highway and about to leave Ollague to head back out into the Atacama Desert, I saw a tiny road sign with a picture of a petrol pump and 'Calama 200km' written underneath.

Given that there was no petrol in Ollague, and none for the next two hundred kilometres, I wasn't quite sure what to do. I headed back into town and spoke to the hostel owner. She confirmed that there was no petrol station in the town, but that there was one about twenty minutes back over the border, along a different road. I didn't fancy spending the day going back over the border process twice just to get petrol, so I asked if there was another solution, and she said she'd ask around. After a few minutes she came back and said that yes there was a lady who had some petrol that I could buy, and she'd be right over, so I waited outside the hostel. The lady lived about fifty metres down the street, and I saw her come out of her house and start walking my way. But after a few metres she noticed a friend walking the other way and stopped to chat.

Fifteen minutes later, she casually walked over and asked me how much I wanted. 'Just enough to get to the next town' I said, which given that it was two hundred kilometres away, was quite a bit. 'Fifteen dollars for five litres' she replied and I countered with an offer of twenty dollars for ten litres. A tough negotiation ensued, but I eventually got her down to fifteen dollars for five. The price was seven times the domestic Bolivia price, which is what I assume she paid, as the border was right there, but only three times the Chile price so it wasn't too bad under the circumstances.

Another few hours desert riding took me to Calama where I ate lunch and filled the tank. It was a good route, because it followed a set of strato-volcanos that sit on the border between Bolivia and Chile, so I had a nice view. The road surface was good too, a couple of major pot holes here and there but mostly just smooth, solid asphalt. By evening I'd reached San Pedro de Atacama, one of the darkest places on Earth, a magnet for stargazers the world over, and one of my bucket list items for South America. I checked into a hostel and put down my bag, then went out for a sunset ride near Valle de la Luna. The weather was ideal for biking, and it was bliss to ride past the dark red rocks on either side of the road minus my luggage and riding gear, just enjoying the cool breeze that was rapidly eating up the desert heat of the day. There's a hilltop near San Pedro with a fantastic view of the Valley, and they have dedicated minibuses that ferry hundreds of tourists up there for the sunset. It was well worth the couple of dollars to park close to the hilltop, and I watched as the sun sank behind the high mountains.

To me the sky looked flawless the next morning when I went to ask about a stargazing tour, just blue as far as the eye could see. But I was disappointed to hear that that week had been terrible for amateur astronomers. There's actually quite a bit of sand and other air pollutants that kick up over the town occasionally and ruin the view, and this week had been particularly bad. The really dark parts of the Atacama are quite a way out of town where the observatories are, but you're not allowed to just wander in, you need to book tours way in advance. I went out anyway in the evening with my trusty binoculars just to take a look, but it was just like they said. I don't mean to say you couldn't see anything, you could actually see the whole milky way which to someone from a well-lit town in Britain is always impressive. But I'd seen that view every night for the last three weeks in Bolivia, so was really looking for something more.

There is another reason to visit San Pedro though, and that's the Geyser field about eighty kilometres north at El Tatio, so I decided to take a trip out there. What followed, and you won't believe this given what I've already written about Peru and South Bolivia, was the most uncomfortable and probably dangerous day of riding of the journey so far. The problem was that to appreciate the geysers at their best you had to get there by 6am, and out in the desert at 6am it is very, very dark, and very, very cold. The darkness was particularly challenging because if I have one complaint about the otherwise excellent Apache, it's that the headlight is a bit underpowered. It's fine for city streets, but on a dark night in the darkest place on Earth, it was always going to be a problem. I checked the map and, assumed, that because the roads had been excellent so far in Chile, that this would continue up to the popular tourist attraction of El Tatio. Nonetheless I still gave it a generous two hours to get there, because I always expect a few unplanned stops or problems, and I left at 4am.

After only a few kilometres the paved road disappeared and was replaced by my nemesis, or one of my many nemeses, a dirt track suffering from an extreme case of washboard road. If you haven't ridden on these ridiculous natural phenomenon, then it's really something you need to experience to understand. Rocks, sand, water, oil, pot holes, I can handle it all, but washboard roads shake your bones to the core and are a great way to get into an accident. I thought they had something to do with the wind and several people have told me that on the road, but then I looked it up online and apparently they're inevitable on any well used dirt road in a dry place. So given that I was on a dirt road in the middle of the driest desert in the world, there wasn't much to be done. The problem is formed when car tyres

103

displace the dry sand and then compact it. It happens uniformly because once a small ridge is formed the next car will compact it more and displace sand to a short distance in front of the last ridge. For someone in a big car with good suspension they can reduce the bone shaking by just going faster. But although that smoothes out the experience for them, it actually makes the compacting problem worse. By the time I got to this road near El Tatio, it really did look exactly like an eighty-kilometre-long washboard and gave my bike, and my body, the drubbing of a lifetime.

I tried going faster like the cars, but it was impossible and although the ridges are compacted, they're still fragile enough to give way and push the narrow front tyre sideways, sending you flying. Then I tried going slowly, but I just couldn't go slow enough to stop the pounding. I was riding through the desert at 4am in sub-zero temperatures, with only basic winter kit, in the darkest place on the planet with a headlight that even a moth wouldn't bother with, and I was getting my bones shaken to pieces. I needed a boost, so I checked my progress on the map, which was difficult with frozen fingers that could barely operate the touchscreen, and saw that I was over half way, but my progress was slowing down. I wanted to stop and go back more than at any point on the journey so far, but I couldn't. The only option was to continue, not knowing if the road would even be passable for me if things got worse. Then I realised that I'd done another stupid thing, and hadn't checked the elevation. The road just kept going up and up the side of a mountain, and although I couldn't see anything, after two hours I knew that it was high because I could hardly stand the cold. At that time of year and at that altitude, it would have been way below zero degrees. I didn't descend again until I was close to

El Tatio, and arrived at the guard house barely able to speak. While the other tourists jumped out of their warm mini-buses saying things like 'OMG it is f***ing freezing!' I went straight to the bathrooms and turned on the blow dryer.

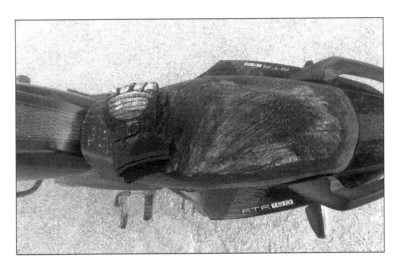

Once I'd recovered enough to handle paper, I bought the ticket and continued the couple of kilometres down to the geyser field, parked up, and walked straight over to a geyser and basked in its heat. I put my hands on the ground to warm them, and stood as close as I could to the opening without falling in, because they're literally boiling hot. They're also incredible natural phenomenon and dare I say it, well worth the journey. I took a few videos of the bubbling and gurgling geysers, and watched a few dramatic eruptions, then went back to check my bike. Both the seat and my gloves had frozen over. I can laugh about it now, but it was a stupid thing to do, I should have gotten much more information about the route.

On the way back to San Pedro, in daylight now and with a temperature nearing thirty degrees Celsius, I saw there were fields either side that had been torn up by 4x4 vehicles avoiding the road. I hopped over a ridge and settled into one of the tracks which took me most of the way back to where one section of washboard ended. Then I enjoyed a thirty-minute blast back down the mountain on a flat section, narrowly avoiding hitting a fox and several llamas, before a final bone-shaking on the last few kilometres before San Pedro. I would meet my arch nemesis, The Washboard Road, again on the Jesuit Route as I rode back through eastern Bolivia into Brazil, but for now I just enjoyed the flat streets of the town.

From San Pedro I rode all the way across the whole country! Which isn't actually that far because Chile is very narrow, and I reached the coast at Antofagasta by mid-afternoon the next day. After eating an Octopus empanada for dinner, I went straight to bed. The next morning, I rode another 470km South through the desert to the beach town of Caldera near the Bahia Inglesia which I'd heard was the best beach in Chile. But on the way a very odd thing happened. As I was riding along through mile after mile of nothing but desert sand, I saw in the distance less than a kilometre in front of me rising out of the ground, a giant hand. Although it hadn't yet fully broken through it was already more than ten metres high from the tip of its fingers to the middle of the palm. The first thing that crossed my mind was how vulnerable I was on my tiny motorcycle riding through one of the largest and driest deserts in the world. The hand could just scoop me up and crush me to dust that would blow away and mix with an infinite number of sand grains. I thought it must be a mirage so I slowed down and pulled over near where the hand was rising for a closer look. It turned out to be the Mano del Desierto, a sculpture by Mario Irarrazabal, placed far out in the middle of the desert and intended sure enough, to emphasise human vulnerability.

The Bahia Inglesia was just as gorgeous as everyone was telling me, apart from a slight chill in the air, and in the water, because this is after all the Pacific Ocean not the Caribbean. A fine sandy beach surrounded by rocky inlets and crystal clear water, and the hotels and restaurants on the beachfront were nice too. After a couple of days' rest, I headed back inland and covered another 470km to my second major destination in Chile, Vicuna. If you're getting the feeling that this story is moving a bit too fast, you'd be right, because I was covering enormous distances now to visit only a few highlights in Chile. I really needed to slow down a bit, and decided to spend a few extra days in Vicuna.

Vicuna is the gateway town for the Elqui Valley, another of Chile's pre-eminent stargazing locations that was certified as a Dark Sky Sanctuary in 2015. Unlike San Pedro though, the skies here during my visit were perfect and even just walking around town the first evening the sky was full of stars. The valley is a wine region famous for sauvignon blanc, and for one of Chile's most popular drinks, Pisco brandy, and it was here that I also managed to find one of the best hostels that I've stayed in on my journey. It was set within a glorious flower filled courtyard, and offered a buffet breakfast of homemade jams, breads, cheeses, hummus and coffee. What a wonderful place to spend a few days.

After sleeping like a log the first night and spending an hour over my delicious homemade breakfast, I took the bike out for a spin through the Elqui Valley, stopping at a couple of villages along the route for lunch and to look around. I followed the valley all the way to the end of the road where there was a big sign that read '*This is the End of the Road'*, before the road ended, then headed home. The weather was just right, warm but not too hot, and the road was just right too, winding around the mountains enough to make the ride fun but not so much that I needed to slow down. The vineyards, surrounded by the mountains of the valley, were beautiful and it was just one of those perfect riding days that make a difficult motorcycle journey worthwhile. Obviously wine and pisco do not mix well with a riding day though, so I picked up a couple of bottles and saved them for dinner. When I got back to the hostel I got chatting with a German girl who was staying in the next room, and we shared dinner and a drink.

In the morning, after another luxurious breakfast, I asked the hostel owner about a sky gazing tour and we got talking about the area. I asked him how he ended up here in Elqui, and he told me how he'd been a translator for the US Army back in Lebanon before finding Elqui on a holiday once, and falling in love with the place. I wasn't surprised, the weather and climate are unique and it's another one of those places that are known for having a special energy. Or maybe it's just the pisco. There were lots of private sky gazing tour options in people's back gardens around Elqui which looked really fun, but I opted for the Observatory tour at Mamalluca including a go on the massive observatory telescope. It was the first time that I'd looked through such a powerful telescope, and seeing the craters on the moon close up was phenomenal. The guide was good too, a really funny guy who made the whole thing enjoyable and also helped us to take moon photographs with our own mobile phones. He had a clear deep interest in astronomy and if I remember correctly also a PhD, and knew everything about Mamalluca and the Large

Telescopes around the world. He gave us fun facts like how the mirror on the largest telescope in the world took two years to polish on a constant polishing machine before it was the correct concave shape. And how half a million people would visit Elqui during the next solar eclipse. He also showed us how to navigate using the stars which I thought might come in handy one day if my GPS failed during the journey. Let's see if I've remembered correctly. So Polaris is due North if you can see it, or you can use Orion's arrow which also points North. To find South, you need to find the Southern Cross, South will be four times the length of the cross, past the end of the cross. Actually I've no idea if that's correct, I haven't tested it out yet and I'm not even sure you can see these things outside Chile. I'll stick with the GPS for now.

I had a splendid few days in Elqui and only two bad things happened. The first was that I felt a fairly strong tremor from an earthquake. It shook the building and the ground moved, but it only lasted a few seconds and there was no damage. Chile is notorious for earthquakes and although this was the first, it wouldn't be the last time I felt a tremor. In fact, they're so common that I'd probably felt other tremors since I entered Chile at Ollague, just without knowing what they were. The other bad thing that happened, was that I got bitten by a dog, which was a shock because I love dogs and came across hundreds of strays on my journey who were as good as gold.

Stray dogs have a bad reputation because they're tough and steal food, and because it's true there's a tiny risk they might have rabies. But on the other hand they're rational and won't bite you unless there's a reason like you're trying to take their food or hurt them. Pet dogs are different, sure they might be regularly checked for diseases, hopefully, but on the other hand half of them live very odd and isolated lives, have mental illness through inbreeding, and spend their days barking at themselves. Whenever you hear about dangerous dog attacks it's usually a pet Pit Bull who's been kept in a small apartment and abused by its owner, not a street dog. If you're a street dog in a pack and act out, then you probably won't last very long.

But the thing is that as much as I love dogs, they really, really love motorcycles, in the sense that they think bikes are a kind of antelope or llama and would be delicious if they could only catch them. A lot of dogs go bananas when a motorcycle rides by, especially if they're in a pack because then they really fancy themselves to take down the prey. But although they love the chase, when the dogs get close to a bike they've no idea what to do. They can't bite because it's all hot exhaust and engine noise, so they just kind of lose interest. Unfortunately for me this particular dog noticed my juicy calf sticking out and had a little taste. Every motorcyclist will have a ton of stories about being chased by vicious, and sometimes not so vicious, dogs but it's pretty rare that one of them follows through. Anyway the bite I got was only a little nip, and I don't blame the poor thing he was just doing what comes naturally. I'm sure if I'd have stopped the bike and spoken to him he'd have snuggled up for a pat on the head.

The mystical energy of Elqui called me back for another leisurely ride through the valley, before I headed off the next day to Valparaiso. I had a fierce headwind in my face the whole five hundred kilometres there, but still arrived in good time. Valparaiso is famous for its graffiti, and like most towns famous for graffiti it has a slightly rebellious, slightly anti-authoritarian reputation that is probably undeserved today. The graffiti has been completely embraced as part of local culture to the extent that there are festivals and streets given over to extensive pieces of street art. I went on a city tour, and saw one street that was totally covered in professional graffiti all except for one house that was immaculately painted in plain green. When I asked the tour guide why, he said that that person didn't like the graffiti and refused to be part of it, he objected to being told how to paint his house and chose to protest by painting his house in the plainest way possible... *Viva la revolucion!* Valparaiso also has the largest individual piece of graffiti art in South America outside Brazil, which covers one entire side of a tall building near the port. And from a nearby hill it's possible to see several small, and striking pieces of graffiti in the foreground, while at the same time looking at the building art behind.

Tagging, that annoying non-graffiti that consists of simple letters and nicknames with absolutely no artistic merit, and that plagues most European cities, is a problem here too. But I must admit, if I'm totally honest there's a kind of tagging here that I do find pretty impressive. Most of the tall buildings in Valparaiso have tags right near the top, even thirty storey high office blocks. They were put there by kids who challenged each other to put the highest tag possible not by taking an elevator up and hanging out of a window, but by climbing directly up the outside. Not everyone's cup of tea, but you have to admire the guts needed to hoof it straight up the side of a building just to prove a point, and putting that kind of intensity and meaning into even a couple of letters passes the threshold of art for me. Graffiti art in Valparaiso has also been popular for such a long time that it's matured along with the artists themselves. There's a married couple that's been creating joint pieces for decades each bringing their own unique style into a union of colours and shapes that is immediately identifiable. And there are all female crews who have stripped the form of its masculinity to create pieces using gentler natural themes, and messages of hope.

Before I left Valparaiso I also paid a visit to the impressive cemetery, and heard a gruesome story. Apparently the local community used to bury their dead in the hills around the city, until there was a landslide one day, and all the coffins and bodies spilled out into the city centre. Anyway on that note, next stop Santiago. I mentioned earlier that in Guayaquil, Ecuador I met up with Luis my classmate from the Cambridge MBA. Our classmates included three more friends from Chile, and so I arranged to meet up with them in Santiago. Valparaiso is only a short hop to the capital so I spent a long time over breakfast the next day, before taking a leisurely ride over.

When you think of a typical city in South America what comes to mind? Traffic and car horns? Loud voices? Markets? Heat and dust? I'm sure that this image comes from British traders and missionaries living in Lima, Peru during the 1800s, but the cities are, of course, as varied as those in Europe. Santiago still has the dust and some of the bustle like Lima, and it's still low rise, but there's something a bit calmer about it that I liked. It's also surrounded by mountains which gives it a dramatic setting, and desert which gives it a frontier feel. It definitely doesn't feel like you're at the centre of a huge conurbation that goes on for miles and is home to seven million people, although I guess it depends on exactly where you're standing. There are some fine neighbourhoods in the city centre by the river that I'm sure cost a fortune to live in, but that also have some reasonably priced hostels, so I found a place there. My quiet street was lined with boldly painted houses and the park at the end of the road was an oasis from the hot midday sun. One interesting thing about that park was that it was tolerated for people to live there who didn't have homes to go to, and several couples where living in tents with all their living equipment neatly stowed inside or nearby. It would be much better if the government would provide housing to people in need of course, but at least it's a step up from the torture inflicted by some local authorities elsewhere.

Meanwhile on the opposite end of the spectrum, I went to meet my classmates in one friend's elegant house outside the city. What a magnificent dinner, a ton of BBQ meat cooked exquisitely and followed by a huge cream and caramel dessert, all homemade. I had told them that I was headed to Argentina, and I think they wanted me to understand that Chilean meat is the best before I was exposed to all those cheap, beef toting charlatans across the border. I was actually getting a bit skinny from all the long biking days and constant moving about, so the banquet sorted me right out. Who knows what they'd been discussing about my trip, and perhaps my state of mind and body, in the days before the dinner. Because after we took a photograph to remember the evening, the wife of one of my classmates said to him 'How does he look so smart after months on the road?' I wasn't quite sure what she was expecting, but I'm glad I made an impression. Anyway the answer to the question *How does he look so smart after months on the road?* is that the hostel had a washing machine, I carry boot polish, and the shirt was non-iron, thanks M&S. We had a good old chat after dinner and put the world to rights in our way, trying not to let our diverging world views conflict too much, and agreeing on most of the basic problems of humanity. And then one of my friends suggested we go horse riding the next day in the hills outside the city.

I did a bit of horse riding back in the day, but only a bit. It was while I was living near Cheltenham in England, and the rolling Cotswold hills were just as perfect for a Sunday morning horse ride, as a Saturday morning blast on the bike. It's also the home of the Cheltenham Gold Cup and an important place for horsey types generally, so I thought I'd get into the spirit of the place. I wasn't very good. I'm fine to get on and potter about, but when they start jogging along I lose my rhythm completely. It's really similar to riding a motorbike, slower speeds are awkward and difficult to balance, but as soon as you get up to cruising speed the momentum pushes everything back into place. I worked my way up to galloping and enjoyed a few months of pleasant riding through the hills. But that was now eighteen years ago, and I hadn't climbed onto a horse since, so my friend made me wear a little safety helmet that I tried to ignore as I pretended to be a Gaucho cowboy riding the desert hills of Santiago de Chile. But the fantasy didn't last long. As soon as I tried to do something more than mosey around I just couldn't keep my balance, and I'd clearly forgotten everything I learned. It was a lovely evening though, and I enjoyed the ride/walk around the dusty hills admiring the city view.

Now I had a difficult question to answer. To the south, way to the south, was the incredible region of Patagonia and the question was whether I would make the long trip down. It would definitely involve going all the way, and reaching the southern tip of South America at Ushuaia, because who goes half way there and doesn't reach the end. On the plus side I would get to see some of the most impressive mountain scenes in the world. On the negative side, I just spent three months going back and forward over the Andes and ridiculous as it sounds, I was a bit fed up of mountains. In the end I decided to head east across northern Argentina, to Buenos Aires. I would leave the Torres del Paine for a future hiking expedition, and I'm super glad that I did because now the thought of heading back there for a couple of weeks hiking fills me with excitement. If I'd have pushed hard to do it on my motorcycle just to tick a box, now I wouldn't have that feeling and the worst thing you can do on a long journey is tick boxes, I've done it plenty of times and always regretted it. If you ever went somewhere and thought that it wasn't quite as good as people said it was, then you know you've just been ticking a box. It doesn't matter what happens on a trip, except if you suffer some illness or other misfortune obviously, but apart from that, you get out what you put in, and if you go in the right frame of mind you'll always find the magic that other people talk about.

After another long riding day through even more mountains and passing the challenging 21 Curves Road, or was it 210 Curves?, that takes you into Argentina, I arrived in Mendoza. The border crossing was fine and the only problem was having to wait for another group of motorcyclists taking some impressive Harleys and Ducatis through the frontier, I was definitely back on the motorbike trail now. By the way, vehicle insurance is a legal requirement in Argentina, but they don't sell it at the border so you need to buy it beforehand, very annoying.

6
You've done
what you came to do:
ARGENTINA

Some sentences are just very difficult to translate between languages. For example, the Spanish sentence 'Argentina es el pais de habla espanol mas grande del mundo, es famoso por ser excelente en el futbol y siempre ha incluido Las Malvinas.' Is a tough one but a reasonable interpretation might be 'Argentina is the largest Spanish speaking country in the world, it always cheats at football and definitely doesn't include the British Falkland Islands.' Unfortunately, I don't speak Yaghan or have any Fuegian friends, so I'm not sure how it would translate into the first language spoken on the archipelago, but I'm sure it's equally as tricky.

Argentina is actually the slightly shorter, but much wider country to the east of Chile on the map and occupies most of the Southern Cone. It really is the largest Spanish speaking country in the world, and they are, at the time of writing, still very good at football. They used to be the 7th richest country in the world per capita, but were unlucky with Presidents in the 20th century. And when the wife of one President *inherited* the title in 1974, the USA took advantage of the resulting unrest to install a brutal military dictatorship as part of Operation Condor. Since the 1970s they've suffered periodic economic downturns and under current President Mauricio Macri have recently been through yet another difficult time. But despite all of this, Argentina has always managed to remain amongst the richest and most developed nations in South America. As far as I know it's not quite as biodiverse as Colombia or Peru, but it does contain the highest point in the Southern Hemisphere, Mount Aconcagua, which you can see just after you cross the border from Chile.

By the time I got to Argentina there was no doubt about it, I wasn't a beginner at this anymore. Apart from the three months across Europe in the Spring, I'd now crossed six countries of South America. Not just a two-week blast down the highways of Chile or the Cusco route in Southern Peru. I'd jumped head first into a full-on transcontinental marathon, and conquered high mountains, desert expanses, and deep jungle, on my own, on a tiny little 160cc urban motorcycle. I also spoke a decent level of Spanish by now, and felt completely confident on the continent. There was nothing more that could intimidate me, and it was no longer the alien and uncomfortable place it had seemed when I looked at my globe back in England.

Although I never really had a set plan of how the trip would progress, at some point early on I decided that the cosmopolitan city of Buenos Aires in Argentina would be the endpoint. It's on the east coast so I could get a cheap flight back to the UK, and I could probably sell the bike there for a good price. But now as I entered Argentina, the last country on my journey, and headed closer to Buenos Aires, instead of having a feeling of euphoria and a sense of nearing completion or having achieved my goals, my mind was turning the other way. I kept struggling with the decision all the way to the city, but I already knew in my heart that I wouldn't be ending my journey there.

After crossing the border from Chile I continued on yet more sweeping mountain roads to the laid back city of Mendoza. Mendoza is famous for the wines produced in the surrounding countryside and I took the opportunity to try some of them out. They're fantastic in my opinion, but then I'm really no wine expert and don't really see the problem with wine out of a box, so don't take my word for it. It was also in Mendoza that I met a group of local slack-liners who were practising in the park. Slack-lining is like tightrope walking but with slightly looser lines that allow for much more expression and creativity in terms of movements and sequences, making the sport a whole lot more interesting than just a balancing act. My first attempt was terrible, as was my second attempt, but slowly, slowly, after a couple of hours of focused practice, I found that I was...still not able to even stand on the thing for more than two seconds. I've no idea how on earth they do it, as soon as you step onto a rope you're going to fall off it's just basic physics. But anyway they seem to have worked it out and so I stayed for a bit longer just watching them walk, run, and jump along a piece of fabric perhaps two inches wide. One of the guys gave me his Instagram and on there he had pictures of people from the group doing basically the same thing, but on a line tied between two sides of a huge ravine hundreds of metres high. I promised myself that I'd find out more about the sport back in the UK, and maybe one day I'll be walking on air between the mountains, as well as riding through them on a motorcycle.

After overnight stops in San Luis and Villa de Merlo, I reached Cordoba and found a lively hostel on a street in the middle of town. You can't choose your neighbours, and anyone who's ever stayed in a hostel, small hotel, B&B, cruise ship, tent or caravan will know how important it is to be lucky with the people who are sharing your space. In Cordoba I stayed in a shared room for eight people, and as I was checking in I noticed that two attractive Spanish girls were in the same room, this was going to be an exciting couple of days. They moved out twenty minutes later as they were heading to the airport, and were replaced by a couple in their mid-fifties and their elderly mother. This was going to be a quiet couple of days. And it was, but they were lovely people, and were taking the mother to a hospital in Cordoba for medical treatment. That's another thing I love about South America, it's not just a stereotype, everyone really is very family oriented.

The next day I met up with Agata, who is from Cordoba but who I originally met in Ecuador because she was volunteering in a hostel there. We kept in touch and I followed her amazing journey as she moved from place to place finding work like volunteering, selling snacks, or waitressing. She would stay in a place for a few months before moving on, and had seen most of South America that way. We ate empanadas and drank wine in the grand tree lined garden of her flat, talking about the best places to live on the continent, and trying to calm down her dog who went nuts when he smelled the meat snacks. The next morning, I set off early again and I was moving quickly now through Argentina. To be honest I was really just focused on getting to Buenos Aires, but before I got there I took an overnight stop in Rosario.

Rosario is the birthplace of Che Guevara, and also the starting point for one of the most famous motorcycle journeys of all time. Would you believe that I've neither read the book nor seen the film, but I've read about the Marxist revolutionary's life and he sounds like an amazing person. A young doctor who treated sick people including Lepers that he met along the way, before devoting his life to fighting for what he believed in. When I was at University I was just focused on getting a job afterwards and thought that would be hard enough, but I remember seeing Che Guevara posters a few times on dormitory walls. I didn't know who he was or what he represented, and I'm pretty sure neither did most of the people who had the posters, but since then I've gotten much more interested in how the world works.

You may have noticed that I didn't write much about the riding from Mendoza to Rosario, and it's because the roads where, to be honest, a bit boring. Extremely well–constructed and very safe, but a bit boring. The road from Rosario to Buenos Aires was similar, and I got so bored that I decided to see how far the Apache could go without refuelling. I'd been meaning to try it out, and this was the ideal place with such safe roads, plenty of people around, and petrol stations on every corner. I made sure that the fuel tap was set so I'd definitely have a little in reserve, then didn't refuel again all the way to Buenos Aires. By the time I reached BA I'd covered 547 kilometres since the last refuel, which must have been somewhere before Cordoba, and the Apache still seemed to have a bit left in the tank, unbelievable.

Buenos Aires, the capital of Argentina and without doubt the most developed and beautiful city in South America, was everything that people said it was. Clean, cosmopolitan, diverse, the weather was good, and the parks and gardens were lush and well maintained, what a place. I rode straight into the middle of town and found a hostel high up on the 10th floor of a stunning old building, looking directly at another similar old building across the street, in the embassy district. They didn't have parking, but frankly I was happy to leave the Apache out on the street because it was a decent looking part of town and there were lots of other bikes, so I wasn't concerned. As usual I didn't use a lock, and hadn't done since my old lock got stolen somewhere in Ecuador, which was a bit ironic. To be fair it was my own fault though, I couldn't be bothered to keep unpacking it so I just started looping it around one of the pillion handles, and they probably just slipped it off. Not sure what anyone would want with a lock and no key, but there you go. After parking the bike, I went for a late lunch, then back to the hostel to catch up on some Spanish learning. And I got to practice not only my improving Spanish, but my Chinese too, when I heard a guy in reception struggling to communicate with the Argentinian receptionist. I went over to help and ended up translating for twenty minutes while they spoke about taxis, travel cards, and supermarkets. It was a lot of fun, and the best practice I could have hoped for, so I didn't bother with the language app for a while after that. Then over the next few days I worked my way through the classic Buenos Aires Tourist Itinerary, including the Modern Art Museum in San Telmo, the grand avenues, and the Costanera Sur ecological reserve. It was all incredible, and the city is so full of interesting things to do that it's almost worth a visit to South America on its own. But this is a story about a motorcycle journey, so from that perspective, the most interesting thing that happened in Buenos Aires was that I met up with my old friend Dustin, the real biker who I met in the motel near Palmaseca, Colombia.

Dustin had continued his journey all the way down through Patagonia to the End of the World in Ushuaia, and was heading back up the east coast of Argentina, so we agreed to meet up in BA and share some stories. He'd also found another hostel with parking so after a couple more days enjoying the sights I went over to join him. It was great to see Dustin again after months on the road. When we first met although I'd been all through Colombia I was still only a couple of weeks into the tour and at that point, you never really know what will happen. Since then we'd kept in touch and swapped the occasional picture of torn up roads and mountain views from Peru but frankly speaking, he takes much better photos than me and his Instagram is excellent. Whenever I went to a famous tourist spot I couldn't help checking if he'd been there too and taken a better photo, and he always had. I think part of me also liked keeping in touch with him about the trip just in case I was doing something truly insane. For a couple of weeks, we followed roughly the same route through Peru with me a week behind having spent more time in Ecuador. So if Dustin came across some challenge that even he found difficult with the adventure bike and a full set of tools, perhaps I might have had second thoughts about attempting the same thing. But I never did, and in fact the one time he did send photos of a landslide ruined road that he and a group of four other bikers struggled to cross by lifting their bikes, it just made me more curious about the place. Although by the time I got there the road had been given a makeshift repair and I sailed across, still balancing on a mud construction only a metre wide next to a mountain slope, but no need to stop.

Dustin was camping the whole way, and after a couple of months in hospedajes (hotels), I was jealous, and keen to spend more time in the countryside. I didn't bring a tent for the same reason that I didn't bring tools. Staying in hotels or homes pushes you to interact with people and you learn much more about a place that way, but that can also be exhausting. I'd been meeting new people every day for months, and although you do get a lot of alone time on the bike, you're constantly concentrating on the road. It's not the same as finding a peaceful spot in the countryside to pitch a tent and just enjoy the silence and nature, seeing sunset and sunrise, breathing clean air. So when Dustin told me that he wanted to reduce his pack weight for the flight home and offered me his excellent Kelty tent, I couldn't resist. Other than a broken door zip which I later sewed shut because it already had two doors which seemed a bit redundant, the thing was perfect. And from then on I was completely free to ride and stop wherever I wanted, even if there was no village, although I didn't camp all the time, just when I found some beautiful area that I wanted to enjoy. At this point I also realised that I'd been packing very loosely because the tent, plus a new sleeping bag and airbed, all fitted inside my backpack. It was a bit stuffed after that and the bike's handling and balance changed, but not too much.

Dustin and I bought some one litre beers and spent the rest of the evening talking about crumbling roads, mountains, landslides, tents, and police stops. He told me about all the wonderful things he'd seen in Southern Chile and Argentina including whales swimming as he cruised along the east coast back to BA. So I was super jealous and thoroughly regretted skipping that part until I remembered that if I had gone, we wouldn't be having this conversation. There's nothing worse than trying to tell an adventure story when the other person's already been to all the places you're talking about. They'll just be thinking about what they saw and won't be able to engage with your impressions. You might say 'And then I saw this incredible view from the top of the mountain!' and they'll be like 'OMG that's amazing' but in their mind they'll be remembering that it was a bit grey when they went and they stubbed their toe on a rock. It's the funniest thing ever to hear two people trying to tell each other an adventure story about places they've both been. It turns into a very precise conversation about specifically what each person did, just looking for some tiny difference that they can use to open up a proper conversation flow. Anyway all this talk about the south was making me even more excited about a future hiking trip down there so I definitely made the right decision.

Dustin packed up his bike and flew back to the US the next day and I continued on my way, heading north for the first time. At first I was just planning to check out Uruguay then return to BA, still clinging to the idea that I'd be ending the journey in Argentina before selling the bike and flying home. But my friend Jana called me from Sao Paulo in Brazil and took about three seconds to convince me that I should extend the journey by another few thousand kilometres. As I said earlier my heart was already on board, and I was really just waiting for a destination, so now I had one, Sao Paulo.

I've read a few travel journals before and they always talk a lot about food. I do have a few food stories and I'll get to them later. But I have to say that throughout Colombia, Ecuador, Bolivia, Chile, and even Argentina, maybe with the exception of one or two meals in Peru, and of course the meal with my friends in Santiago, I just wasn't that impressed with the food. It's probably because I've been spoiled by living in China for eight years. I could write a thousand-page book about the fabulous food in Beijing and there's a good reason why Chinese people are famous for annoying airport security staff with bags full of their own natural ingredients for cooking when they travel. But at this point I have to give a special mention to one of the best desserts I've ever eaten. An Alfajor, that I bought from a little shop in Buenos Aires full of the most delightful cakes you could imagine. Absolutely no airs and graces, and it wasn't so expensive, just a little shop full of cakes like you'd find in a Dickens novel attracting little kids to squash their faces up against the windows. Actually now I feel guilty because I forgot to mention another five-star dessert that I had in Medellin, Colombia. It was Dulce de Brevas in a classic Colombian cafe downtown. Syrupy figs, arequipe, and salty cheese. Not everyone's cup of tea, but I loved it.

Although it's possible to shoot straight over to Montevideo in Uruguay by boat, I didn't fancy that route and wanted to see more of rural Uruguay. So after leaving Buenos Aires, first I headed north along the border on the Argentinian side to Gualeguaychu. It was a nice little town, clean, well planned, with some local fruit markets and a butchers, a pleasant stopover before the border. I stayed at a place that I found on an overlander website that bikers use to find places with parking, and in the hostel I met an Argentinian biker just beginning a trip to Alaska. Judging from the photos online he's going to be taking a long time over the trip, because he's still in northern Argentina, but even if it takes him a year he still wouldn't be the most committed adventure motorcyclist that I've heard of. That would be a guy Dustin met in Mexico who'd been riding a tiny 125cc motorcycle around the world solo and unsupported for seven years. Although I suppose technically he's no longer an adventure motorcyclist, but a Traveller, in the Gypsy sense, just using a motorcycle to get around. I'm not sure where the dividing line is but presumably not less than six months around South America.

Anyway my Argentinian biker friend from the hostel was another well prepared adventure motorcyclist, and had a compressor, a small version of the one at the petrol station for pumping up tyres. And on the morning I was due to leave, as we were checking out the bikes, I noticed that my front tyre was looking a bit soft. At first I thought it was a slow puncture because a few days before I'd pulled quite a large stone out of the rubber, but then the guy asked me when was the last time I'd pumped up the tyres and I realised that in the few months I'd been on the road, I hadn't done it once. We hooked up the compressor and the tyre was solid again in a few seconds. My theory that as long as you talk with people that you meet on the road, that you can do this kind of trip with very little bike knowledge, was proven yet again, kind of. Next stop Uruguay.

7
The World Cup Stadium, but it's closed: URUGUAY

The Oriental Republic of Uruguay is the second smallest country in South America. About one third of the people live in the capital Montevideo, and 82% of the land area is focused on farming. It's a tiny country sandwiched between two giants, Brazil and Argentina, and its history reflects the competition between the two. Uruguay suffered under a brutal US supported military dictatorship in the 1970s, like most other countries in South America during Operation Condor, but this ended in 1985 and since then they've enjoyed a period of relative stability. Despite the fact that it's one of the richest nations per capita, Uruguay is famous for having *The World's Humblest Head of State*, Jose Mujica, who was President until 2015. He was a former guerrilla fighter who famously rejected the trappings of high office, and donated over 90% of his salary to charity. Uruguay is also famous for being probably the most liberal corner of South America, and was the first country in the world to semi-legalize Cannabis, but it's not quite the free for all that you might imagine.

Although I chose Gualeguaychu as a stopover before crossing the nearby border into Uruguay, I actually crossed at the Colon frontier post about a hundred kilometres further north after advice from the owner of the hostel. The road from there to my destination in Tacuarembo was a bit quicker she said, and in any case there wasn't much difference between any of the border posts linking Argentina and Uruguay, they were all quite efficient. I was heading to Tacuarembo because it's out in the middle of the great plains, about as far from Montevideo as you can get before you get close to the Brazilian border, and I really wanted to see more of Gaucho culture, the cowboys of South America.

Guachos are just as famous, and just as important to South American culture as Cowboys are in the US. They played a similar role, bridging the gap between static agricultural societies and nomadic hunter gatherers as they competed throughout the continent and today hold a similar position in rural society. The northern part of Argentina has a strong Gaucho culture too but when I saw that 80% of the land in Uruguay is given over to cattle related industries, I decided to head straight there, and I wasn't disappointed. Well that's not quite true, I was very disappointed when they told me at the border post that not only was vehicle insurance legally required, but that it wasn't sold there at the border. I'd need to go more than ten kilometres further into Uruguay to a bank office in a nearby town that sold insurance, then come back for the bike. What should have been a twenty-minute border crossing turned into a wasted afternoon as I waited for a taxi, went on a magical mystery tour of the surrounding countryside with the grafting taxi driver, then got pushed from pillar to post as I tried to find a bank that would accept international cards, because the insurance agent would only accept payment in cash. Not the best start to my journey in Uruguay, but it could have been worse and I was on my way in a couple of hours.

The road to Tacuarembo was pleasant enough, and very straightforward to navigate, but like most of the ride across Argentina, there's really not much to write in a journal. The country is incredibly flat, the roads are perfect, and there are very few towns, so the most exciting thing to report is that I met my first real local Gaucho ranchers as they we're riding along the road and I was taking a rest. We only said a brief hello though, and the look on their faces said 'shouldn't you be riding a twisting mountain road somewhere in Colombia or Peru?' or so it seemed to me. I arrived in Tacuarembo in the mid-afternoon, and found a working farm with a boarding house to spend the night. The house was setup for groups, and had a large kitchen, dining room, and comfortable lounge with an open fireplace, but as I was the only guest I had it all to myself. The farm had some cows and chickens, but was a small holding and surrounded by much bigger cattle ranches, so later in the afternoon I took a long walk around the area. It wasn't quite the Wild West, but it was still great to watch cowboys on horseback in the fields taking care of the land. As I walked back to the farm, the animals who lived there formed a greeting party so I was joined by one large Alsatian, three collies, a black puppy, and a cat, and they walked with me all the way back to the gate. I spent the rest of the early evening chatting with the farm manager before heading back to my spacious accommodation and settling down with some hot chocolate in front of the open fire. I did take out my Spanish book with good intentions, but did more snoozing than reading until around 9pm, then went to bed.

The next morning after an organic breakfast with the farmer and his wife talking about living and working in the countryside, and dreaming about packing up and moving to this remote and beautiful part of the world, I went into town on a mission to buy a belt. But not just any belt, I wanted a real Gaucho/cowboy belt, and not from just any tourist shop, I wanted a real gaucho shop that served real gaucho customers. It was easy, the farmer told me about a corner shop where he bought boots, and Tacuarembo is so small that it was simple to find. In amongst the spurs, the knives and the leather boots, I saw a rugged black leather belt with blue canvas details that was perfect.

Travellers are always chasing authentic experiences, and purchases, but everything stands in their way. Unless you're a full on explorer you're probably following some kind of route that people have followed before, and if the places are attractive then people will have noticed and put up infrastructure like hotels, restaurants and shops. The facilities then draw you in to the tourist web, because they're the easiest to find, and often dominate the places that you want to see. It's easy enough to step off the tracks if you really want to of course, but you're stepping into the unknown, and by that I don't just mean dangerous, much worse, it could be boring.

Tacuarembo treads the fine line well, and although it's the main city in this part of Uruguay it doesn't feel touristic at all. The people are warm and friendly, and when I noticed that my motorcycle drive-chain was getting a bit loose again, I looked for someone to help. Luckily there was a guy walking out of a shop wearing a motorcycle helmet, so I asked him if there was a motorcycle mechanic nearby. He not only confirmed that there was, but took me there himself, he knew the mechanic and we had a lively conversation about

Tacuarembo, motorcycles, and my journey, before he tightened up the chain. I offered some cash but he refused so I said I'd put his garage on Instagram instead, I didn't tell him that I've only got eighty followers.

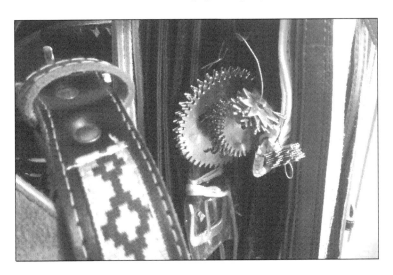

From Tacuarembo I headed south to Montevideo and stopped off in Durazno. I really didn't fancy another city hostel, and instead found a spot in a forest campsite just outside town. Waking up in the dancing morning light of the forest and listening to the sound of birds singing, was the perfect way to start the next day. And then it was another completely uneventful two hundred kilometre ride on smooth asphalt roads down to the capital city, Montevideo. I arrived shortly after lunchtime, and settled into a place near the port.

The only reason that I'd come to Montevideo was to see the Estadio Centenario, the stadium that hosted the first FIFA Football World Cup in July 1930. The world looked at bit different back then and the USA and Yugoslavia made it to the semi-finals while Uruguay beat Argentina 4 – 2 to win the Cup, watched by seventy thousand people. Since then football has grown to become an integral part of world culture and so the Centenario has become an important historical monument. But it's also a living monument and the Uruguay national team still play there, in fact they're almost unbeatable in their home stadium as Brazil have learned over the years. If you're looking for an authentic travel experience, then the Centenario would be hard to beat. There's almost no touristic infrastructure built around the stadium and they've left it in the same basic format as it was then, no fancy new stands, covers, or shopping malls, just a plain concrete stadium, and a little museum.

Unfortunately, there wasn't a match on that week, at least no internationals, so I couldn't watch a game. Instead I settled for just a regular stadium visit, so I could try to imagine what it must have felt like to be there in the stadium, during the First World Cup. But double unfortunately, and my authentic travel experience was starting to get a bit too authentic now, I forgot that it was Sunday. All of South America closes on Sundays, no matter how historically significant the monument, so the huge metal gates of the stadium entrance were shut tight. I was planning to stay in Montevideo a bit longer and come back the next day, but then I noticed an open door as I walked round the side. Nobody was around, so I went inside to take a look at the pitch. There's not really an awful lot to see in a football stadium, but it was fun just to sit and imagine the cheering Uruguayans with tears of joy in their eyes as they watched their team win. Blissfully unaware that it would be their neighbours to the north, Brazil, that would go on to dominate the competition.

The next day I continued up the east coast and arrived in Punta del Este, a leafy green town that feels more like Germany than South America with thatched roofed houses and a cool climate. It's actually right next to the best beach in Uruguay so overall it's a beautiful place, and I spent a few days relaxing by the sea before continuing on again to Punta del Diablo. Again another decent beachside town, and fantastic if you're into surfing, but I only stayed one day before getting back on the road again, and heading north.

I liked Uruguay a lot, it's the most developed corner of the continent and would be a comfortable place to live, but it's in a funny sort of location. Buenos Aires over the river is a far bigger and more cosmopolitan city than Montevideo, and Brazil up the coast has far better beaches. I got to see an important part of South American culture when I visited Gaucho country, and I went to the Estadio Centenario, but other than that the country's pretty flat, and there's not much to see as you ride along the beautifully maintained, and very straight, highways. The country is also tiny so it took less than two weeks to cross, and before I knew it, I was already racing north into Brazil.

The border process was again quite straightforward, just the usual questions and documentation. But they did spend a long time emphasising that I couldn't sell the bike in Brazil, without going through the long and expensive Permanent Import Process. It's the same in most places in South America, and the idea that you can just buy a bike in one country then sell it at the end of your journey is only true for very specific, and very popular, routes. Most adventure motorcyclists either ship the bike in and out, a very expensive option, or sell to another foreign traveller and in that case the new owner needs to leave the country before the temporary import permit expires. Even that's not legal everywhere, but works on the route down to Ushuaia in Argentina because it's super popular, and there's a good chance that a biker will be looking to head back north within the time window. If on the other hand you want to sell to a local, then you need to go through the process of permanently importing the vehicle to the country. It's a very big deal, not always possible, and often costs more than the bike is worth. Neither of these options were suitable for me, but in any case, the Apache had long since paid for itself. The cost of renting even a small engined motorcycle in South America would have been around 40-50 dollars per day, and I was enjoying incredibly low fuel and maintenance costs. I did intend to sell the Apache at some point but it was a problem that could wait, and for now I told the border guards that I'd be riding back to Uruguay in a few weeks, but I don't think they believed me.

8
Cuidado, boa viagem:
BRAZIL

At over three million square miles in area, Brazil is three times bigger than the next biggest country in South America. It has borders with ten countries from Venezuela and Colombia in the Caribbean, to Argentina on the Southern Cone. In fact, the only South American countries that it doesn't have borders with are Chile and Ecuador. The inequality is also huge, and at Gini 53.3 it's one of the most unequal countries in the world. It's second largest city, Rio de Janeiro, was officially the capital of the whole Portuguese Empire for a while, before the territory gained independence in 1822, and since then it's flirted between democratic and authoritarian rule. They didn't need outside help to get a Military Regime in the 1970s, because they already had one, but US interference ensured that the brutality continued, and Brazil didn't recover democratic governance until the 1980s. Given that they've recently elected a far right President who admires the old military rulers, the story may not be over yet.

The six hundred kilometre ride from Punta Del Este in Uruguay to Porto Alegre in Brazil took nine hours including the border crossing, and I arrived at night, only to spend the next couple of hours searching for a hotel. The two decent looking ones that I'd found online were both closed, so I ended up asking around, and in the end found a beauty, nice area, parking, and a good atmosphere. The only downside was that before I realised there was parking inside, I had to deal with the dodgy guy running the on-street parking racket outside. I've come across his type before and he was all 'this is a very high crime area' and 'that is a really cool looking bike, how much did you pay for it?' We agreed that I'd come back later once I'd settled in to the hotel, and he gave me a look like death when I reappeared after a couple of hours and pushed the bike inside the gate.

To say that Porto Alegre, Happy Harbour in English, is a gay friendly place would be quite a major understatement. The city has been famous for decades as a hub for progressive thought, and more than half the couples that I saw on the street near my hostel on the first evening, were same-sex. Not every place in Brazil is so tolerant though, and the country is struggling to define the right approach. This is perfectly illustrated by the fact that in February 2019 the President, Jair Bolsonaro, at a time when he was curiously both condemning, and also supporting homosexuality in Brazil, took leave of his senses. He shared on his social media account, an account followed by millions of people of all ages, a graphic sex act between two men. It wasn't a hack, he really did that, The President, and admitted it, although he said he only did it to show how bad it was, fascinating country.

Porto Alegre is also unfortunately quite violent, as are most port cities in South America, but Porto Alegre is exceptional and it's currently the 43rd most violent city in the world. So despite the city's name, a good part of the population is probably not very Happy at all right now. I only stayed one night, and in the evening went for a drink in a place called Soho with a Brazilian girl from the hostel. The police presence was stifling, but I also got my first taste of Brazilian style bars, and the music was incredible. MPB (Musica Popular Brasileira) is so famous that it has its own acronym and the mix of bossa nova, samba and jazz is infectious. I like Salsa too but after four months living in Colombia and three months on the road, it was starting to get a bit repetitive. Also being rubbish at Salsa dancing always put me off a bit.

After shooting through tiny Uruguay in less than two weeks, the sheer size of Brazil was beginning to feel overwhelming. I'd already travelled over 500km from the southern border to reach Porto Alegre, and Sao Paulo which on the map looks like it's way in the south of this giant country, was still another 1500km away. Luckily it wouldn't all be in a straight line though, and my next stop was the Serra do Rio do Rastro, a mountain range about 350km north of Porto Alegre near the Atlantic coast. I would be crossing it on the famous Route SC-390 which is about as good as they come for motorcycling, or it would be if it wasn't also as good as they come for caravans and SUVs.

SC-390 starts off as an unremarkable offshoot from the main highway where the most interesting thing that I saw was a guy riding a small motorcycle very fast, lying face down with his legs pushed out behind him like Superman. But then it gives you a hint of what's to come as you pass through broad plains and traditional villages, and begin to see the mountain range in the distance. There's a section made of polished cobblestones that is nice to look at, but tough on the suspension and not the best for grip, and then there's one of the bendiest sections of road that I've ever ridden. It's so curvy, that it's listed as one of the most dangerous roads in the world.

I've read that overall there are about three hundred curves on SC-390 with an average gradient of almost 10%, but that seems to me like an underestimate. It's a very, very challenging road to ride but you get rewarded almost constantly as you pass wide canyons, cliffs, and mountain views, one after another. The area is prone to fog so you need to be lucky with the weather, but on a good day you can see all the way to the Atlantic Ocean. When I was there it was a real mix, foggy, then clear, then foggy again, but I got more than enough of the views to make it worth the effort. Traffic is the only downside, and you meet the traffic just about the same time that the good bit starts. It's super annoying to come through miles of straight highway seeing barely a moped, then hit a caravan car-park once the mountains get interesting. The traffic is also one of the reasons SC-390 has an infamous reputation. To sit behind an SUV for two hours as it slowly negotiates the curves is just not an option and your judgement on the acceptable amount of space for overtaking gets worse and worse. I must admit to a couple of close calls as I leaned in and passed in a way that I probably would not have on another road.

At the top of the Serra is a well-developed viewpoint with cafes, shops, a police station, and a ton of other motorcyclists to share your experience. If you look hard enough you'll also find, a few hundred metres down the road, one of the most beautiful camping sites that you could wish for. Down a dirt track into the national park area, past the guardhouse and on the right. It's a working farm with a small hillside surrounded by trees where you can pitch tents, and that overlooks the mountain plateau, and I was joined on the hill by a couple from Sao Paulo, and a biker from Porto Alegre riding a Harley Davidson. The fact that he'd managed to get his heavy Harley over a few kilometres of rocks and dirt road was impressive enough, but the fact that he'd ridden the thing until the front tyre was completely bald was just amazing. Definitely not the midlife-crisis, sitting in a garage all week and only ridden on Sundays, fate that awaits most Harley Davidsons. And I learned another thing about Southern Brazil on the farm, that you can pay for things in US dollars and Uruguayan pesos, which is what I had to do when I realised that I'd run out of Brazilian Reales and there was no ATM.

The whole area is just stunning and early the next morning I woke up at dawn with the birds, and set off for a morning ride through the national park, and then on to explore the nearby Canyon da Ronda. You can't ride directly into the canyon unfortunately but it's only a ten-minute walk from the road, and what a reward for a short walk. Standing at the top you have a view directly down through two vertical mountains with vultures and eagles soaring overhead. It was so quiet that you couldn't hear a thing except the loud swoosh of the eagles as they passed. Another one of those places that you just want to sit and look at for hours, and I would have, had I not been rudely interrupted by a loud gang of Brazilian motorcycle hooligans in leather waistcoats. Luckily they were just taking selfies on the mountaintop, the motorcycle equivalent of a coach tour I guess, and after a short time they left me in peace to enjoy the view.

They did also remind me that I had places to go though, so I didn't stay much longer and when I walked back to the Apache the whole lot of them were still there. They were standing around wide-eyed and open-mouthed looking at the 160cc Colombia registered motorcycle with a backpack tied to the wheel arch. I told them a bit about the journey as they were putting on layer after layer of Harley branded motorcycle gear, before I got on the bike and headed back down to the main road. Colombia was now 5000km away in a straight line and almost 20,000km away by road.

My next stop was Florianopolis on the Atlantic Coast, which is famous for having some of the best beaches in Southern Brazil. But it was raining cats and dogs when I arrived so I didn't stay long, and after a couple of days I headed to Curitiba. There I got to eat home-made Chinese food for the first time in over a year for which I'm very grateful to Chen, the Chinese lady that I met in the hostel, who was bravely travelling Brazil alone for a few weeks before heading back to Beijing for a new job. The food was delicious, and even the traditional Brazilian meat buffet that I had the next day couldn't compete with authentic *xihongshichaojidan*, and *wuhuarou*. The stories Chen told me later on about missed buses, 3am arrivals in dark city centres, and dodgy guys on the street, made me think that my own journey was a real walk in the park. We kept in touch though and she did eventually make it back to China, safe and sound.

By this time, I'd been in Brazil for about ten days, and had long since used up the pure gasoline that I filled up with just before crossing the border from Uruguay. The

Apache was now running on Brazilian style Gasolina Comun, which contains 25% sugarcane ethanol. I knew that biofuels were common in Brazil, but at first I thought that I was still choosing normal petrol, because there was a much cheaper Ethanol Fuel option at the pumps. It was temptingly cheap, but 100% ethanol might have been going a bit too far even for the indestructible Apache. Brazil is the world leader in the use of bio fuels and although the USA produces more base product, they make it mostly from corn which is less efficient, and only use it in light blends of up to 10%. Here in Brazil they've taken advantage of a strong domestic sugarcane industry to adapt the whole fuel system to cater for richer blends, and there are far more pumps.

Once I'd realised how much ethanol I was putting into the engine, I started to get a bit concerned about performance and damage to the bike. Brazilian engines are modified to take the heavier biofuel blends, but the Apache was designed for use in Colombia where they only have up to E10 (10% blend). I had noticed that the acceleration was not quite as sharp as it was before, and that there was a tiny bit of chugging at certain engine speeds, but otherwise I didn't think that it was too bad. So I continued using E25 (25% ethanol) all the way through Brazil, with the occasional splurge on a luxury con-aditiva blend with cleaning agents. In the end though, it probably did do some damage, because I had to replace the carburetor when I reached Boa Vista in the north at around 27,000km. The replacement was super cheap though and in fact the reduced fuel price more than made up the difference. So there you go, when I said that I didn't have much bike knowledge, I really wasn't joking. I didn't even know what fuel I was putting in the bike and I still managed to survive, so a motorcycle journey can't be that difficult, can it?

My next stop was without doubt one of the most beautiful places I've ever been, the Ilha do Mel, or Honey Island, just off the Atlantic coast of Brazil. It's a gorgeous place with fine sandy beaches, gentle water currents and, at least during the time that I was there, perfect weather. I couldn't take the bike unfortunately but the boat transport was all quite straightforward. I found a boat hire place that would store my bike for a few days at about half the rate of the expensive port-side carparks, then bought a ferry ticket, and was on the boat within an hour. The campsite where I pitched the tent was ideally located, just off the beach but in a small forest to give some shade from the hot sun. There was one problem though, mosquitoes, millions of them, and they attacked me as soon as I started putting up the tent. I quickly setup the inner compartment, attached the outer shell then sprayed the entrance, and myself, with repellent. It all took less than ten minutes but I still came away with red polka-dot arms. Spraying the entrance of the tent is a genius trick and it works really well to keep the mosquitoes away from the door while you open it to get in and out. That way you avoid the problem of a lucky mosquito sliding in just because he was hanging out near the zip. Once I was inside the tent I happily got on with sorting out my stuff in peace while the hungry mosquitoes buzzed around outside.

The next morning, I woke up at dawn and went straight over to the beach. I'd been for a swim and a walk with another traveller the evening before, but I wanted to see just how beautiful the place would be in the morning light. Actually that evening walk was quite interesting because I found out that the lighthouse on Ilha do Mel was built by a Scottish company. I imagined for a moment the guy sitting in a cold office, on a damp winter's morning on Main Street in Glasgow, being told that he'd have to hot-foot it to Honey Island off the coast of Brazil to build a lighthouse. 'Damn my terrible luck, oh the things I do for this company.' was the dour response, I'm sure. The morning light didn't disappoint, and after a quick run I dived into the still cool sea for a long swim, then stayed in the water for a while watching the sun rise further and feeling the heat build. The best thing about the whole experience was that there wasn't a single other person on the beach, I had it completely to myself. The same was true for the ferry, and the shops and there were never any queues. Travelling off-season certainly has its challenges, especially the rain, but it has its advantages too. Next stop Sao Paulo.

Sao Paulo is absolutely huge. And remember I didn't just fly here straight from a small village in England, I've lived in Beijing for years so I know what I'm talking about. Whereas London is a packed city centre surrounded by far less populated regions, Sao Paulo is surrounded by urban sprawl and in total the built-up area has a population of 30 million people. The city throbs with the energy and hustle of all these people, but it also suffers from a very high crime rate, and in May 2006 Sao Paulo experienced the worst peacetime violence that Brazil has ever seen. Over 150 people including forty police officers were killed during a period of just a few days, and in order to stop the violence the city had to bring in over 100,000 police officers from across the state. The tragedy mainly affected people and businesses trying to get on with their lives in the less developed districts, and it's unlikely that a traveller would get caught up. But it's definitely still important to take care when motorcycling through cities in Brazil.

My offline GPS assisted map was working like a dream as usual, so I easily found my friend Jana's apartment which was close to a famous bus station. And after a couple of hours' rest, we went out to explore the city on the Apache. Sao Paulo is indeed huge, but surprisingly easy to navigate and the traffic flows far better than in some of the other cities that I'd travelled through. The traffic was heavy, but at least almost everyone was obeying the rules and heading in the right direction. We rode along Paulista avenue, over bridges, and along city parks and gardens admiring the twinkling lights of the skyscrapers as the temperature went down along with the sun. Then we found an excellent little cafe, and stopped for some dinner before picking up ingredients for making chocolate Brigadeiros. It's a Brazilian speciality, which basically consists of melting down condensed milk with cocoa powder and sugar before setting it into small round chocolates. Then we gorged on them while watching a film.

The next day I had to go into town to buy a screw because the original one had worked its way loose from the exhaust cover. I say *worked its way loose*, I suppose in reality it was greatly helped on its way by the repeated falling over but in any case, it needed a new screw. We found a mechanic specialising in Indian bikes on the map, and off we went. Unfortunately, I got a bit lost, again, and we ended up in a rundown area that was home to some of the unluckiest of the unlucky of Sao Paulo's population. When I stopped to ask for directions Jana almost broke my arm with her right hand while simultaneously, furiously, pointing further up the street with her left, she didn't even want me to stop there. Sao Paulo is clearly not taking good care of its own people and to let a neighbourhood get to that state is shocking in such a wealthy place. The next street we went down had four military police vehicles and around twenty armed officers standing around, responding to what, we didn't find out.

We eventually found the mechanic and it was great to learn that he was from Paraguay, so I could finally communicate with someone in Spanish. He didn't have the exact same screw, but said that he had plenty with the same thread diameter and fitted one for free. We stayed and chatted with him for a while as he fixed a couple of other bikes, and I asked him about selling the Apache in Sao Paulo. Bad news, there was no way someone would accept a Colombia registered bike in SP without a very heavy discount. Once you add in the complication of registering for permanent import, and paying the high import taxes that they'd told me about at the border, the bike was worthless. 'However...' he said 'you should be able to sell without any of those problems...in Ciudad del Este, Paraguay' and that's how my journey got extended yet again. Jana and I went home and finished off the brigadeiro chocolates, then went out to see some more of Sao Paulo's famously vibrant nightlife. The next morning after breakfast, we said goodbye, before I got back on the bike and set off towards the highway heading west, to Paraguay.

The southern part of Brazil is actually quite narrow compared to the immense north, so the route to Paraguay is only around a thousand kilometres. But that still means at least one stop along the way. So I looked at the map and saw that there was a city called Londrina in the state of Parana, a city named after London that was founded by British people. Actually I didn't know that at the time and only chose the city because it was half way between Sao Paulo and the border, but it was a nice coincidence. In any case although it was founded by the British, it was the Japanese and Germans who really built up the city, so I'm not sure there's anything *London* about it anymore.

145

As I raced along through the terra roxa (red earth) that characterises this incredibly fertile part of Brazil, I couldn't help thinking that the hills and trees looked exactly like a part of Bedfordshire, England that I know well. Just north of my home town, Luton, in a beautiful area of the Chiltern Hills. The ground there is more white chalk than red earth, but otherwise the flora looked just the same. Ancient sturdy trees, fields separated by low wooden fences, and rolling hills planted with flowering crops. Then just as I was daydreaming about whether it was the British settlers that made it look that way, or if they settled there because it reminded them of home, a huge 4x4 driven at speed passed me so close that my bike swerved. The heavy truck skidded to a halt a few hundred metres down the road, and two men got out. They both drew guns, and pointed them somewhere between my head and the road between us. I slowed down as fast as I could without skidding, and quickly flipped up my visor to make eye contact. They motioned me to pull over, and I parked up behind the 4x4. It wasn't the first armed police stop of my journey, nor even my first guns-drawn police stop in Brazil. But the speed that it happened, and the look on the officers faces before I flipped the visor, was something different. This was not the usual calm, random check and I had no doubt that they would have shot me dead if I hadn't stopped. They probably wouldn't have, I hope, but it wasn't something that I was willing to test, even though I've ridden straight through hundreds of checkpoints on the route without even looking at the guards. Once I had pulled over I raised my hands high above the handlebars until the policemen holstered their weapons, although one of them kept a hand on the pistol butt, and I said 'Buenos dias' I'd forgotten that I was still in Brazil and said hello in Spanish, rather than the usual Portuguese

'Bom dia'. And I was hoping that it wouldn't be another little black mark against me, along with whatever had made them pull me over. But to my relief the slightly older looking officer responded in fluent Spanish, now looking much more relaxed, and asked me for my documents.

'Are you Colombian?' he said,

'No, British.' I replied.

'Soo, why the Colombian number plate?'

'Because I bought the bike there, and rode it here through nine countries.'

[long pause] 'On your own?'

'Yes.'

[another long pause] 'Are you insane?'

'It's possible.'

And for the next twenty minutes I took the officers through the details of my journey and how I came to be in this part of Brazil, while they looked at me in disbelief. I completely emptied the entire contents of my bags and pockets onto the road and took out not only the usual passport, license, and ownership documents, but my import documents and insurance too. Then satisfied finally, that I was, who I said I was, but clearly disappointed from not having caught a master criminal, the two officers said I could go. Feeling a bit more relaxed now and having got all my stuff back in the bag, I asked them why they'd stopped me, but they didn't answer. As they got back into the car the older officer turned and said, 'Cuidado, boa viagem' (take care, and have a good journey). Perhaps the reason for the stop was just because I was on the road that leads directly to the Paraguayan border, which was why they spoke fluent Spanish. They have issues both with stolen bikes, and general cross−border criminal shenanigans in the region so fair enough, a Colombian plate was probably worth a stop.

Eventually I did make it to Londrina (Little London), but the people weren't wearing bowler hats and carrying umbrellas like I expected, and nobody said 'Sorry' when I deliberately bumped into them on the pavement, so I quickly moved on. There was one more place in this part of Southern Brazil that I couldn't miss before I crossed into Paraguay, and that was Foz de Iguazu, one of the most impressive waterfalls in the world. Well I say waterfall, it's actually a whole national park full of hundreds of waterfalls, that spans the border between Brazil and Argentina. And on the way there, I passed another milestone on the journey, 20,000km. I spent my first night in Foz de Iguazu in a hostel before going to visit the Iguazu national park the next morning. And it was only then that I discovered a wonderful camp site less than five hundred metres from the ticket office. The expensive parking near the entrance, which was the same price whether you were driving a truck or a moped, cost more than a night on the camp site, so I decided to move. I went back to the hostel to check out early, then rode to the campsite and found a spot under some trees at the back of the field. The walk back to the ticket office took less than ten minutes and I had a ticket in my hand within another five. Sometimes travelling is almost too easy. Then in the queue for the bus that takes you to the actual falls, I met Alexie who was from Cambodia, and we carried on up to the falls together.

Foz de Iguazu is a major tourist destination and as you might expect the whole experience was very well managed. There's a walking route along the mountainside overlooking the falls that is just hard enough to get you breathing deeply, but not so much that you'd quit. And the falls that you see along the way are just impressive enough to keep you amazed, but not so much that it ruins the finale. The downside of this is that you start taking millions of pictures as soon as you step off the bus and see the first set of four waterfalls cascading down the mountainside. Walk a few hundred metres and you see the same falls but from a closer and better angle, and click click click go the cameras and phones again. Another few hundred metres and there's a much closer one where you can feel the spray. You pass a few more viewing points of ever increasing beauty and just as your camera's about to run out of memory, there it is, the huge curtain of water that is the main waterfall. The viewing platform goes right out over the water flow, right into the spray, so everyone spends a few minutes at the start putting on their waterproof jackets, and no doubt clearing a bit of space on their memory cards.

Iguazu is impressive and in the middle of an especially ferocious rainy season it was even more so. Heavy torrents of water poured over the brink and looked like they were frozen in mid-air as they hung together tightly before getting torn apart by the air resistance as they accelerated downwards. The sheer amount of water moving underneath the platform was breath-taking and if you just stood still and watched for a few seconds it literally made you feel dizzy. The falls continued out from under the platform and fell again another hundred metres down to their final resting place in the river that ran between the mountains. The sound was overwhelming and the roar of the water as it rushed past the rocks was immense, I couldn't hear myself think let alone hear Alexie when she asked me to take a picture. Obviously the most important thing when you're in such an awe inspiring place is to get the perfect Instagram selfie, and while I went with a cool pensive look out across the water, Alexie went with a classic smile. Then we went for a coffee, wind battered and soaked to the skin despite our waterproof jackets.

In the evening I met up with her and another traveller from her hostel and we went out for dinner, then to a couple of bars, before I rode back to the campsite alone. And as I approached the ticket office, and turned on to the dirt track that went to the campsite entrance, I realised just how dark the whole place was. I've mentioned before about the Apache's less than impressive headlight, and I could barely see anything as I crawled and slid along the muddy path back to the site. When I finally found my tent at the back of the field, sitting there in complete darkness, not a soul around, I started to imagine all the creepy crawlies and bigger things that might emerge from the forest during the night. I slept like a log though, and the morning was glorious. I was again woken by dancing beams of sunlight streaming through tree branches as my tent began to warm up. Then the birds sang me a little tune while I ate my breakfast, and I was soon on my way to Paraguay.

9
Kjenn jie noch Plautdietsch?: PARAGUAY

Paraguay is commonly known as the Corazon de Sudamerica (Heart of South America) because of its position right in the middle of the continent. Like Uruguay it's pinched between the two giants Argentina to the South, and Brazil to the East, and in 1864 it went to war with both of them, at the same time, with devastating consequences. The Paraguayan War was the most brutal ever recorded in the history of South America and over 70% of the adult male population of Paraguay died, while they lost over 1/3rd of their territory. The next time Paraguay went to war they chose a slightly more realistic opponent, Bolivia, and took control over most of The Chaco region. The expected oil resources from The Chaco never materialised, but that doesn't matter because Paraguay now generates so much electricity from hydro that it exports much more than it uses. Paraguay was also the location for some of the largest Jesuit Missions built by Christian missionaries as they tried to convert the local Guarani population. The Missions have been lovingly restored, and are now one of the main reasons to visit.

It's an amazing history, but I didn't know any of that when I crossed the border from Brazil. I was really only interested in seeing the capital Asuncion, and selling the Apache for a better price than the zero dollars I would have gotten in Sao Paulo. And I thought I was going to sell it within two minutes of entering the country, right at the border post, when I found that all the customs guys where big bike fans. They were asking me all about the displacement, brakes, spare parts and everything, and I found out that although the TVS version is not available in Paraguay they had seen a very similar bike under different branding. It was a much more pleasant experience than I'd had at other border posts and they were super friendly, but the casual nature of it all was a bit concerning. Initially I had gone into an official looking office to the right of the border crossing, but was told to check with one of the ten or so non-uniformed men hanging around outside. The first guy I checked with pointed me to another guy, and he pointed me to yet another who took me into a small unmarked wooden cabin. He pulled out a wad of template forms, so that was good at least we were starting to look a bit more formal now, and then proceeded to take out and eat from a huge plate of empanadas. He did offer me one though, so I can't really complain.

Then all the other guys started coming in for empanadas and some of them sat down to watch for a few minutes while eating. Once I started telling the story of my journey the visitors began staying longer, and after twenty minutes the office was full. Six or so empanada eating guys laughing and joking about leaving their wives and riding a motorcycle to Colombia. It was a fun conversation but as I said, the casual nature of it did make me wonder how much control the senior customs officials had over the process, and if it might all result in some unexpected special fees. It didn't, and I was soon on my way to navigate through the chaos that is Ciudad del Este, and out onto the highway. By this time, it was still early so I decided to push on all the way to Asuncion, the capital of Paraguay, 350km to the west, which is actually quite a nice place for a capital city, and feels smaller and more laid back than others. But almost as soon as I arrived it started to rain, and when it rains in Paraguay, it really rains. Torrents that were equal to anything I'd seen in the amazon jungle in Peru started to fall on the city and it got so bad that the road outside the hotel turned into a flowing river. We checked on the internet to understand when on earth it would stop, but it went on for the whole evening, and most of the next day. Given that I was stuck inside with nothing much to do, I started to read a bit about Paraguay.

Paraguay is not a common destination for tourists, and while it's also not a remote backwater it's unlikely to feature on most people's travel itineraries. Argentina yes, Brazil yes, Chile yes, maybe even Bolivia or Uruguay depending on the route, but Paraguay sits right in the middle of them all. There's just no reason to pass through, and no Machu Picchu, Buenos Aires or Salar de Uyuni to bring people in. But as I read more about the history of the country and in particular the northern part of Paraguay, I was captivated.

Earlier I wrote about the massive war that killed off half the population and the subsequent smaller war with Bolivia over a region called The Chaco. Well it turns out that during and after that period, the Chaco region was populated not only by native Guarani, and mestizos of mixed native and Spanish descent. But also by light skinned people of German and Russian descent, the Mennonites, who did not speak Spanish, but a dialect of low German. And the really incredible thing is that they

153

are still there today, still working the farms, still speaking German, and still looking like they just stepped off the boat from Friesland. The reason that their culture has remained so strong for over a century is partly related to the Menno religious foundations, and partly due to geopolitics. I know I'm supposed to be writing a fast paced story about a motorcycle journey, but forgive me a few paragraphs about this history, it's truly fascinating.

Mennonites are a Christian religious group, they are pacifists and believe that the one, and only route to heaven is through hard, lifelong devotion to agricultural work. This belief is so strong that many Mennonites don't own mobile phones or drive cars, choosing instead to use the same horse and buggy contraptions that were tearing up the dirt highways a century ago. Their absolute conviction to pacifism led them into conflict with both Catholic, and Protestant societies in Europe that wanted them to fight in the countless, pointless wars that ravaged the continent from the 1600s to the 1800s. So they began moving.

The Mennonite branch that ended up in Paraguay moved first around Europe through Germany and Russia, then when Russia introduced military conscription, to Canada. Other branches moved back through Germany and across to Argentina and Bolivia along with thousands of Nazis after the World Wars. The Nazis mostly changed their name to Juan and got jobs improving the manufacturing techniques of Argentina, while the Mennonites formed colonies across the region. Unfortunately for the Paraguayan Mennonites as they would come to be known, Canada then decided that everyone had to speak English in school, so they started looking for a new place to go. And as luck would have it, just at the same time, Paraguay was getting nervous about Bolivian activities on its Northern border, because the Chaco region was a sparsely populated arid desert and difficult to defend. There were rumours of enormous oil and gas deposits under the surface that needed protecting, and so the Mennonites made Paraguay an offer.

They would populate the Chaco, and using highly efficient farming techniques developed over decades, turn it into a fertile area that could sustain a local military presence. This would allow Paraguay to defend the Northern border, and potentially also feed the rest of the country. In return the Mennonites would not be asked to betray their pacifist beliefs and fight in any future wars, and they would be left to govern their own affairs. The Mennonites, being Mennonites, were not lying nor even joking, in fact they probably underestimated what was possible in the Chaco and over the decades they turned it into one of the most productive regions in South America.

Once I'd read this history there was no way I was not going to The Chaco. It was a 450km ride north, but I was at the end of my journey in any case, and one long trek from there back to Ciudad del Este to sell the bike would not be the end of the world. I started asking about the possible routes into the region, and the weather and road conditions in the north, but the feedback wasn't great. First of all, the Chaco is about as remote as a populated place can get. It's not desert any more but the vast estates that now cover the region are immense, and you can go 200km along a straight road without so much as a village to get supplies. There are homesteads dotted here and there but I wouldn't fancy testing out the Mennonites pacifist beliefs by knocking on their door at all hours. The roads are also a problem and although at some point some intelligent person did manage to get them covered in asphalt, they may have underestimated the forces of nature that would attack them. In places there are long stretches of mud, enormous pot holes, and fragmented piles of asphalt where the roads used to be.

All this would not necessarily have been a huge problem, the Apache had seen worse, but then there was the rain. It hadn't stopped since I arrived and I found out later that it had been going on since March, two months before. My relatively dry run from the border had been pure luck, and we were hearing on the news that the Chaco had had much heavier rain than even Asuncion. The Paraguay river had been completely overwhelmed and the entire area was now underwater displacing more than 40,000 people and closing the main, the only, road linking the region to the capital. There was a Brazilian couple in the hostel who had been delayed over a week waiting for the waters to recede so they could continue their cycling tour of Paraguay and Bolivia. I joined them waiting, and eating, and reading even more about the Mennonites.

The rains stopped in Asuncion later that evening and the next day we heard on the news that the main highway had reopened. The Brazilian couple decided to stay put because although the road was technically open, the whole area was still experiencing floods and things could change at any moment. They were also familiar with the after-effects of flooding and expected the road to be covered in sediment and mud. Not the kind of thing you want to ride through, but also not enough to stop me getting on with my journey so the next morning I set off on the long haul north. But before I left I went to pay the hostel, or rather ask if I had already paid because usually you pay upfront but I couldn't remember handing over any money. Unfortunately, they didn't keep a record either so we had a bit of a problem, which was only solved when the manager asked me if I wanted to flip a coin for it. I lost that gamble and paid up, then prayed that I'd win the next gamble on the weather as I headed north to Filandia.

The first two hundred kilometres out of Asuncion were fine. It was raining as usual but nothing major and the roads were in good condition. The only problem I came across was a local protest where the protesters had blocked Ruta 9, and were not letting anyone pass. But after twenty minutes or so when, for some reason, they let one other small motorcycle pass, I lifted my visor, tried to assume the most pathetic and unthreatening look that I could, and tail-gated him through. The road continued in good condition but just as I was beginning to relax and believe that maybe the waters had already receded, I noticed that some of the local houses were surrounded by water. Another few kilometres, and almost all of the houses were surrounded by water, this time much higher and much closer to the road. Given that the problem had been going on for two months, I was beginning to understand what some of these protests might have been about.

We get some flooding in the UK too and I used to live in an area near Tewkesbury in England that suffers quite regularly. There's nothing to be done, cars don't work, trains don't work, even doors don't work. The water is not pure rainwater that cleans everything up, it's the opposite, dark dirty water filled with heavy and destructive sediment, rocks and mud. It's the sediment and objects in the water that do a lot of the damage as they're picked up and accelerated by the water flow. They crash into houses, trees or other property, which in turn get broken up and turned into even more destructive material. Eventually when the waters do subside you're left with an almighty mess and it costs the economy billions, not to mention the risk to people's lives.

Here in the Chaco region some of the people living by the side of the road had clearly seen it all before, and not only had they built their houses on short stilts, but some had small boats tied up to the verandas. Others didn't, and sat together on plastic chairs on top of small mounds in their front gardens with water all around them. The damage wouldn't be limited to houses either because the whole region depends on an agricultural economy driven by crops and cattle that would suffer tremendously. I continued, and eventually the waters covered the road, so at this point I had a decision to make. The water was not very deep so it would be possible to carry on, for now at least, but I had already noticed a few pot holes in the road and if I did continue there was no way of seeing where they were. Hitting a massive pot hole at anything more than 30kmph and coming off the bike in the middle of a flooded area would be a disaster. And if 30kmph was to be my average speed from here to Filandia, well I wouldn't make it to Filandia, I'd have to find somewhere else to stay for the night. On the other hand, I was already two hundred kilometres from where I set off, and up until this point on my journey I'd only been fully stopped in my tracks once, by the landslide in Peru. Well also by the chain falling off in the Amazon, but in that case I did actually continue forward when the bus came along, whereas the landslide forced me to go backwards. So I continued on, and for the next ten kilometres I slowly edged my way through the floods, spraying water up into my waterproof trousers, as I felt the road crumbling beneath my tyres. Every few minutes, bang, I'd hit another pot hole, and it was never just one. You get a whole series that bounce you up and down like a jack in the box for a few seconds, shaking your bones before letting you go. The surface water did eventually start to clear, and I was left with a damp, wreck of a road. But within ten more minutes of that, the rain started up again.

Despite the rain, which had only just begun to fall, I had a relatively dry road now so I increased my speed to make up some time. I started to crash into the pot holes rather than just bounce on them, with the poor Apache taking all the punishment as I held on for the roller coaster ride. I hit even more when I was trying to avoid patches of muddy, slippery, sediment, choosing to take a hit on the suspension over the probability of dropping the bike. The conditions got worse and worse, and after another twenty kilometres or so I came to a long stretch that was just annihilated. Pot holes had stretched completely across the road destroying any last traces of asphalt, and there were so many that they'd all joined up. Although the grass banks on either side still showed you where the road was, it was just a muddy, rocky, uneven mess. Also the rain turned into a torrent and so I had to slow right down again and my average speed went back to around 25kmph. But even this put me in the fast lane compared to the huge trucks that were transporting goods to and from the colonies in the north. They had to take each pile and each ditch like a speed bump, 10kmph or less to protect their cargo. And it must have been massively frustrating for the drivers more used to storming down the highways at 100kmph. Although I guess some, if not most of them, would be quite used to it on this road. With my average speed down to 25kmph and still a hundred kilometres from Filandia with no towns in between, I realised that there was no way I was going to make it by nightfall. I was going to break my Golden Rule again, *never ride at night*, that had helped me to plan my days and avoid the worst disasters throughout the trip. But there wasn't much I could do about it, so I continued on. Then the road conditions started to improve, a bit, the rain stopped, again, and I began to hope that maybe I would make it after all, if only there was no more flooding.

As each vehicle came onto the horizon I started examining it closely to check if it was a small car or motorcycle. Anything that could prove the road was actually passable by something less than a truck. But there were none, every single vehicle I saw was either a massive cargo lorry or a 4x4, and I started to get a bit concerned. I got even more concerned when I saw the still living remains of a huge black and yellow snake that had just been run over. Not that I have a particular fear of snakes, but I could have done without the reminder that this was snake country, when I might be forced to camp by the side of the road in a few hours. More roadkill followed, but this time it was an anteater that judging by the state of the carcass had been there a long time. That was evidence of the floods, because the body would not have stayed there long in the dry with so many vultures about. Come to think of it, it's strange that I haven't mentioned these vultures earlier because if you ride South America they'll be your constant companions, and they'd been following me about since Colombia. I'd seen a group of fifty of them picking at what was left of a very unfortunate former dog.

The rain returned, yet again, shortly after that, and with immaculate timing, the zipper on my rain jacket broke and the wind pulled it wide open. I was left with what looked like a superman cape, connected only at the top, flapping around behind me and completely useless against the torrents. I hadn't been in the best mood to put it mildly for the last few hours, but when the zipper broke, there was nothing I could do but laugh. Hysterically I mean, as the rain continued to batter my helmet and soak my denim jacket and jeans. I took a mental step back to properly assess the situation. This was not the mountains, and it was not cold, I was well fed and the bike was working fine. The worst case scenario assuming that I could avoid a crash, which was not 100% certain in such conditions, would be a very uncomfortable night. Soaked to the skin, sitting in my tent, somewhere far enough away from the road to avoid any trucks, but close enough to avoid the snakes. Not ideal, but not the end of the world. The rain continued to drench every layer of clothing that I was wearing for another twenty minutes or so, then all of a sudden, stopped dead, and the clouds parted just enough to see the last few rays of sunlight.

The final fifty kilometres to Filandia was not straightforward. The road was flat now, but still full of muddy sediment and I could only make my way at a relatively slow pace, slipping and sliding through the mud. And as I approached the town I started being overtaken at speed by the much more confident 4x4 trucks. But the rain stayed off, which was important because it quickly got dark and my visor was, after four months of abuse, now scratched to pieces. Not a problem during the day but hellish at night, because it diffuses all the light from oncoming headlights into a blinding mess. Rain would have meant that I needed to keep the thing shut, but in the dry I was able to lift the visor for periods to keep my bearings. I had originally intended to reach what sounded like a beautiful farm hostel on the outskirts of the city, but the road there was slightly uphill. It was covered in more than six inches of sediment and mud, and impossible to navigate for the Apache. So I settled for an hospedaje on the high street that looked to have plenty of parking in a yard at the back. Literally within one minute of my putting the bike away and walking back round to reception to check-in, the heavens opened, and the rain came down in torrents, yet again.

Luckily the hospedaje also had a connected restaurant so there was no need to venture out again in the evening, and I went in to order some food. There was a very large man with dark hair, but a fairly light complexion, sitting behind the counter and I asked him in Spanish 'what is there for dinner here?' He looked at me in a puzzled way and responded in a language that I didn't understand, but in a way that I could at least get his general meaning 'Kjenn jie noch Plautdietsch?', Don't you speak Plautdietsch, I'd just been mistaken for a Mennonite. Of course I didn't speak Plautdietsch and the guy's Spanish was surprisingly basic. So I made exactly the same judgement as he had done, and assumed that because he looked a bit like me that he might speak English 'Don't you speak English?' I asked, genuinely shocked, and he said no. So Spanish it was, and I did eventually manage to order some meat and mixed vegetables. Then after a few minutes a lady who I later learned was the man's daughter came out, and she spoke flawless Spanish and some English too, so no more problems with communication. She was clearly the one who usually dealt with the customers, most of whom I believe were Guarani or mestizo Paraguayan. After a long day fighting through the rain and floods I washed my face and collapsed into bed, the next thing I knew it was 6am.

Whereas the day before had been dominated by the rain, the morning was dominated by an equally fierce sun, and it was already hot by the time I left the hospedaje at 10am. My clothes had completely dried out in the couple of hours that I'd hung them in the sun to dry, and so had the bike thanks goodness. After a bit of a cough, the engine started and purred nicely. Not only was it a glorious sunny day, but I had an easy day in front of me and all I had to do was get from Filandia to Neuland Colony, a Mennonite settlement just twenty kilometres away. Then I would check into a room that I'd found online, on a farm run by a German couple, The Martens. When I arrived on the farm there was no-one around, and I was greeted by two huge dogs who barked a lot, but otherwise didn't come any closer as I stepped off the motorbike. I could tell they were lovely dogs just protecting the farm so went over to see if they'd let me pat them on the head. They actually didn't initially and kept edging forward to take a sniff of my hand then backing away again and having another bark, until Mrs Martens came out of the house to say hello.

From the moment I met Mrs Martens I knew that this would be a great place to stay, she was fantastic, gentle and kind, but professional too. She showed me the summer house where I could use the kitchen and bathroom, and the small field in front where I could pitch my tent. Then we spoke for a while about the town and how she had ended up here in Neuland. I didn't actually write any of this down in my journal so I really hope I've remembered it correctly, but as far I can remember, Mrs Martens had come to Neuland because her husband's family were related to the Mennonite community. Her brother in-law had come first a few years earlier, followed by her father in-law and then finally she and her husband. Mr Martens had found a job managing a large cattle estate nearby that belonged to a Mennonite man, who now lived in Canada.

By the time I'd put up my tent and spent a couple of hours snoozing in the summer house, Mr Martens had returned from work. He told me more about the colony and his job on the estate, and it sounded like hard work, but what a wonderful life. We mainly spoke in Spanish despite being two blond haired north Europeans, because while Mr Martens spoke completely fluent German, Plautdietsch, and Spanish, he was not confident in his English. In fact, I think his English was really much better than my Spanish, but we swapped between the two anyway. As we were talking I mentioned that I'd been looking to sell my motorcycle in Ciudad del Este and was going to head back there afterwards. He said that a friend of his sometimes bought bikes here in Neuland as they were difficult to get, and might be interested. He took a few photos of the Apache and sent them to his friend just in case. I also asked him where I could buy something to cook for dinner and he told me about a supermarket in town, so I took a couple of hours to see the sights before going to buy some supplies.

I bought wine in a box, that turned out to be excellent, and one of the best slices of beef that I've ever eaten. All I did was cut the thing into pieces and gently fry them along with some onions, but it was just amazing. The whole region was so clean, and everything was completely organic, so I barely showed the meat to the pan before serving it. Mrs Martens brought me some cheese filled buns that were leftover from a batch she had baked in the afternoon, and a papaya, that I had for dessert. As we were talking I mentioned that the zip on my tent had broken the last time that I'd used it, and I was a bit worried about mosquitoes. She told me that I should probably worry more about the snakes, and that I could stay in the summer house for the same price anyway. I finished the wine with the fruit and settled down for another amazing night's sleep.

In the morning I woke up early, completely refreshed. The Martens had already been awake for hours of course, and Mr Martens was heading out to work when he popped over to the summer house to say good morning, and wish me well. I told him that I was intending to push all the way to the border with Bolivia if possible. 'Bolivia? I thought you were going back to Ciudad del Este, to sell the bike?' said Mr Martens. And it's true, that was the plan originally, but the night before I'd had more time to kill, and started reading about the Jesuit Missions circuit in eastern Bolivia. It was only a few hundred kilometres away, so I woke up with a new idea. In any case I hadn't heard anything more from my contacts in Ciudad del Este, so I thought I might as well continue onwards and maybe sell the bike in Sucre.

Mr Martens cautioned that the weather was not predictable recently, and I should really have some backup ideas in case I didn't make it all the way to the border. I was pretty sure that it wouldn't be a problem because the sun had been burning hot for almost two days, more than enough to dry out all the new rainwater, and the floods had already been receding. But I took his advice and worked out a couple of places on the route where I could stay if things didn't go to plan. Then I wished Mr and Mrs Martens and their children well, said goodbye, and headed back out onto the highway towards Bolivia.

A few kilometres out of Neuland, the highway started to deteriorate again and I found myself slowing down to 40kmph to avoid the potholes and the huge cracks in the surface. Then after another hour, the rain started, and just like two days before it came down in an absolute torrent. Everything was soaking wet again within twenty minutes, and suddenly I was in motorcycling hell yet again. Battered from above by the rain, battered from below by the broken road surface and barely able to see anything because my visor was now so scratched up. But I'd have chosen this battering in a second, over what came next. Uncomfortable as the destroyed asphalt was, at least my tyres were able to find grip and I could move forward at something more than walking speed. But the next section of road was made of the smooth red earth that makes the Chaco so fertile, and it hadn't been remade during the couple of dry days. So it was still in the same condition as it had been two days before, churned to pieces by the heavy trucks after days of torrential rain. If you look up Dirt Road on Wikipedia, the picture you'll find will be of cattle walking along a dusty, muddy track in some remote out of the way place. The picture is from Paraguay, right there in the Chaco, so here I was riding a dirt road in the home of dirt roads.

Throughout the journey I'd chosen to stick with regular road tyres, and I think overall that was the right decision, but on this particular day I was really wishing that I'd had full on mud-terrain tyres. There was no grip, and rather than pushing forward I was just rolling, with my feet down ready to regain my balance at any moment, at a ridiculously low speed, and with a minimal amount of engine power. I was giving it just enough to keep me moving, but not enough to cause me to change direction in any way, because if that happened I'd have fallen straight over on the unbelievably slippery mud. After a couple of kilometres, I saw a car that had done just that, and ended up in a shallow ditch by the side of the road, unable to move without spinning the wheels. A large 4x4 had stopped to help, so I kept on moving, but as I rode by I asked the 4x4 guy how much further, and he said just a few kilometres.

He was right, and the road turned back into asphalt so I was beginning to make up for lost time when about 10km outside the town of Mariscal Estigarribia I ran into some roadworks. The main highway had been closed for resurfacing and a side road, again made only of earth, had been opened for the traffic. The side road hadn't been re-flattened after the heavy rains so it was still in a similar condition to the bad section that I'd just ridden through. Only this time the road was in a kind of large ditch and the mud was deep, very deep, and absolutely torn to pieces by the trucks. The main highway itself had recently been scraped ready to receive a new layer of asphalt, and would have been rideable had I been able to get over to it, but that was impossible, so I carried on.

As soon as my tyre touched the mud I slid two metres across the road, and would have dropped the bike if I hadn't put my boot down ankle deep into the sopping wet red earth. But I was still moving forward and at this point I thought, hoped, prayed that it may only be a kilometre or two, so I carried on. In hindsight I should have asked the workmen who were standing at the start of the section but I didn't think of it as I passed by. Now I was using both feet constantly to keep my balance, but still moving forward, barely, so I carried on this way for about one kilometre. Then the inevitable happened, my rear tyre completely lost all traction and started spinning in the mud, and the Apache stopped dead. I tried pushing forward, and I tried rolling backwards, I even tried stepping off and wheeling the bike for a bit adding just a tiny bit of gas, but nothing worked.

That one kilometre of pushing through along this churned up dirt road had completely covered my wheels in a thick layer of the clay−like earth. It stuck fast to my tyres but wouldn't stick to anything else. The mud was so thick that the wheel arches were completely full, making sure there was a fresh supply of slippery mud should any small pieces fall off. I was properly stuck, over a kilometre from the asphalt road behind me, and who knows how far in front. And it was still raining, so there was no chance that this mud would dry out, my good mood of the morning sank along with my boots in the mud. Without any idea how bad it might get further on down the road, and with the rain starting to get heavy again, I decided to try and slide back through the one kilometre of mud. I planned to get back onto the asphalt road, head back to Neuland, and come back once the rain had stopped. There were other options on route but if I was potentially going to spend some time there until this road dried out, why not stay somewhere pleasant. It's never easy to make the decision to go back on yourself on a motorcycle journey, but I really liked the Martens and the thought of heading back to the farm wasn't so bad.

First I let the bike roll back into another smaller ditch by the side of the road so that I could at least put down the side-stand. That was risky because I might not be able to get it back up the tiny slope again, but had to be done. Then I went into the bushes at the side of the road, and found a stick that I could use to attack the mud. I spent the next ten minutes cleaning out some of the mud from under the wheel arch and from the tyres, then got back on the bike. By now the rain had turned into a torrent, again, and was helping to get rid of a bit more mud off the tyres, but also making the ground even more slippery. I started up the engine and turned the throttle the tiniest amount possible, but it was no use the wheels started spinning again.

Then I noticed that even further down the small ditch at the side of the road was a little section of, basically more mud, but with tiny blades of grass growing out of it which meant that the mud might possibly hold together if I could get my tyre onto it. I let the Apache slide back even further into the ditch, at the risk of not being able to get it out again, until my rear tyre was on top of the grass. I pulled and pushed the bike as much as I could to get it pointing the right way, then gave it a little gas while standing over the bike and pushing with my feet. The tiny bit of grass did its job and I started moving. And although it took all the strength in my left leg to keep the bike upright, I did make it back onto the road, pointing back in the direction that I'd come. I'd even managed to get a little bit of momentum, and landed directly back onto the slightly less slippery section that I'd just ridden on.

The odyssey wasn't over yet though, because at the start of the muddy section, a kilometre back down the road, I'd ridden down a much steeper slope. And I had no idea what would happen when I tried to go back up. After another ten minutes of rolling slowly through the mud, I arrived at the slope and immediately decided not to try and just ride all the way up. There just wasn't enough grip and I needed to make a slight turn halfway up the slope. Instead I got off the bike, turned off the engine, put it in neutral and moved onto the tiny, rocky, and much steeper section next to the road. Then I pushed with all my strength until I got the bike near the top. I got back on and started the engine, and was filled with relief when I found myself coasting back down the asphalt. I was exhausted.

By the time I arrived back in Neuland it was already mid-afternoon and the dirt track leading to the farm was soaked. I spent the next forty-five minutes slowly navigating the track in the same way I'd done on the roadworks. Only this time the mud was shallow and didn't accumulate under the wheel arch, so I managed to crawl all the way there. Mrs Martens said that she was surprised to see me again, but something in her eyes told me that she wasn't. They had seen the rain and must have known the tough time I'd have getting through to the border. As I put my things back into the summer house I was paid a visit by two of the cutest of the Martens six children, bringing the meat, eggs and vegetables that I'd left in the refrigerator the day before. I cooked the same simple but delicious dinner of beef and onions, with fruit for dessert, then settled down for another glorious night's sleep.

The next day I did absolutely nothing, except read, and enjoy the cool breeze blowing through the summer house annex which had mosquito nets for windows. There was a fat old leather chair, and a hammock, so I split my time between the two. And I was still practising my language skills, so I read a few pages of Treasure Island in Spanish between snoozes. In the evening I very cheekily asked Mrs Martens if she had a sewing machine, and would it be possible to sew shut the door of my tent. I'm not sure why the idea didn't hit me sooner, after all the tent had another door on the other side, so I didn't really see the point of two doors anyway. She smiled and said it was no problem, and when I offered to pay something she said no. I didn't even bother to check the weather conditions for the next day, because I knew I wasn't going anywhere, it would take another full day of scorching hot sun and no more rain to dry out the roadworks enough for me to pass.

Mrs Martens reminded me that tomorrow was Sunday, and invited me to join them at Church, which I accepted. She also told me that another traveller had booked to stay the following night, a biker like me, so I'd have some company in the evening in the summerhouse. Then she told me some sad news, her brother-in-law who had been the first to move to Neuland, would be leaving to move back to Europe, and his goodbye party was tomorrow if I'd like to join. I couldn't think of anything I'd like more than to spend the day with these lovely people so I accepted.

The next day I woke just after dawn and made myself some scrambled eggs on toast for breakfast, with a glass of milk made from the trusty milk-powder that I always carry. I also had an orange left over so wasn't left wanting for a nutritious breakfast. Church was at 08:00 so I had a couple of hours to kill and retired to the hammock again to read Treasure Island. Although my Spanish reading is very slow and constantly interrupted by dictionary checks, it's still a marvellous story of travel and adventure, the perfect novel to read on a motorcycle journey to stay motivated. My clothes had now completely dried, yet again, on the makeshift washing line I'd suspended between two trees by the summerhouse. The Marten's bundled myself, themselves, and six children into the van and we started out on the drive to church. About three minutes later, we arrived, because it was in fact less than five hundred metres down the road. We'd taken the van because the mud was just too slippery and deep for the children to walk on. The small hall that served as the church was empty and we opened up the windows and had a quick tidy up before the congregation arrived. I've been to some of the grandest churches and cathedrals in the world, but this was easily one of the most beautiful. Mr Martens opened up the piano, grabbed some song books from the shelf, and put the large heavily marked up bible from which he would later read, onto the lectern.

The congregation consisted of just one other family, that of Mr Marten's brother in law who would be moving on soon, but he had a big family too so overall there were over fifteen people and it felt quite lively. Once everyone had settled down and taken a seat, Mr Martens led us through some readings from the bible, and some songs. He was sometimes accompanied by his sister-in-law and her daughters on guitar, sometimes by the other Mr Martens on trombone, and sometimes he would play piano himself. I'd never seen such a completely genuine display of love and affection both for each other and for God, it was very moving and one of the daughters was overwhelmed. She left the room for a moment in tears after singing, but returned a few moments later to her guitar. Most of the service was of course given in German but Mr Martens gave a basic translation so I could keep up. The choice of songs, readings and points for thought were chosen to help all of them think about, and process, the news that one of the families would be moving away. Thoughts about the importance of family, how distance was really no barrier to strong relationships, and how God would always be with all of them wherever they were.

After the service I helped to clean up a bit, and move the benches into a 4x4 that would take them to the other Mr Martens house for the leaving party. And while we were doing this I got another reminder about the importance of having a working zip on your tent. Mr Martens pointed out a centipede on the floor and said 'If that thing bites you, it will hurt like nothing you've ever felt, and you won't sleep for 3 days' Well noted.

I joined the whole family back in the van for the two-and-a-half-minute drive over to their relative's house, and we set up the benches on their porch. There was already a barbecue pit being prepared outside, and we setup the benches and tables for about thirty people. More guests would arrive later on, so we had some time to relax. I got talking to the different members of the family and it was clear that the move back to Europe would be a challenge. They were all excited about the social and educational benefits of living near a city in Germany, but also incredibly sad to leave their well-ordered and secure lives in Paraguay.

When the other guests arrived the BBQ got into full swing, and once again I got to taste the incredible local beef, that the Marten's modestly called scraps of meat. In reality the scraps in Neuland were the kind of thing that would cost a small fortune in an upscale supermarket back in the UK. But here it was just a normal part of life that you'd eat the very best, completely organic beef. Maybe it was true, maybe they really were just the scraps, and each evening the Martens sat down to eat the meat of another kind of super-organic cow that I hadn't seen yet, but I was more than happy with what was served. Some of the guests had baked various kinds of party cakes, and all of them were bursting with flavour. My guess would be because of the milk, which came from cows on the estate. And for drinks we had little bottles of sugar masquerading as orange, apple or pineapple juice, some things are the same at parties the world over.

This was not going to be just a food-fest though, and a complete itinerary of field games had been prepared so that we could enjoy the gloriously sunny afternoon. There was R*unning along with your child in a wheelbarrow;* there was W*hich child is bravest and can* *climb furthest up the water tower;* there was a *Cake hunt;* and there was *Which team can wear the most layers of clothes in two minutes.* It was all completely absurd and enormous fun, and both families seemed to forget the sadness of the moment for a couple of hours. While one of the games was going on I spoke some more with Mr Martens about his job on the estate, and The Chaco region in general. He was a big expert on farming, cattle management, and everything you'd expect from living a rural life. He told me how the Algarrobo tree puts nitrogen back into the soil, and that's why I was seeing so many in the area, and how the torrential rains have been welcomed with both fear and joy.

Usually the summers in the Chaco are fiercely hot and dry, and it's so extreme that they even hold one of the world's most famous rally competitions here, right next door to Neuland colony, the Trans-Chaco Rally. It's most famous for the amount of dust that the cars kick up, and the number of cars that overheat and don't make it to the end. Quite a different challenge to the deep mud and rain that I was facing on the little Apache. So the same rains that had flooded the area and forced 40,000 people to relocate, are also essential to balancing out this extreme heat, and the combination is what has enabled the Mennonites to turn what was once desert, into the most fertile area in the country. To drastically oversimplify the story, they built an extensive irrigation system which stores the torrents when they do come, and distributes it evenly over the region. Combined with excellent knowledge about crop rotations and things like the Algarrobo tree, they've managed to do all of this without some of the modern chemicals and more damaging farming techniques used elsewhere. But as Mr Martens also told me, the dramatic changes in weather can take a toll. His first three years in the Chaco saw drought, and nothing would grow, cattle died and crops wilted. He was one of the lucky ones though, with another job and more secure income, while many farmers who were relying completely on their small holdings, suffered more.

Once the afternoon's festivities had finished I returned with the Marten's to the summerhouse and shortly after that, Ewan, the other biker who was staying on the farm that evening, pulled into the driveway. Ewan was riding what would, for the average adventure motorcyclist, be considered quite a small machine, a 250cc. But it was fully kitted out with expanded fuel tank, GPS system, and all terrain tyres, and he had all the tools you could wish for. He was also wearing full canvas biking kit compared to my everyday denim. So although I wasn't jealous on that baking hot afternoon, I would be later when sliding over some rocks in eastern Bolivia. After yesterday's ordeal trying to get my road tyres through the thick mud, the one thing I definitely was jealous of that day were the AT (all terrain) tyres. They would have helped a lot, and I might even have been able to save a day by riding slowly all the way through to the border with Bolivia. Then again, given that I'd just had one of the best days of the journey, perhaps getting turned around was not such a bad thing. Ewan and I chatted about all the usual biker stuff and he laughed when I told him about trying to do all this on a 160cc TVS. I think perhaps he was more used to people on six–fifty Suzuki's wondering how on earth he was doing it all on a two–fifty.

By this time Mrs Martens had done a supreme job of helping me to sew shut the tent door, and also my broken rain jacket. She'd even added a large button at the top so I could button it tight against the rain but also open it a bit more to take it off, as it now didn't have a zipper. I pitched my tent and Ewan pitched a few feet away while we both used the summer house for the bathroom and kitchen. We cooked a basic pasta dinner and swapped stories about our journeys, plus a few tips on routes and conditions. Then the next morning we both woke up early and started getting ready for the long road ahead.

Ewan was also riding to Bolivia like me, but our paces would be very different. Whereas Ewan liked to cover about two or three hundred kilometres every day, finish by lunchtime, and enjoy a free afternoon, I preferred to cover much more ground up to 600km, but then take a day off. In order to cover such a long distance, I often needed to wake up early, especially in the beginning stage of this journey because I'd started with a rule about finishing any ride before 3pm. This would give me plenty of time to find a hotel, settle in, and see some of the sights. But as time passed this rule had morphed into *never ride at night*, and I'd already broken that one about ten times, luckily without serious consequences. My basic principle now was just to ride full on until around three or four pm, then take stock. If I was confident that the road ahead would be good then I'd continue, if not I wouldn't take risks and I'd find a nearby place to stay. After a few hours pottering around getting ready, but really just waiting for the tents to dry out, I set off much later than normal, and Ewan would set off about half an hour later.

The weather was glorious, and although there was a little bit of light rain, the sun was beginning to get hot. I navigated the dirt road up to the highway then twisted the throttle all the way back hoping to cover as much distance as possible while it remained fairly dry. Unfortunately, when I did this, I noticed that the chain was loose. I'd actually noticed it in the morning and

Ewan had offered to help with the adjustment as he had all the tools. But like many times before on the journey, I decided that it was better to pay a mechanic and have the benefit of a visual once-over from a professional. So I took it easy for a while until I reached the next town, trying not to hit too many potholes and bounce my chain off the sprocket. That would have been exactly the same kind of breakdown as the one in the Amazon jungle, only now it would be here in The Chaco, two months later. One time makes an interesting story, but two times would have been embarrassing.

When I reached Mariscal Estigarribia, which was my backup town to stay as per the advice of Mr Martens when I first set out for the Bolivian border, I pulled off the highway to look for a mechanic. It was super easy to find one, and I stopped at a professional looking place with Yamaha branding just a few hundred metres from the highway. Unfortunately, by now it was lunchtime and the place was closed, but the manager helped me to find a smaller independent place with a young mechanic, who would be open. The younger guy was great, although he hadn't seen a TVS before it was all familiar to him from similar bikes and he tightened and greased the chain in seconds. As it was lunchtime I thought I might as well eat while I was stopped, and had a quick lunch in town. I also replaced the bungees that were holding my bag on the back and were getting a bit worn down, before heading back out onto the highway. My newly tightened chain felt brilliant and I quickly covered the next thirty kilometres up to the point where I'd been turned back a few days before. I was locating and swerving around the surface damage much more easily now that I'd ridden the road once already, and the weather stayed dry. If it wasn't for the nightmare ride a few days back I'd probably be describing this day as hell, pot holes as big as cars and everything! but it's all relative, and I was feeling quite relaxed. Then just as I was approaching the point where the highway turned to mud, who should I see about two hundred metres further on, but Ewan, standing taking photographs of the road, while his bike was parked up by the side in the mud.

The road was much drier than last time, and I was able to roll onto the muddy part without problems as long as I kept the speed down around 30kmph, but it was still greasy. As I got closer to Ewan I could see that his canvas protective clothing had been doing its job, he was absolutely covered in mud from head to toe. I couldn't help laughing when I pulled up alongside, and luckily he could see the funny side too. He said that basically he'd entered the muddy part way too fast, and although he was able to keep the bike upright for a couple of hundred metres, eventually he just lost it right in the middle of a massive puddle. So there you go, all terrain tyres are definitely the way to go if you're going to be on the mud a lot, but they're not going to reach out and grab a tree branch if the ground is really slippery. I didn't feel so bad about my choice of regular road tyres after that.

We looked around and noticed that the deep mud by the side of the road had dried out a lot since I was last here, and it was now possible to ride across to the new highway. So we got back on our bikes and crossed over to the area that was in the middle of being built, and had been scraped ready for a new layer of asphalt. The new road had ruts all along it from the scraping process and this time Ewan's thicker AT tyres really did make a huge difference. He went speeding off while I struggled as my narrow tyres got caught in the ruts, making me swerve all over the place. It didn't last long though, and after about ten kilometres I was back on smooth asphalt. I'd lost quite a lot of time by keeping my speed down for the terrible road surface and because I'd taken quite a long lunch-break to fix the chain. So there was no way I was going to make it to Bolivia, especially because once I'd crossed over the border it would be another couple of hundred kilometres before I got to the first town, Villa Montes. I needed to find a place to stay the night and there were a few places nearby, but I decided to go a bit further on because I was heading into a National Park on the border between Paraguay and Bolivia. And it would be much more fun I thought, to find a place to camp.

I knew that I'd reached the national park area when I started to notice more and more armadillos crossing the road, and tried to remember all the chicken jokes that might work with an armadillo instead. Then I noticed a massive shadow moving in front of me that at first I thought was some kind of aircraft or drone, before realising it was a huge eagle. I learned once years ago when I did a bit of gliding that asphalt roads can absorb and store a huge amount of heat, slowly releasing it during the day. This means that a road can provide a reliable thermal lift, and that's why you see so many big eagles and vultures following the bike as you ride. Either that or they were waiting for me to take a fall, so they could eat something different from armadillo for a change.

Anyway the trouble with my camping plan, was that in this particular National Park Reserve, there were no places to camp. No petrol stations, no parks, no national park entrances. Nowhere that I could pitch a tent far enough away from the road to avoid the dust, pollution, and risk of being hit by a truck. I checked an app that I'd downloaded to my phone for overland travellers, and found that there was, thank goodness, one roadside refuge. It was another twenty kilometres further along the road, and had been tagged by a French traveller a few years before. It was called Refugio Carretero Canada el Carmen, and I know that because there was a huge wooden sign above a makeshift entranceway about six metres high, presumably to keep out some of the larger trucks. Other than that there was nothing around, not for a hundred kilometres back along the road nor for a similar distance into Bolivia, so that's where I would be staying the night. Border crossings themselves can be another safe option as there are guards, but remote crossings often close quite early in the afternoon, and I preferred this place because at least it was surrounded by beautiful forest. The refuge itself had all the basics including a parking area that had been asphalted, and some cleared areas under the trees to pitch tents. And it was about forty metres away from the road, so all in all it was perfect really for a refuge, but eerily quiet. It clearly hadn't been maintained for a long time and was completely overgrown. As I pulled in on the Apache I noticed that it was also the site of an historic battle from The Chaco War, and there was a touching sign that talked about the brothers on both the Bolivian and Paraguayan sides that perished. Of course Paraguay won that war, so they can afford to be generous, and I didn't notice similar signs about the Brazilian brothers who died in the fierce Triple Alliance war that lost Paraguay half of its territory.

Now I'm going to try and describe this Refuge without making it sound too much like The Blair Witch Project. Because it's actually quite a good place to stay, and I wouldn't want to put you off. But the fact that it was the site of an historical battle where thousands of people met a gory death, and the fact that it was a hundred kilometres from anywhere, was slightly unsettling. I don't believe in ghosts, but if I did, I'm sure you'd find them here in this lonely spot far away from the lights, and the bustle of any town. Not only that but it's in the middle of a national reserve park absolutely bursting with wildlife including puma, and alligators. Then add in the risk of psychotic, homicidal, axe wielding truck drivers, or drug dealers looking for a quiet place to ditch bodies before crossing the border, and you get my drift. It's for days like this that most people do motorcycle journeys in groups, and although I'm not the kind of person that gets lonely, I do know when it would be better to have some other people around.

Once I'd set up my tent where it wasn't visible from the road, I went for a walk in the forest, but that probably wasn't a good idea, because what I found there made things even worse. In the overlander app the last traveller to stay here said that there was a farmer living nearby. But I've no idea what he could even have meant by that, because there were no visible signs of any house or compound. The only thing I found was a small hut that had been abandoned years before, some fencing that separated this area from the huge adjoining estate, and a shipping container. There was nobody around, and it was completely silent at that moment, even the birds were quiet, so I opened the door of the shipping container and found inside an old desk, a chair, and some tattered clothes. Someone was, or had been, living there.

I closed the container and looked around a bit more outside. There was a fire pit where someone had cooked, and in and around the fire I found the jawbones of sheep and capybara. Nearby there was a basic fishing spear with a sharp splayed point like a crown. The strange thing was that all of this stuff looked well-used, but also hadn't been used for a long time. They were placed as if someone was expecting to come back for them, but they were all covered in dust or dirt like they hadn't moved in years. Why would someone make a spear then leave it, why would someone put a desk and chair in the shipping container then just abandon them? And why would someone do that over a hundred kilometres from anywhere?

As I was standing looking at the remains of the sheep and rodents in the fire-pit I heard, coming from the forest, a deep growl. Not so close that it would make me panic, but not far enough away to ignore. Sometimes cows make deep throaty noises so it was probably that, but I didn't want to stand there and find out, and quickly walked back to my tent. The sun had already long since set, and the mosquitoes were starting to bite, so although I would have preferred to keep an eye on both the highway and the forest path, I had to get back into my tent and settle down to sleep.

When I woke up the next morning I was relieved to find that I'd not been eaten by the puma, nor axe-murdered, nor even haunted by the ghosts. Far from it, I'd slept well and it was another glorious sunrise, so after I'd eaten some bread and jam for breakfast, I gathered my things and rode up to the border post just as it opened. The crossing was straightforward and I found myself in Bolivia by around 9am, but it would be a long day. I'd arrived so early that there didn't seem much point to stop in Villamontes after only one hundred kilometres, and I decided to push on all the way to Santa Cruz for a total of 572km. A very long way, but I'd already ridden much longer days and the weather conditions looked ideal.

10
God's soldiers & wild dogs: BOLIVIA (Second leg)

The highway leading from the frontier post into Bolivia was just as remote and deserted as the Paraguayan side. But the road surface was better, so I just buckled down and cruised on auto-pilot all the way to Villamontes, then turned north. When you're riding a motorcycle you're never 100% on autopilot of course, because there are just too many things to look out for. Pot holes, roadkill, oil patches, the list of potential dangers is endless, and things that are an annoyance in a car can be fatal on a bike. If you've ever had the experience of driving a car exhausted, and nodding off for a second before waking up startled, imagine doing that on a motorcycle. Bikes are fun because the steering is so responsive and direct, but it also amplifies mistakes. So to be on the safe side you need to stay alert, and it's always good to plan your days, and be finished riding by a reasonable time to get some rest. It's different for everyone, for some people it's a couple of hours, others can go ten hours without stopping, and I'm sure some motorcycle couriers do much more, you just need to know your own limit.

After Villamontes the road began to deteriorate again quickly. Nothing as bad as I'd seen in the Chaco, but enough to slow me down. By 12pm I still had almost four hundred kilometres to go but had been riding for a few hours and needed some rest. So I stopped in Boyuibe to get some lunch and an oil change. I spent way too long messing around with different mechanics and looking for an ATM to withdraw Bolivianos, and by the time I'd sorted it all out and eaten lunch, it was already past 2pm. As I said, my usual rule was to keep going until around 3 or 4pm then take stock, so I continued on my way. After Boyuibe the road improved again, but the same pattern of speed-up, slow-down for the damaged sections continued, and the route was now monotonously straight. It was turning into a frustrating day's ride, and I think this had something do to with my, frankly very poor, decision making in the afternoon.

By 3pm it should have been clear that I wouldn't make Santa Cruz de la Sierra by nightfall. The roads had been basically fine for a while but they were just bad enough to mean that I couldn't race along at full speed, and needed to constantly slow down for damaged sections. I should have planned for an overnight stop, and there were some options around the mid-way point, but because I was so frustrated with the stop-start ride I didn't do that, and chose instead to push on and take stock again at 4pm. I'd gotten it into my head that I'd be making it to Santa Cruz, and this was turning into a bit of a thing, an important objective, the road was just about good enough to give me hope.

Then as I was forced to go slower, and slower, just to stay upright on the ever-deteriorating road surface, the more frustrated I got, and I started thinking about how late I could push the ride. 5pm was fine, 6pm would still be light, 7pm might be dark but there would still be people around. What about 8pm? Riding at 8pm is not something that I would have considered earlier in my journey. I started with quite a firm rule about being done by 3pm because if you do have a problem, that gives you a few hours of daylight to sort it out. And although I did drop that rule after a while, I was still for the most part super cautious about being out on the highway at night. It's fine in a well-lit town in England, although some bikers are even cautious about that, but out here in a remote part of South America it's insane. You won't be able to see all the dangers in the road, potholes, oil patches, even tight curves or crossings because there are often no signs. The driving standards are even worse than in the daytime, and crime is an issue.

It's heavily advised not to travel even by bus at night because of crime on rural roads, so alone on a motorbike you might be asking for trouble. If you had a breakdown, no good citizen would stop to help, because they'd think you were planning a robbery, so you'd really be spinning the roulette wheel in terms who you'd meet, and what could happen. But as I pushed further north on this maddening road that seemed to give me just enough good asphalt to get up to speed before throwing a huge crater in the way, I started to do some mental gymnastics, and suddenly 8pm didn't seem so bad.

I only learned the phrase *mental gymnastics* later when I was on the internet and trying and get more information about these games that your mind plays when you're in a difficult situation. I was experiencing *cognitive dissonance*, to use another technical phrase, where the cold hard fact of time could not resolve with my utter belief that I would achieve the objective of the day. As they came up against each other, it was the facts that gave way, not my belief. So 5pm came and went,

6pm came and went, and I was still over a hundred kilometres from Santa Cruz when I realised that I was starting to find it hard to see through my scratched up visor as the oncoming cars turned on their headlights. It was now 6:30pm and the sun had set. My mind's stranglehold on the facts continued for another twenty minutes as I sped-up and convinced myself that the road into Santa Cruz would have more street lights, would be less damaged, and I just needed get through the next few kilometres. Then the facts came crashing down on me like a bucket of cold water. Still more than sixty kilometres away from Santa Cruz, and now in pitch black darkness without street lighting, I ran into more roadworks.

Again not the kind of roadworks that are well managed with decent, although reduced, lanes, with working traffic lights and clear signs, and with street lighting. No this was the kind of roadworks where the road is torn to pieces but still open to traffic, where there are traffic lights but people ignore them because they often don't work or there's no one around anyway, and where you can't see your hand in front of your face because of the dust. I had to pull over for a minute to let my mind catch up. What on earth had I done, and why the hell was it so important to get to Santa Cruz today. I could have just stopped in the last town and carried on in the morning, what difference would it have made? But now I was over two hundred kilometres from the last stopover with a hostel, and I couldn't even remember seeing any buildings for the last hundred kilometres.

The cognitive dissonance started to resolve itself again, properly this time, and the facts took over while my belief sat in a corner quietly, feeling like an idiot. There were no good options. Head back into the darkness on a fast, narrow, and crumbling single lane highway when I could barely see through my visor, looking for some kind of place to stay along an unlit road a hundred kilometres long that as far as I could remember didn't have any towns. Or continue on into what I already knew would be the absolute worst few hours of my journey so far. I knew exactly how difficult and dangerous the muddy, destroyed road would be in the dark. I knew exactly how I'd keep raising my visor just to be able to see, then slamming it closed again as the dust got in my eyes. I knew that I would come across trucks that had ignored the traffic lights, and were bearing down on me while I prayed that they could at least see me with my inadequate headlight. And I knew that the cars behind me would be tailgating, and unable to slow down if I did drop the bike. But I also knew that I would at least find a place to stay in Santa Cruz, and that the speed on this stretch of road would never get above 60kmph (40mph). And I knew that I'd have some kind of reference for where the road was despite the lack of street lighting, because there would be other cars and trucks going through the route along with me. So I took off my helmet, cleaned the visor as best I could, checked the bungees were still holding my bag securely onto the back, cleaned my headlight, and set off.

The change was immediate. As soon as I pulled back into the line of traffic and moved onto the unmade surface I started to hit potholes. I just couldn't see them, they were always hidden behind the car in front until the last second so I didn't have time to respond. And even if I did have more time I probably still wouldn't have seen them because of the scratched visor. As the traffic started to speed up, I started hitting things hard and getting my bones shaken just like the washboard road in Chile. Only this time not in a predictable forward motion, but getting my front tyre pushed and pulled this way and that, depending on the shape and angle of the hole, or the rocks. I had enough grip to keep moving forward, but never felt secure enough to trust it. And every few seconds I felt the tyre sliding down a slope or moving across a patch of sand, and I'd be praying to just keep the bike upright. My hands where already aching after riding all day, but I had to use them almost constantly to adjust the brakes and throttle, and just balance the bike. Whenever I slowed down to get a better view of the road, and give myself more time to think, I'd feel the truck behind me right on my rear wheel. Honking the horn and pushing left and right to see if it could get past, despite the fact that the car in front was only a few metres away.

The dust got thicker as I got further into the roadworks, and at times it was difficult to make out the line of cars. You could only see the car in front, and the opposite line of traffic. The worst parts of the road were, in a way, actually the best, because the trucks had to take them so slowly that I could pass them and have a few minutes' respite with a clear bit of road, able to see all the rocks and holes. But then in places the road surface would smooth out just enough to encourage the trucks to drive fast, but not enough to make it safe for me on the bike. These were the worst, because as my tyre slid here and there across the road and I kept crashing hard into crevices, I just couldn't keep up the pace with the cars in front. As I slowed down the trucks behind would get even more impatient and start pushing again left and right to force me to pull over and let them pass, but there was nowhere to pullover to. And what was I supposed to do anyway, wait two hours for the hundreds of trucks to pass, sitting there on my bike in the dust? I'd only have to pull out again into exactly the same conditions, so I continued on.

I was cursing the fact that I'd bought a brand of helmet that was only available in Colombia, and I'd been trying to get a replacement visor for over a month in Chile, Argentina, Brazil and Paraguay, with no luck. I should have just bought a new helmet, but here I was struggling with a scratched up visor flooded with diffused light from the oncoming headlights, and I could barely tell when the car in front was speeding up or slowing down. Several times I hit the bumpers of other cars, but they didn't even notice in the chaos, and the cars were doing the same acrobatics as my bike as they went over the rocky ground. After a while I couldn't bear the feeling of constantly worrying about a crash, so I lifted the visor. But it only took a few seconds for the dust and dirt to start filling my eyes, and I flipped it back down, plunging back into blindness. This open and close game carried on for an hour until finally I came to another set of traffic lights. At this point I took advantage of the one benefit of being on a motorbike in this situation, and once the traffic had stopped, I weaved in and out until I reached the front of the queue. I just wanted to be out of the flow, out of the exhaust pollution and dust, able to see the road in front of me, and potentially move away more quickly just to keep away from the cars. It was fantastic to be at the front of the queue, able to breathe properly, and to take a rest, but then I made another stupid decision.

I mentioned earlier how in South America motorcycles are often allowed to just continue on through red lights at roadworks, presumably because they wouldn't block the lane and can move out of the way of oncoming traffic. Well when the workman signalled that I could go, even though the lights were red and the cars would have to stay put, I decided to go for it. It took less than ten seconds to regret the decision,

190

when after riding around the signs and onto what looked like a smooth section of road, I heard the workman shouting frantically behind me. And when I looked into my side mirror, I could see him raising his hands above his head. In the darkness I'd ridden straight onto a newly asphalted lane, and I started to feel the bike slowing down as the tyres got stuck in the black viscous mixture. I could hear the hard lumps that were being thrown up onto the wheel arch, thick black balls of asphalt with rocks and sand holding them together. I turned quickly, and luckily was off the sticky liquid before I slowed down so much that I needed to put a foot down. But now my tyres were covered in what was essentially black glue, and they were picking up every bit of rock and sand that they touched.

Asphalt's wonderful when it's dried and set, but when it's first laid as a hot liquid it's seriously dirty stuff. It's as strong as superglue, and impossible to wash off without strong chemicals. There was no way I could use my hands or anything else to clean the tyres, I'd just have to continue in the hope that it would eventually rub off as it stuck harder to the rocks and sand, than the rubber tyre.

Back on the unrepaired lane now, I hit around twenty more potholes before reaching a stretch of road that was much smoother. So I started to speed up, and reached 60kmph even though I could barely see twenty metres in front of my front tyre. The thick dust in the air meant that I couldn't see where on the road the different lanes started and finished, so I just stayed roughly in the middle of the road and kept up my speed. I was trying to get to a better, wider part of the road before I met the traffic coming from the other direction, which had the right of way. But it was too late, I started to see the headlights of oncoming trucks, and was forced to move further to the right, and the road was so narrow that I really wasn't sure what lane I was in. It was while I was hugging the right hand side of the road trying to keep away from the oncoming traffic, blinded by the dust, but travelling now at 60kmph, that I crashed.

If I had kept to a slower pace, I would have had time to react when out of the darkness and the dust, I saw a metal drum container about a meter high, right in the middle of what I thought was the right hand lane. I crashed into the heavy drum head on, without slowing down, and before I knew what was happening I was flying into a ditch at the side of the road. Miraculously, I managed to stay upright for a couple of seconds which saved me from sliding along the old asphalt, but then finally I dropped the bike. My left hip took the full force of the impact and the bike landed on my left leg. I lay motionless in the ditch, invisible to the road that was two metres above me, not feeling any pain at all but breathing heavily because of the shock and adrenaline. My bike's engine was still running but the light was shining into the dirt, I was in darkness. I heard voices above me and thought I saw someone moving the drum that had been knocked directly into the path of the oncoming traffic, but no-one came down into the ditch to help. The first thing that ran through my mind as I was lying dazed in the dirt was that my health insurance had run out months earlier in Colombia, and I hadn't renewed it. As I tried to work out if I'd done any damage to myself and the bike, I was thinking in terms of the cost of hospital treatment, something that I'd never had to think about living in the UK.

I started coming to my senses just as the traffic started moving again. I'd been lucky, very lucky. Although I couldn't move because of the weight of the bike I knew right away that no bones were broken, I felt pain but nothing intense, just the kind of thing that would remind me of the accident for a few weeks or months. I tried to pull my leg out from under the battered Apache but it was useless, the full weight was on my leg and no matter which way I twisted or pulled, it wouldn't budge. The bike was slightly above me on the incline of the ditch so I was pinned to the bottom and I couldn't get my other leg into a position to try and push. I was able to reach the ignition so I turned off the engine in case any fuel had spilled, then spent a few seconds just looking at the bike and wondering what on earth I would do. I didn't shout curses into my helmet this time, actually I'd already taken my helmet off to help me breathe. I just sat there in awe of how monumentally stupid I'd been to ride fast in those conditions, but also wondering who on earth had put a huge metal drum in the middle of the road. The speeding was easy to understand, I was rushing. Rushing to beat the traffic coming the other way because I thought I might be in the same lane as them. Rushing to get out of the hellish road conditions, and rushing just because it was 8pm and I was still out on the road. But the metal drum, I've still no idea about that.

If you laid me down on the floor right now, gently placed the Apache onto my leg and told me to lift it up, I'm pretty sure I'd find it impossible. It's not a heavy bike, in fact compared to the giant BMW touring bikes it's as light as a feather, but when you're pinned underneath it on a slope it feels like something Atlas couldn't move. So I think it was purely down to the adrenaline that the next time I reached forward and just pushed with everything I had, I was able to lift it enough to slide my leg out from underneath. My jeans were torn to pieces, and my leg was covered in blood, but I could walk without acute pain, so I breathed a huge sigh of relief.

I looked at the poor Apache covered in asphalt and mud and rocks and sand, lying in a dark ditch in the middle of Bolivia, and thought the worst, I'd be leaving it here and hitch hiking to Santa Cruz. It was pitch black because the oncoming lane of traffic had passed and the trucks coming from my own direction hadn't arrived yet. I brushed away some of the thick layer of mud that covered my denim jacket and jeans, tried to clear the mounds of mud that covered the front of the bike, then lifted it up onto its wheels. I couldn't feel anything heavy hanging off, and the bike supported itself, so I began to have a bit of hope. I got back in the saddle, and tried to start it up. No luck. The ignition switch turned and the sidelights came on giving me a bit of light, but the engine wouldn't start. I let it sit for a moment in the upright position then tried again, and this time it started up and the engine began to tick over as normal. I wasn't yet sure that it was rideable, but was feeling a lot more confident.

Once I got the bike pointing in the right direction, I gently turned the throttle and was soon bouncing along the bottom of the ditch at around 10kmph, over the rocks and debris. Then I saw a space where the side of the ditch was lower and the ground was smooth, and accelerated. The Apache sailed up over the edge, and back into the road, just as the trucks which had been following me in the traffic were arriving. I must have been quite a sight as I emerged from the darkness, clothes covered in mud, leg covered in blood. There was no place to pull over out of the way without going back down into the ditch so I just started riding along again in front of the line of traffic. I rode slowly with the trucks honking behind me, but I ignored them and after ten minutes or so when the road widened out again I pulled over for a proper look at the bike. As far as I could see it looked fine. Plenty of surface damage including a scratched up headlight, an indicator hanging off, a missing crash bung, but nothing structural. I tested all the vital things, brakes, lights, steering, then cleaned the headlight again and set off. Later on I found out that the Apache did indeed have a much more serious problem, a twisted steering column, but it was so slight that I didn't notice as I rode the remaining twenty kilometres, under the same terrible conditions as before, into Santa Cruz.

Sometimes you arrive in a city keen to explore, and sometimes you just want to find a bed. This was obviously one of those days when I just wanted a bed, but the first couple of hostels that I found were either closed or full. It took me another hour, but eventually I found a fantastic place with lots of parking, buffet breakfast, and even a swimming pool. I parked the bike behind a secure gate, took off my torn jeans and filthy denim jacket, then took a long shower. I was exhausted, but used my last bit of energy to make some pasta to help my body recover during the night, then went to sleep.

The next day I woke up absolutely aching from head to toe. I had a splitting headache, my left arm ached, my left hip ached, and I had a bruise that was just getting started but was already covering my whole thigh. My left calf hurt and for some reason, my feet hurt. My hands ached partly from the impact of the crash, but also partly from the thousands of gear changes, braking, and accelerating that I'd done over thirteen hours of riding. My body had long since used up the pasta, so I went to work on the buffet breakfast devouring great piles of eggs, fruit, wholemeal bread, and pastries. Then I poured gallons of hot chocolate and fruit juice down my throat, before going back to bed for more sleep.

I woke up again around 10am, and went down to check the Apache in the daylight. The bike now clearly looked like it had been in a crash, and there was damage to the headlight and indicator. But because of a neat little design quirk, the bodywork around the fuel tank and wheel arches was untouched. Some genius at TVS had positioned the crash bungs so well that they took almost all of the impact, and protected the delicate bodywork. I'd already ridden the bike at least thirty kilometres since the crash, so was quite confident as I took it out into the street ready for a morning test run. My initial optimism quickly evaporated though when I started up the bike. It made an awful sound, something like a tiger after it's been trapped in a noose for a week without food and water, and is barely clinging to life, still a growl, but hollow and weak. It was at least rideable though, so I found a street nearby full of mechanics' workshops and took the bike there.

Choosing a mechanic is a real art form. If you know your stuff you could ask questions, but in that case why not do the job yourself? You could look at the workshop and always go for a clean professional looking outfit with a big Yamaha or Suzuki sign above, but then they might be several times the price of an independent. And even a nice looking workshop is still no guarantee, I've had a professional looking mechanic leave my clutch rod undone after a repair, in Germany, so you never know. Anyway on this particular day I got it badly wrong and chose an absolute rogue. I thought that despite the fact the workshop was small with no branding, that because he had two customers waiting outside, he might be well known locally. And nine times out of ten that would be reasonable logic, but it didn't work this time.

He was quick enough to get my bike up onto the sidewalk-workshop and take a look, and to be fair he went to the trouble of taking it for a test run around the block, so I was feeling quite relaxed. But then he started installing a ridiculous little fuel filter that looked like something out of a Christmas cracker. He couldn't get the thing to sit right next to the carburetor so he cut the rubber fuel line in half to make it shorter. Then he bent the remaining fuel pipe backwards on itself, he literally folded it like he was doing origami, and started to put the other parts back together. 'Whoa, wait,' I said 'there's no way that's going to work, how will the fuel get through?' 'No it's fine,' he replied confidently 'I've done it lots of times before'. So I reluctantly went to pay, and it was very cheap considering he'd spent an hour working on it, but I still thought that I wouldn't make it two blocks. I started up the bike, which did sound a lot better after all the cleaning and tinkering, and rode away. But I was right, it didn't make it two blocks and after about one minute the engine cut out, so I pushed it back the few hundred meters to the mechanic, and told him to take out the filter. Now you'd think that he'd be mortified at his shoddy work, hugely apologetic and embarrassed that the exact problem that I'd told him about when he was fixing the bike had caused the breakdown. But he just said 'OK, no problem' like I was asking for an upgrade. Then after he removed it, he just stood there like a lemon with the filter in his hand, presumably waiting for me to leave so I said 'I've paid for that filter, it didn't work, I want my ten bob back' 'OK, no problem' he said and we walked to the counter. Along the way he kept pointing to the rubber fuel pipe attached to the filter that he'd cut to make fit, but I had no idea why. Then at the counter he said something that I didn't understand to the guy who was clearly the owner of the shop, and he gave me back only five bob, about half the cost of the filter. We're only talking about fifty pence so it wasn't about the money, but I couldn't believe the cheek of it, they were trying to charge me because the idiot had cut the pipe when he was trying to force it into place. I ranted for a minute or so until they gave me back the other five bob, but let them keep the sixty bob for labour, because the bike really did sound a lot better after all the meddling.

My rush to get to Santa Cruz was, of course, ridiculous, but it's even more so when you remember that Santa Cruz was not even my final destination. What I really wanted to see in Bolivia was the Jesuit Circuit further north, near the border with Brazil. But as I was here in Santa Cruz anyway, I decided to go for a walk to a nearby produce market and see a bit of the city. Also the bungees holding my bag onto the bike had gotten covered in sticky asphalt that was impossible to clean, so I needed to buy some new ones, and also get my torn jeans fixed. I found a tailor on the fourth floor of the market building where I went to buy lunch, and I found the bungees in a small shop on the second floor. The tailor asked me what kind of material I wanted and I said 'the strongest you have, I don't care how it looks, just make it strong', and she said OK. The result was excellent, in my opinion, because she didn't make any effort at all to hide the damage and rather made it into a feature with huge zigzagged stitching across the outside and a thick piece of denim on the inside. The vertical and horizontal gashes that opened up when the jeans took the impact of my fall, once repaired, formed a perfect Chinese character, *shang*. Which means to go up, or improve, for example your driving skills, so very appropriate.

On the way back from the market I went on a detour, and took a walk through the Mennonite area of Santa Cruz. For two blocks all I saw was men wearing exactly the same uniform of black boots, dark dungarees, a light shirt and white cowboy hat, and women wearing traditional and highly conservative dresses with ankle socks and neck covers. The enclave was even more homogeneous than Neuland in Paraguay, so I thought there'd been some kind of event, but I asked someone and they said no, it's the same every day. Can't argue with that, it's not so different from the City of London where everyone wears the same black suits, it's just that for Mennonites, almost all the time is work time.

After a restful couple of days in the hostel, letting my body recover from the crash and planning my route through the Jesuit Circuit, I set off. Not on a loop that would end back in Sucre where I could sell the bike as originally planned, but a more linear route that would take me east, all the way to a remote frontier post on the border with Brazil. I'd changed my plans again as I was looking at the map trying to work out a route through the Missions, and got distracted by the huge expanse of lush green that started only a few kilometres to the north. It was the Amazon Rainforest, and the immense green area continued from here all the way through Brazil and into Colombia. There were parts of the jungle that you definitely couldn't ride to, that only boats or aircraft could reach. And although I'd already experienced the amazon in Colombia, Ecuador, and also Peru, the idea of taking a boat deep into the Brazilian Amazon still seemed special. As for selling the bike, I'd already done almost 23,000km across some of the worst conditions on the planet, and crashed it into a ditch, so how much could it even be worth now? Also I read online that the Port of Manaus free trade zone in northern Brazil was another good place for selling bikes, cars, and all kinds of things.

I was justifying a decision that my heart had already taken, and I was heading back into the Amazon. But first, the Jesuit Circuit of Bolivia, and my first stop would be the mission at San Jose de Chiquitos, the most developed and well preserved of the missions, and the easiest to get to by road. The rest of the missions are located further North and each one, would you believe, has its own airport. Many of the tourists have some kind of connection to Jesuits or the Christian faith and they fly in from Santa Cruz or even directly from overseas to one of the airports then take organized 4x4 tours around the circuit. The Missions themselves were built in the 17th century when the Jesuits, funded by some rich Spanish Catholics, set out to convert the last remaining parts of South America to Christianity. Far into the interior of the continent between the frontiers of Spanish (West), and Portuguese (East) South America. And if you're thinking that sounds like a tough mission, then you'd be right, but the Jesuits were tough people. Catholic missionaries who'd sworn vows of chastity, poverty, and obedience to the Jesuit Society, they were expected to accept any mission, anywhere in the world, under any conditions, and are commonly known as God's Soldiers.

With this kind of funding and determination, it's no surprise that the Missions were successful in their conversion objectives. Then again, when the alternative for local people at the time was slavery at the hands of Spanish and Portuguese settlers, the bar was set pretty low. The Missions were built as fortified towns that actively fought against other powers in the area, and protected the inhabitants. Local people could live in the settlements, learn Spanish language and culture, undergo conversion, and find work in return for the Missions protection. But a hundred years later it all stopped, when the Spanish elite decided that they didn't like the Jesuits any more, and the settlements were abandoned by the missionaries. The buildings survived though, and in the 1970s a Jesuit architect from Switzerland started a programme of restoration. Then in 1986 a film was made about the last days of the Jesuits, starring Robert de Niro, which brought the area to global prominence. The rest as they say, is tourism—industry history.

The Mission at San Jose de Chiquitos is incredible, a real beauty and a credit not only to the original Jesuit designers, but also the local craftsmen who built it. Not to mention the Swiss architect who restored it, and the native craftsmen's great—grandsons who re—built it. I arrived just in time for sunset and didn't even bother checking—in to a hotel. I went straight there and watched as the sand coloured outer walls turn to warm pinks and reds, before the sun disappeared behind the leafy park outside the front gate. It was another one of those completely visual experiences, and I didn't move for an hour while I watched the colours change, before the lights came on and turned the walls golden. As you might expect, the missions are quiet places of contemplation, and I was relieved to find that there were virtually no other tourists on that day. Perhaps it just wasn't tourist season, but in any case I took full advantage, and the next morning came back to spend another few hours inside and outside the building, just enjoying the beauty and tranquillity. The next stop on the circuit was San Ignacio de Velasco, two hundred kilometres to the north.

Although I hadn't done a huge amount of route planning on this journey, the Jesuit Circuit was one place where it really was essential. The roads are entirely made of earth, and there's no asphalt north of San Jose, although some sections are finished with gravel and other hard materials. This means that the weather will make a huge difference to riding conditions on the route. If it's dry then the road will be solid and relatively easy to navigate, but you might have problems with excessive dust, slippery sand patches, or the dreaded washboard road. On the other hand, if it's wet, then the road could be impassable for anything less than a 4x4 or motorcycle with full mud terrain tyres, and even then it wouldn't be guaranteed. Apart from two days of heavy rain while I was in Santa Cruz, the weather had otherwise been dry since I entered Bolivia, and the reports indicated another massive dry spell. Five full days of scorching hot weather with zero rain, so this was definitely the right time to do the circuit, and I needed to complete it within five days. If I didn't then I might find myself stuck in one of the towns in a rainstorm, with impassable mud roads for two hundred kilometres in every direction. And who knows how long it could take for them to dry out.

The first day's riding had gone excellently and I arrived in San Jose ahead of schedule, but that was on smooth asphalt highways. The route out of San Jose towards San Ignacio was the first narrow, dirt road section of the circuit proper, and it started as soon as I left town. I calculated that the 211km between the two Mission towns would take me around three and a half hours at an average speed of 70kmph. And I estimated the 70kmph based on an average of half the distance at 90kmph, and half the distance on rough sections at 50kmph, plus thirty minutes for water breaks and any rocky parts where I'd need to slow right down. So I left San Jose at around 10am and expected to be in San Ignacio around 1:30pm in the afternoon. Just in time for lunch, and hopefully to spend a long afternoon visiting the Mission and enjoying a coffee next to the park. I knew there'd be a park because all the buildings were restored in the same style, with a city park opposite, where people could relax and enjoy the architecture.

The first hour out of San Jose was fine, just about the best dirt road you could hope for in such a remote area, and 90kmph was no problem. Then I hit a rough patch, and just as expected I was down to between 30 and 60kmph, so an average of 50kmph seemed just about right. Some more fast road was followed by a rough patch, and a few rocky sections, but I was still on schedule. The only problem was the dry heat, it was ferocious and there was absolutely nowhere to hide. While I was doing ninety it was just about bearable with a hot breeze, but anything less than 50kmph was like a dry sauna. The bike wasn't enjoying it all that much either, it sounded tired, and I could feel the heat coming off it warming up my legs even more. Then all of a sudden I spotted in the distance my arch enemy, who I hadn't seen since that cold dark morning in the Atacama Desert...Washboard Road. Even before I'd reached the sand ridges I could feel my bones quaking in fear of the complete destruction they were about to endure.

It was every bit as bad as expected. Even though I'd slowed down to 50kmph I was still slamming into four ridges every second, and it went on for so long that I started to get concerned about breaking down again. These were very remote roads, and I'd seen only a couple of 4x4 tourist vehicles since I left San Jose. Such a fierce shaking could not be good for any of the thousand components that could shake loose, and in this heat, that seemed all the more likely. No matter how slow I went, I just couldn't stop the battering, so I decided to try fast again. Back in El Tatio, Chile, going fast had not been an option because my thin road tyres were cutting into the ridges, forcing the bike sideways, and throwing me around. But perhaps here with the fierce heat, the ridges had been compacted more and I might be able to skip over them like the 4x4 vehicles that were now overtaking me at 90kmph. So I pushed harder, and endured an almighty battering up to around 70kmph. Then my tyre did, as expected, get caught in a ridge and was pushed sideways, throwing me into a massive wobble and skid across the sand. I managed to control the bike, but slowed back down to forty. There were tiny periods of respite, like when I went across some big rocks, or sandy sections where I was constantly having to put my foot down, but not many.

The washboard road lasted around two hours, at which point the road returned to just flat dirt, and I could get back to cruising speed. My whole body ached once again but the final 90km to San Ignacio were beautiful. The flat road meant that I could keep up a respectable speed, and the speed meant that I could keep cool with the breeze. And because I didn't need to concentrate every second to avoid an accident, I could look up and enjoy the landscape. I arrived in San Ignacio at 15:00, an hour and a half behind schedule, but still with more than enough time to see the Mission and enjoy a coffee before dinner.

Around 5pm I started to think about a place to stay. Usually this is the first thing I do, but at both towns I chose to go straight to the Mission, then spend a couple of hours relaxing and eating. It was just so easy, they were tiny places with only one major attraction next to the main park, which was also always the location of all the cafes and restaurants. I could walk around the mission then pop over to the cafe and park my bike right outside, anywhere I liked on the wide empty roads. So that's what I did in San Ignacio, and after a huge lunch at an excellent local restaurant, I checked the map. I'd been staying in hostels for a while, and the weather was perfect, so I checked for places to camp and, Bingo! there was an unofficial campsite next to a lake just two minutes' drive from the town centre.

The location was great, a small grassy area right next to an open lake and as the sun was beginning to go down you could tell it was going to be another stunning sunset. There were still quite a lot of people around because it was a Saturday, so I just enjoyed the view, read my book and thought about where to pitch the tent. There was an ideal location that looked like it was almost made for camping, a flat piece of ground a couple of feet higher than the surrounding lawns so it wouldn't flood, with soft short grass on top. Now that I knew where I'd be setting up, I waited for the last few groups of people to leave, but they didn't show any indication of moving on. Remember this was not an official campsite, I was wild camping in a public place and didn't want to draw too much attention to myself, so I waited a bit longer. After another thirty minutes one group of people sitting right next to where I wanted to pitch, were still not showing any sign of leaving, so I looked around and found another spot that wasn't quite so good. The grass was rougher and there were a few stones, but it still had a lake view and probably wouldn't flood, so I just pitched the tent there. Then about thirty minutes after I'd finished setting up, the people left, and I was cursing the fact that I hadn't been more patient. I considered moving, but in the end just stayed where I was and settled down to sleep. It was the best decision I've ever made, because a couple of hours later at around midnight, long after the lights had turned off and it was pitch black, a jeep came flying into the parking lot. It weaved around some benches and a playground, then drove directly through the spot where I was thinking of putting the tent.

Once it reached the water four men got out of the jeep, along with an amplifier, and started to play loud music on the lakeside. They'd brought a few cases of beer which they unloaded next to the car, and started to walk around. One guy went on his mobile phone, while another started dancing on his own, and a third moved like he was going to dance, but then looked over at me and smiled. He just stared for a few seconds, then bent over and started to vomit the entire contents of his stomach onto the grass. Just as suddenly as they'd arrived, they packed up the amplifier and left. Two guys helping their sick friend into the car before they drove off again, right over the spot where I was going to put the tent. The next morning, I woke at sunrise feeling exhausted, but once I saw the colours on the lake, and heard the birds in the trees, I was re-energised. A capybara and her three young swam silently up to the lakeside, then walked straight up onto the grass. They stayed for a moment until they realised I was standing not far from them, then quickly slipped back into the water, what a way to start the day.

I'd already decided that I wasn't doing the normal circuit that takes you back to Santa Cruz or Sucre in Bolivia, so my next stop was the Brazilian border post at San Matias, three hundred kilometres to the east. The Jesuit Mission Circuit itself is already a challenging road in a remote part of South America, but taking a 300km route away from the circuit and into who knows where, was quite an exciting prospect. The continent is so huge that it's easy to become blase about these distances, but that's the equivalent of London to Leeds, on a narrow dirt back-road, with only a few villages on the route, in searing semi-desert heat.

My mental gymnastics went to work again assuring me that at some point the road must turn to asphalt, because it led to a border post. If I broke down there must be at least one car or truck within a few hours, because people would be bringing stuff into the area from Brazil. But I was forgetting the much larger border post on the main highway linking Southern Brazil to Santa Cruz, and there wasn't even a petrol station at the frontier between Bolivia and Chile at Ollague. After the Capybara had quietly gone back into the lake, I ate a quick breakfast, packed up the tent and set off. Usually I'd wait for the tent to dry out because it always gets wet from the dew, but the road to the border would be so hot and dry that this wouldn't be a problem. And it was a good idea to set off earlier, because the washboard road started again less than thirty kilometres out of town.

My bike had already taken a beating when I crashed near Santa Cruz, so when the bone shaking started up again it was a real concern. Every little component, every nut, bolt, and screw, every rubber cap, the light filaments, the fuel filter, were all being shaken to death and I was just waiting for something to go wrong. I wasn't so much worried about breaking down because there were a few villages along the route, and I had seen a vehicle coming into San Ignacio from this direction as I left town. It was more that I didn't fancy having another accident out here in the baking heat. There were hundreds of small lagoons on either side of the path, and the jungle was right behind those, but here on the road it was dry, dusty, and fiercely hot. The washboard road went on for hours, thud thud thud thud, as I hit hundreds of ridges every minute and I had to slow down again to less than 30kmph. There were flatter sections, but they had slippery sand slopes that made me paranoid about getting caught between two impassable inclines. And by now I wasn't even looking up at the road ahead, let alone enjoying the landscape, because I had to keep my eyes on the ground constantly, watching as the tyres swerved and pitched through the sand. It was during one of these periods of intense concentration as the thud thud thud of the washboard shook me to pieces, and I had my eyes firmly fixed on the ground directly in front of the bike, that I realised I'd just passed a huge, fat, alligator.

I passed the giant reptile within three metres, about the same length as it's body including the tail. But I wasn't even aware of it until we were side by side and it turned violently in my direction and hissed like a snake. I instinctively revved the engine which usually keeps any kind of animals at bay, and carried on riding for twenty metres, praying that this wouldn't be the point that one of those components finally broke. But then my curiosity overcame my caution and I stopped the bike to turn around and take a look. I wouldn't have done that if I'd have thought it was going to be sitting there waiting for me. But I couldn't hear anything and I couldn't see anything in my mirror, so I was pretty sure it had gone. I kept my engine running as a precaution, and turned around only to see the end of a tail vanishing into the undergrowth. The fact that it had escaped rather than taking an interest in me, and the fact that I had a loud motorcycle engine to scare it off, hopefully, if it did come back, gave me a bit of confidence. So I slowly rode back to take a look, but there was nothing, not even the sound of it moving through the reeds. For the next few minutes I rode along laughing to myself like a lunatic with the joy of having had such a beautiful experience, until one of the bungees that was holding my backpack onto the back of the bike, snapped. The bag didn't fall to the ground, but was left hanging off the side so I needed to stop and deal with it. I always carry a spare so it only took a moment to get it out of the backpack and tie around, but I spent the whole time looking over at the undergrowth between me and the nearest lagoon.

Usually it's always in the back of my mind that even if the worst happened, I could always pitch my tent and wait, overnight if necessary, for a vehicle to come along. But this wasn't the place to do that. The fact that an alligator would just brazenly walk along the road in the middle of the day meant the place was full of them, so breaking down or falling off here would be risky. Not to mention the fact that this was a narrow dusty road, between thick undergrowth and lagoons. There was simply no place to pitch a tent, without the risk of getting hit by any cars that did happen to come this way. In any case the road quickly flattened out, and I was soon back up to 80kmph again, cooling off slightly in the breeze and only slowing down for the occasional wooden bridge. On one bridge I saw people fishing, and when I looked closer noticed that they were carrying heavy duty equipment and had a big truck. My guess was that they might be tourists hunting alligators, but who knows. I reached the frontier at San Matias around 2:30pm, with plenty of time to complete the border procedures and, assuming the roads across the border were asphalt which they had been in the south, make it to the first town in Brazil.

You never really know what you're going to get at a border post. Sometimes they're super-efficient, no queues, knowledgeable staff, and your done and dusted in twenty minutes. When I walked into the Bolivian police station in San Matias and saw that there were no other travellers and just one policeman on reception, I thought this was going to be one of those, but it wasn't. First of all, the migration guy was at lunch, and wouldn't be back until around 3pm, not the end of the world so I waited. He really did come back on time so all was still looking good, but then he told me that the customs office was across town and reminded me that it was Sunday so it might be closed, although unbelievably, he wasn't quite sure. San Matias is tiny and it was only a ten-minute ride, so I just went straight over, but sure enough it was closed. I went back to the migration office and asked if there was any other way, and they said there was a customs point on the actual frontier line 20km further along the road, but it would definitely be closed. So finally I asked the officer if there was anywhere in San Matias that I could pitch a tent, and although he initially said no, he remembered that there was a football pitch nearby that I could try. With nothing to do for the rest of the day, I took a long lunch then bought some fruit in the market before heading over to the football pitch around 5pm, to check it out.

There was a game on, and it must have been important because the whole town was there cheering on one side or the other, and the quality was surprisingly good. We were in the middle of nowhere, but then again we were on the border with Brazil so perhaps it wasn't so surprising. The score was 1-0 when I arrived according to the old guy standing next to me, who then proceeded to get more and more irate as the game went on, and it ended in a draw 1 – 1. The game finished around 6pm and the football fans started moving on shortly after that as it started to get dark. I found a place near the small gazebo where the substitutes and coaches were sitting during the game, and pitched the tent. It was a great spot and I parked the Apache underneath the gazebo, so it even had covered parking, awesome. The only downside was that the cleaners weren't coming until the morning, so the place was littered with discarded water bottles and the remains of empanadas and fried chicken.

I got my head down early around 8:30pm, and apart from a few people walking across the pitch to get home, and several horses who'd been let into the field to graze, the place was silent. One of the horses came right next to the tent and started munching the grass really loudly, but it wasn't enough to keep me awake, and I was asleep in minutes. Then around 1am in the morning, I was woken up by another sound, the low menacing growl of what was clearly a very big, and very angry, dog.

I sat up in my sleeping bag and listened for a moment before realising that it wasn't just one dog, but a whole pack. I heard around six different growls, all within two metres of the tent. The football pitch which was empty at night, was clearly these dogs' territory, and I'd gone and pitched my tent right in the middle of it. Not only that but tonight was buffet night, when they'd be feasting on all the chicken bones thrown away by the football fans. At first I tried to ignore it, thinking that maybe they'd get bored when no sounds came from this strange animal that smelt like a human, but looked like a cow lying down on its side. Then after ten minutes or so they started coming closer, barking much more loudly and biting at the guy lines and outer shell. I couldn't just wait for them to tear open the tent and start attacking me, so I decided to do something about it.

This story could have been called *Dogs and Vultures* based on the sheer number of stray dogs and flocks of vultures that were my constant companions on the road. The actual title is a bit clearer, but to be honest when I look back on the journey, the dogs and the vultures are one of the first things that jump out. So it wasn't my first time meeting a dog that wasn't keen to make friends, but it was the first time that I'd been vulnerable, sitting in a small tent asleep, when six of them surrounded me and started growling. Although I knew from cartoons and crime movies that the best thing to do with angry dogs is to throw them a bone, or better still a slice of beef, I didn't have either to hand. And although my second choice would have been Relationship Based Training Methods, there was simply no time and in any case, our relationship was based on them eating me. So I went for the least good option, I'd claim the territory, including the chicken bones.

I looked around the tent for something heavy and hard, and found my motorcycle helmet. The next best thing would have been my boots, but they were sitting outside, and the rank smell was probably what made the dogs angry in the first place, so that wasn't really an option. I picked up the helmet, unzipped the inner shell and started yelling, not at the top of my voice, but in a loud measured tone trying to sound in-charge. Then I unzipped the outer shell and stepped out into the darkness, dressed only in my boxers and holding the helmet at shoulder height, ready to crash it down on the nearest dog. There were two standing right in front of me, and another four behind the tent.

Perhaps it was the shock of seeing me in my underpants, but they all stopped barking for a second and just stared at me, before the biggest one who was standing behind another slightly smaller dog, started up again. The slightly smaller dog ran forward and tried half-heartedly to bite me on my knee before pulling back, and I took the opportunity to swipe at the bigger dog. I missed him by a whisker and he backed off to about twenty metres away, the five other dogs following behind. They didn't run away though, they just stood there growling again. So I started yelling again and ran after them waving the helmet in the air like a barbarian. That was enough, and they ran off towards the edge of the field. I watched them for a while as they milled about, then the big dog ran over to the other side of the football field and started rooting around in the chicken bones over there. I'd successfully claimed this side of the pitch, and they stuck to the agreement until I packed up my tent and left around 8am in the morning. Before I left one of the smaller dogs came back over, but this time in a much better mood, as I was drying the tent in the sunshine. He didn't quite come close enough for me to pat him on the head, just close enough to say hello before rooting around in the garbage near the fence.

The customs office was still closed when I arrived at around 8:15am so I went and filled up with petrol at the station opposite. Then I parked the bike near an empanada stand, put the tent over the bike to dry a bit more in the sunshine, and had empanadas and coffee for breakfast. The lady who served me had been there a while and knew the routine, the customs agents would be here at 08:30, order empanadas then go in to work, which they did.

There is one really annoying thing about the San Matias border crossing, and that's that Brazilian customs is in a city about 80km past the frontier. I was heading north, but the city is to the east so I had to make a huge detour. All in all, the border crossing took about three hours including an extra military checkpoint and the detour into town, so it was lunchtime before I finally got on the road to Pontes-e-Lacerda in Brazil. This wasn't a problem though, because I'm a very patient person. Which is lucky, because the border agent told me that both the Bolivian customs on the frontier line, and Brazilian migration and customs, had all been open the day before. Well at least I'd gotten to see some more Bolivian wildlife.

11
Fine, I'll do it myself:
BRAZIL (Second leg)

The highways in Amazonia were just as well constructed as those I'd ridden earlier when I crossed the south of Brazil. Clearly a lot of money has been spent on asphalt across an absolutely huge area, so taxpayers of Brazil, I salute you. There is one completely understandable exception though, a nine hundred kilometre stretch of road, four hundred kilometres of which has never been paved, from Porto Velho to Manaus. It runs in a straight line directly through a pristine part of the Amazon Rainforest, and it's called BR319, also known as, The Worst Road in the World.

When you first look at the map, it seems as though there's a continuous road all the way from the south of Brazil to Manaus, and continuing up to the border with Venezuela. And it's true, technically there is, but while the majority of the route is decent asphalt, section BR319 is world famous as a graveyard for trucks. The original dirt road was built by the Brazilian military government back in the 1970s as part of a grand plan to develop the amazon region, but it was never maintained properly. As you might expect, the jungle tore it to pieces, and although in 2006 a new internet cable route meant that the road was kept serviceable for company maintenance vehicles, it was never asphalted. The result is that in the rainy season the road gets churned up with mud over a metre deep, and it's become a place of pilgrimage for off-road enthusiasts and monster trucks. My little Apache with standard road tyres didn't stand a chance, and I realised this when I saw a picture online of a monster truck towing a regular 4x4 truck out of the mud.

The alternative is much better, a leisurely cruise down the Amazon, sleeping in a hammock on an all-inclusive river ferry. So now I just needed to get to Porto Velho from where the ferry departed, still more than a thousand kilometres further north, and the roads were so good in this part of Brazil that I was tempted to do the whole route in two days. But fatigue is dangerous when you're motorcycling, fatal probably if you do it enough. So my first priority after the ordeal of the washboard road, the alligator, and the wild dogs, was just to get some rest and do some shopping. I stopped quite early in Pontes-e-Lacerda, a pleasant town just off the highway, and found a hotel where I booked a private room with an included buffet breakfast. Usually I love meeting people and cooking, but I really just needed to rest, and also find a mechanic to do some minor repairs on the bike.

This time I was much luckier with my choice of mechanic, and he turned out to be Colombian. When he saw the bike and heard my story, he said he'd fix the indicator with some super glue and tape for free, and while I was there I also had the chain adjusted and re-lubricated, and bought some new bungees. Then while I was in the hardware store looking for glue, for the next time I dropped the bike and broke the indicator, I noticed a pair of safety goggles that were thin and curved like sunglasses and completely covered the eyes. Not perfect, but a very good substitute for my scratched up visor, they were crystal clear and when I wore them it felt like there wasn't anything in front of my eyes, so I could really enjoy the landscape again. Once I'd finished getting supplies I had an early dinner, then went back to my hotel and just slept right through.

The breakfast in my hotel the next morning was unbelievable, an unlimited buffet of eggs, meat, breads, cakes, yoghurt, fruit, quiches, juices, quality coffee, everything. The lady behind the counter must have thought I hadn't eaten for a week, and actually it's true that I'd skipped a few meals or eaten lightly for a few days, so I just gorged myself. I probably got the full cost of the hotel back in cake alone. Then I rode an easy three hundred kilometres to Vilhena, and had another relaxing day in another quiet hotel, then ate another awesome breakfast. By now I was completely recovered and looking forward to the boat ride into the amazon, but there was one more stop to make along the way. I didn't have a particular town in mind, but after riding for a few hours started to feel tired just north of Ji−Parana, and looked at the map. There was an ecological reserve about thirty kilometres off the main highway, about a hundred kilometres further along, so I pushed on until I reached the reserve, just outside Caucaulandia.

The town of Caucaulandia wasn't even on any of the online maps, but the written directions given in the overlander app were super accurate and took me straight there. What a place, the reserve had been described as paradise on earth and I had to agree. An immaculately tended farm with rooms for twenty or so guests, and a small grassy area by a lake for tents. There were green and red parrots in the trees, geese and a peacock walking around the gardens, and cows grazing in the fields. Hundreds of other breeds of bird were flying overhead or playing on the other side of the small lake. The owner gave me an excellent rate to pitch the tent, and also have use of an outdoor kitchen and showers, there was even a small swimming pool, although I didn't use it.

Once I'd pitched the tent I went and sat by the lake to enjoy the wildlife, and the cool evening air. The place really was paradise, supremely relaxing and I didn't even mind when at 05:30am in the morning, I was woken up by rumbling in the sky. A major storm was less than five minutes away. The owner was much better informed about the weather than me, and he'd asked if I wanted to pitch the tent by the lake or bring it onto the veranda of the guesthouse. I thought it was an odd question at the time because it was so beautiful by the lake, but now it made more sense, he'd just assumed that I knew about the storm. I managed to get the tent and my stuff under the veranda roof just as the heavens opened, then ran out again to push the Apache under the roof of the shower block, which kept it half dry. The storm was just as impressive as the sunset had been the night before, lighting, huge claps of thunder, tremendous rain that caused little rivers of water to run down to the lake, and then it stopped, suddenly, after around thirty minutes. By nine o'clock the bike and all my things were completely dry again, and I set off for Porto Velho.

After another straightforward and uneventful ride along a very good, but very boring, Brazilian highway, I arrived in Port Velho in the afternoon. After checking-in to a hotel I went straight over to the river port to ask about buying a ticket to Manaus. There was a boat leaving in two days, so I bought a ticket for myself and the Apache. It was the most expensive thing that I'd bought for a while, but considering that it transported me and the bike over a thousand kilometres north, avoiding a road that was probably impassable, it was worth it. Also it wasn't just a cargo ship, but a full service boat with three meals a day and entertainment, so it was actually quite good value. And the fact that I'd be sleeping on an open deck in the cool night air, on a hammock, only added to the adventure. They even said that because the boat was already docked in the port, that if I'd like to board a day early and save myself the cost of a hotel then I'd be welcome, so that's what I did. The next day I looked around Porto Velho in the morning, but nothing much to report, it's a nice enough city, but I was really just focused on getting the boat. Then in the afternoon I rode down to the docks and spoke with the ticket officer, who showed me to the right ferry.

The docks were like something straight out of a Jules Verne novel, and I felt like Phileas Fogg as I walked across the narrow, bouncing gangplanks to board the boat, dodging the merchant sailors who were loading all manner of merchandise. I put down my bag on the second deck where I could fix up a hammock, and asked the lady who sold me the ticket about loading the bike. It was at this point that I realised the real pirate was not one of the tough looking merchant sailors running back and forth across the water, but the ticket lady, when she said 'boarding the bike is not included in the price.' What a scam, they sell you a ticket not only for yourself but specifically including the motorcycle, then refuse to load the thing from the port to the boat. After a few minutes of arguing she said that the boat would take care of getting it from the first deck up to the second deck, where it would be stowed for the voyage, but I'd have to pay to bring it across from the dockside.

Now this part is a little difficult to explain, because although it sounds quite simple, getting the bike on to the boat was really not straightforward. There was a winch, but it couldn't reach all the way to the dockside, because there was no dockside, it was just a muddy slope, and there wasn't even a proper gangway. There was just a loose, chaotic arrangement of thin and bendy pieces of wood, that barely managed to support the sailors as they crossed with melons and bags of onions. Basically not something you'd want to use to transport your beloved motorcycle over a span of water. The sensible thing to do might have been to just pay up and look on in wonder as the experienced merchant sailors maneuvered the bike across. But I wasn't in any mood to cave in to a scam, and I'd also been reading a bit too much Treasure Island, so I said 'Fine, I'll do it myself.'

With the dockers and sailors still running up and down the gangplanks, I chose quiet moments to move them into two, almost straight, lines up onto the boat. Near enough together that in theory I could stand on one set of planks, while leaning over and pushing the bike up the other set by the handlebar, simple. It took about ten minutes and quite a few adjustments, but eventually I managed to do it without annoying anyone too much. Then I realised that they were so close together that the dockers were bumping into each other as they tried to pass with wide items to load. So I moved them apart again, and would just have to lean in a bit more to push the bike. I walked back over to the muddy slope that served as a dock, and up the slight hill to where my bike was waiting, then turned on the ignition, and put it into neutral.

When I looked up all the dockers and sailors including the loading manager had stopped loading, and were looking at me as I moved the bike to the edge of the slope. The Pirate Ticket Lady told me later that they were literally taking wagers on how far I'd get across, before I dropped the bike into the water. But it didn't bother me, because I had determination. That admirable quality that had gotten me into a night–time crash in the middle of roadworks in Bolivia, and almost got me killed on a frozen washboard road in Chile. In fact, by this time I was really quite confident, after all I'd ridden full speed over a bridge made of branches and mud almost as thin as these planks while crossing water rapids in Peru.

I pushed the bike down the slope to get a bit of momentum, then straight up onto the first right–hand plank, which bent deeply under the bike's weight. At the same time, I jumped onto the first left–hand one, while leaning over to keep hold of the bike. I leaned in even more to steer onto the second right–hand plank, which I'd laid at a kind of crooked angle, and walked along the left–hand one which didn't actually reach the boat. It was being supported by another piece of wood tied to the right hand plank and when the bike went over that, it made me jump up in the air. That was also the moment when I really had to lean in to push the bike upwards, and probably the point that most of the sailors wagered that I'd capsize. In any case I was 110% committed now and just kept walking, balancing, leaning, pushing until both myself and the Apache hopped down onto the ferry deck. The moment passed in a second, and when I turned around the sailors were back to work, but I did get a few half admiring, half annoyed looks. I'd given them a fun distraction for a moment, but not the fifty Reales they would have preferred. Pirate Ticket Lady was very impressed and told me about the wagers.

Anyway now the bike was safely on–board I stowed my stuff in a reasonably safe corner on the second deck, and went out to buy a hammock. I found an excellent one, well made, comfortable, but also fairly lightweight and it didn't cost the earth. I bought it from the same place that the sailors got theirs. It was a small shop in a side street near the dockside, and next door to the shop was a hardware store where you could buy rope to hang your hammock on the metal hooks along the deck. I found an excellent spot on the second deck near the port side that I thought might give me a good view during the voyage, then lay down to read more *Treasure Island* in Spanish. I imagined that my hammock was fixed not to a ferry on the amazon river, but to the deck of the merchant ship La Espanola, ready to set sail on the high seas.

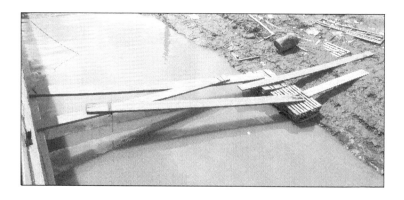

The boat wasn't due to leave until the next day so I had plenty of time just to relax, read, and watch the loading. It was fascinating, not just melons and onions, but also vehicles, and there was another motorbike, a jet ski, and even a couple of the *Google Cars* that they use to drive around filming everyone. I got talking with the Google driver and he gave me and another guy a tour of the car, showing us how many terabytes the little memory cards could store, and showing off the camera quality. I never asked how on earth they got the heavy cars onto the boat?

Another few people started to board, and a Venezuelan lady set her hammock next to mine so we got chatting. Maria had moved to northern Brazil for work, and her young son was living with relatives. Her job sounded tough, handling wood products in a factory, and I admired her ethic a lot. I met a lot of people in China doing the same thing, living hours away from their families to earn enough to get by. There's some freedom to the lifestyle that traditional communities don't offer, but it's mainly just hard, and lonely. You also come across a lot of racism when you've moved for economic reasons, which is understandable. A few migrants bring much needed diversity, but they also directly compete for work, lowering wages and workplace protections, and change the culture of communities. Too many and you can upset a delicate balance, leading to unrest. It's probably one of the main reasons that many people in Britain wanted to leave one of the world's strongest economic blocs.

We were joined by an older Venezuelan man who'd come to Brazil to visit relatives, and we spoke about the situation in their home country. At the beginning of my journey I'd considered visiting Lake Maracaibo and Merida in Venezuela, just over the border from Colombia. But in the end I decided against it because the news was full of chaotic scenes as pro and anti-Government protesters jostled in the streets. By now after talking with Venezuelan people on the road, I realised that most of what I'd seen on the BBC was simply not true. For example, no-one had even heard of the guy that the US, UK, and Europe were now saying was President, and people blamed US sanctions as much as Government policy for the economic situation. People were leaving to get jobs, just like they do in Europe, not because of politics or the level of violence, which is similar to Colombia. At this point I still wasn't planning on going further than Manaus where I was hoping to sell the bike, but it did get me thinking about what might be possible. Maria and I went ashore to get some dinner, then spent the rest of the evening chatting with other passengers on the top deck, and watching the dockers load the last few trucks' worth of merchandise. Then around 10pm the six or so people who had set up hammocks on the second deck like Maria and myself, settled down to sleep. Although we were still only in the dock, it was great fun sleeping in a hammock, swaying gently in the breeze.

The boat set off around 11am the following day, but not before another sixty people had come on board and setup hammocks on my deck. I thought I'd positioned my hammock right next to the port side for a beautiful river view, but apparently not, as one very large lady found enough room to squeeze in. To be fair the deck did feel cosy now with all the coloured fabrics, and it was lovely to read my book nestled among them, but you couldn't swing from side to side, which is the best part of hammock living. At around 6pm we heard a loud whistle, it was dinnertime. I was dreading the food because how good could it possibly be on a low priced river ferry in Brazil, but actually it was excellent. Maria and I queued for a few minutes as one of the crew managed people in and out of the small dining room ten at a time, then we went in to eat. There was only one option, but it was a good one, a fresh, piping hot beef stew full of meat and vegetables, with rice, and sugary coffee on tap, and the best part was, it was all you can eat. The fresh air was definitely good for the appetite and

I ate a ton, then went back to the hammock to sleep it off.

About four hours later we made a stop at Humaita and as I hadn't realised there would be any stops at all, this was a surprise. A good surprise in that I got to watch the dockers trying to load another huge jet ski, and almost dropping it several times while the owners looked on in horror. But also a bad surprise in that another fifty people came on board with fifty more hammocks, and hung them in spaces that we didn't know were there. River boat hammocks are hung two-tier, not one-tier, apparently, and so the new passengers were hanging their hammocks right above the others, but slightly offset. I had to admire the efficiency of fitting so many hammocks in the space, but I ended up with a giant arse, less than a metre from my face. Luckily they wouldn't be serving any spicy food on board.

The next day passed much like the first and I spent most of the time on the top deck reading or enjoying the river views as we passed by villages and docks along the river. I'd brought my binoculars and the wildlife watching was brilliant, we saw dolphins, eagles, and even some monkeys in the trees when we got closer to the riverbank, and I let the kids on board use the binoculars when I wasn't using them. Then in the evening, to my absolute joy and relief, the big guy in the top hammock disembarked and I no longer had to look at his rear end during the night. Day three passed in much the same way, reading and relaxing in the hammock, wildlife watching, and waiting for the mealtime whistles. I'm not usually a package tour kind of traveller but I was starting to get used to the routine, and enjoyed having absolutely nothing to plan or think about. In the afternoon there was a football game on TV so the crew arranged chairs on an upper deck, and setup a barbeque. The meat arrived by speedboat, and we didn't even need to slow down. But the real highlight of the cruise had to be when we passed the famous, Meeting of the Waters, where the dark blue waters of the Rio Negro flow together with the brown waters of the Amazon River, without mixing together, a wonderful sight. It really was a fantastic way to cover the distance between Porto Velho and Manaus, and I thoroughly recommend it.

We arrived in Manaus port in the mid-evening, and before we docked there was a commotion as people untied hammocks, washed faces, applied make-up, and gathered possessions. I gave my hammock to Maria as a spare because she took the boats often and I wouldn't need it anymore, but was sad to see it go after sleeping so comfortably for a few days. It would have made a nice memento, but when you're travelling on a motorcycle you need to be strict about weight. I knew I'd have to wait for the bike so I said goodbye and sat down on the other side of the deck as the passengers disembarked. Then I went to speak to the loading manager about the Apache. At first he was keen to get another bulky item off the boat so he called a colleague and we went immediately to take a look, but there was bad news. The bike couldn't quite fit between a hundred heavy sacks of onions and the side of the ferry, so it had to wait until everything else had been unloaded first. The ferry was absolutely full of stuff, so he told me it could be as late as the next morning.

I thought about doing it myself again, but that might have been a bit tricky from the top deck down to the dockside, three metres below, without a winch. After a bit of pointless debate, I accepted that there wasn't much to be done, and he said I was welcome to stay on the boat overnight if I preferred to stay with the bike. I told him that would be difficult as I'd already given away my hammock, and he thought about it for a moment. Less than a second later, with incredibly bad timing, a young sailor walked up from the bottom deck with his hammock slung over his shoulder. The manager called him over and demanded 'Hey, give him your hammock!' The look on the poor guy's face said it all, his eyes were wide open with a sense of the injustice, but he said nothing and gave me the hammock anyway without complaint.

The hours passed and the merchandise slowly left the boat, bag by bag, melon by individual melon. It was a slow laborious process, but presumably more efficient under the circumstances than trying to install modern machinery in the ferry and port. In other places they'd load all this stuff with forklifts, wide metal gangplanks, and loading bays, but here they were still doing it the same way they would have done a hundred years ago. The only piece of machinery was a traditional manual winch that was used to unload the jet skis and my bike. Then later in the evening around 11pm the loading stopped, the dockers left, and the sailors went back to their bunks inside shared cabins at the back of the second deck. I didn't notice the guy who'd lent me his hammock, but I was hoping that he had a bunk, and wasn't curled up on a hard floor somewhere plotting my downfall.

So there I was, lying in a hammock on the open deck of a boat, close to midnight, in the Port of Manaus, one of the most dangerous cities in Brazil. Manaus had been in the news a lot that week, because it was in the middle of a murderous gang war that had killed forty people across four prisons in the city. And as I watched the pimps and prostitutes walking up and down the dockside calling to the sailors, I was hoping that the gangs were making money from other lines of business, rather than ransacking newly arrived boats full of jet skis and google cars.

The five or so sailors on my ferry, all hard-as-nails looking Brazilians and Venezuelans, were tucked up warmly in their beds inside the gated section at the rear and I was a bit concerned to say the least, when they locked the gate, leaving me outside on the deck. There was a short stairway down to the bottom deck which was level with the dockside, and it would have taken a pirate about three seconds to come up and murder me in my hammock. But luckily they didn't, and I managed to get a few hours' sleep before the loading started up again around 6am.

One of the first things to be moved was a huge set of pallets at the front of the second deck, which opened up a narrow path around all the other merchandise, and back across to the winch. I could easily push my bike around the path, avoiding The Onion-Bag Passage, so asked the loading manager if we could unload now. He agreed, and the Apache and me were off the boat and heading to the port exit within a few minutes. There was one last scam to endure as I left the port, an extortionate port exit fee, that used up my last remaining dollars, but finally I was here in Manaus from where I'd be heading into the Amazon Jungle. By this time, I'd already run out of Brazilian Reales too, so I had absolutely zero cash, and the first thing I did after leaving the port was to find a cash machine before looking for a place to stay. Although the first couple of places I found were full, the third one was another beauty, with indoor secure parking and a pool table.

Routine is important on a long motorcycle tour. It doesn't matter what kind of routine, whatever is important to you, but you need something that you can control, to level out all the ups and downs. I've already mentioned reading, which is the perfect routine activity especially if you're reading an adventure book like Treasure Island, but I also got quite attached to the routine of having a good breakfast. The next morning in Manaus I made my own, and really went to town with mango, avocado, French toast, hot chocolate, and creamy oats. I ate breakfast early, around 7am, because I was hoping to join a jungle tour the same day and when the guides came to pick up those people who had pre-booked tours, I asked one of them if there was any space. My luck was in, and by 9am I was in the car, with a full stomach, on the way to catch another boat to take me on a tour of the Amazon.

I've already used up all the colourful words that I know describing the rain in Peru, Ecuador and Bolivia. So I'm just going to have to say that the rain was heavy, very heavy as we drove back to the port. The rain was so heavy that the ramp leading down to the boat that would take us back up the Amazon river, had turned into fast flowing rapids. It was the kind of rain that you genuinely think might damage the car roof, and it reminds you how the Rainforest got its name. Actually I read that the Amazon produces its own rain from plants and trees, rather than through evaporation from the ocean, so it's especially well named. We spent around an hour on the boat getting to the next peninsula, where we transferred to a classic Volkswagen minivan. Then after another few hours on the road, we transferred yet again, to another boat, for the last part of the journey to the riverside jungle-lodge. The long journey was worth it though, and the place was absolutely beautiful. I jumped straight into the river for a swim after we'd checked in, and within a few minutes three dolphins came swimming by. So technically, I have now been swimming with dolphins, although they were wild river dolphins so probably would have eaten me if we were any closer. The first activity of the jungle tour was yet another boat ride, but it was a totally different experience from the noisy speedboats in the pouring rain that had brought us from Manaus. This boat did have an engine, but we only used it on low speed and often switched it off as we cruised through the reeds and around the islands, spotting all kinds of wildlife. We even went piranha fishing and yes I did catch one, but it's no great feat because they went berserk when we dropped in our meat covered hooks.

Later in the evening we went Cayman spotting, and after an hour on the water without finding any, the guide started to get concerned. After another twenty minutes had passed and still no Cayman, he spoke rapidly to the guy piloting the boat, and we moved to another spot in shallow water about knee deep. At this point the guide stepped out of the boat in his plastic sandals and started walking around shining a torch into the water. Then suddenly he tried to run, but couldn't because the water was clinging onto his flip-flops, and he fell into the water head first. He came up again with a Cayman in his hand, and although I'd rather have seen one swimming naturally on its own, I had to admire his determination. The next morning, we did a hike through the jungle, and the same determined man was our guide. He knew everything about the forest and we did all the usual things like eating grubs that we found in a tree, swinging on vines like Tarzan, and calling to the monkeys. But our guide really proved his worth when as we were walking along the edge of a small stream, hacking through the undergrowth to carve out a path, he was attacked by giant wasps. He didn't tell us that it was wasps, he just started jumping about frantically then running in our direction and shouting at us to go back, go back! He looked so frightened that I thought it must be a Jaguar, and so bravely protected the girls in the group by running faster than them to make sure another Jaguar couldn't attack us from behind, as Jaguars are known to work in pairs.

Anyway one of the giant wasps had flown straight into his nose and stung him, which must have been frightening, but for us it was just quite funny because he couldn't stop sneezing all the way back to the lodge. After lunch I took another swim in the river, and got a fright of my own when I started moving backwards away from the lodge even though I was swimming fairly hard. The current was incredibly powerful after all the extra rainfall, and I only just managed to push back and grab hold of the pier. Then it was time to head back to Manaus. I'd managed to do everything that I wanted to do on my jungle tour in the Amazon in only two days, and was thoroughly happy with the experience. There were longer tours where you camped out in the jungle, but frankly I'd had enough of camping in dangerous places, so gave it a miss.

Back in Manaus I started planning how to sell the Apache, and asked the hostel manager if he knew any dealers who might want to buy it. He recommended a shop that he'd used before that was about a kilometre away and gave me the address. When I arrived I found another of those wonderful places that was just 100% all about the motorcycles, and out front there were eight different mechanics, working on eight different bikes, from eight different manufacturers. The shop had a ton of bikes and gear and tools for sale, and the air smelt of gasolina and smoke. The only sound you could hear was the revving of engines or the clanking of metal tools. I walked up to the counter with my ownership documents in hand to ask about selling the Apache, but then had a change of heart. I wasn't ready to end the journey yet, and asked for a new chain and sprocket set instead.

There were no more easy options though, and the only country left that I had any interest in visiting on this journey was Venezuela. The country that Christopher Columbus mistook, in complete earnestness apparently because he was a deeply religious man, for The Garden of Eden. He'd just travelled through the Bahamas and the Caribbean, yet it was Venezuela that prompted him to make that comparison. But now in 2019 Venezuela was going through a difficult time, and an economic and political crisis made worse by US interference and sanctions, was killing thousands. There were two men claiming to be President, and the whole world was talking about its imminent collapse. I'd seen news articles on the BBC talking about people eating animals out of the zoos, mass murder by rival gangs vying for power where the police didn't dare to intervene, and starvation.

But I'd also met a lot of Venezuelans on my journey, and the stories they were telling me were not of a country in chaos, but one that needed support. A country where there were very few jobs, so everyone was trying to migrate, but where life was still going on as normal, albeit under austere circumstances. I'd also noticed that more than half the people I'd met who were migrating away from Venezuela were not actually Venezuelan, they were born in Colombia, or Ecuador, or Peru. Their journey was not one of leaving, but of returning, to jobs and family and social networks that had always been there. This wasn't a story of refugees fleeing violence and destruction, but one of simple economic migration. So I started to think more seriously about continuing my journey not only all the way up to the Caribbean coast, but all the way back to Medellin in Colombia, a complete circuit.

The Apache felt like a whole new bike with its new chain and sprocket set as I rode back to the hostel. And I'd even found, after five months on the road, that it had a USB connector down near the engine! Not that I'd had any problems with my phone battery, but it was nice to learn that there was another backup, that ran on petrol. Now I effectively had my own generator, just as I was heading into areas that might have power shortages. After cooking some pasta for dinner I sat down to make a detailed plan, for only the second time on the journey.

The first issue to work out was food and water, and I'd heard on the news that the drinking water system in Venezuela was broken, and there was no food in the supermarkets. But the people I'd met on the road had already told me that this was not true, and for anyone with even a modest income, food was not a problem. Yes, many people relied on organised food banks and deliveries, just like in Britain, but as long as I had some cash it wouldn't affect my journey. The next issue was petrol, and I'd heard that there were severe shortages throughout Venezuela. If that was true it would kill my idea of riding a combustion-engined motorcycle through the country, and mean that I might be forced to abandon the Apache. Unfortunately, this one was only confirmed by people I'd met, and especially in the south, people were having to wait days. But as I thought about the reality of the situation, I realised that I had a big advantage here, time. There was no deadline that I needed to complete the journey by, so who cares if I had to leave the Apache in a fuel queue overnight. It was so fuel efficient that I'd only need to fill up four or five times, to cross the whole country. In any case I did some research, and found that the shortages were unlikely to get any worse because Venezuela was refining some of the oil that it would have sold to the US, for the domestic market.

Next I thought about hotels, but this one was easy and it took just a few minutes searching online to find several decent looking, reasonably priced hotels in Caracas. Throughout the journey I'd found that the booking websites showed less than 1% of what was available, so this wasn't a concern.

Then I considered security and although I had no idea about the police in Venezuela, I did have a reason to be optimistic. For years I'd heard people say that the police in Colombia and all of South America were as corrupt as they come, but I'd found just the opposite to be true, in my case at least. I'd had hundreds of interactions with police and military during the journey, and except for a couple of heart stopping moments when they felt the need to draw weapons, I'd found them extremely professional. As for kidnappings, another BBC and British Foreign Office favourite, I couldn't find a single recent case of any foreigner, let alone a British or European person, being kidnapped there. The cases all involved wealthy local people with political connections, a very different kind of problem, and not one that would affect a travelling foreigner on a reasonably priced motorcycle. In any case I'd heard the same things about Colombia, so even if there was a risk, it wasn't a big escalation.

Cash is another issue that I'd heard would be a problem, and I was expecting chaos. I'd been told by other travellers, who hadn't been there of course, that if I went to Venezuela people would kill me for the few dollars in my pocket. When I spoke with Maria, she said that, obviously, this was not true but the hyperinflation meant that I should plan to use cash within a week, by which time it would start to lose value. I'd heard on the news that inflation in 2019 was going to be 1.3 million percent, but in reality, as I checked the daily rates it was changing at around 20% per month. This is still incredibly high, but not something that would affect my few weeks in the country. In fact, one consequence of the economic problems was that Venezuela looked like an incredibly cheap country to visit, so the real cost of things was never going to be an issue. As for availability of cash, Maria told me that ATMs throughout the country were working as normal, but she wasn't sure about international cards. And in any case, money changers were easy to find, so as long as I had some currency in dollars or reales, I'd be fine.

I did some research on the roads, but I needn't have worried. Venezuela made massive investments in infrastructure before the current crisis and has some of the best roads in South America. As for protests or other things that might block those roads, I checked local news sites for all the places on a possible route, and there was nothing recent, so fingers crossed. Given the situation, I also took the precaution of checking both opposition and government affiliated news sites, but both gave a similar picture. Borders were another issue, and although I knew the Brazilian border was open because I'd met people who'd just come through, the western border with Colombia was still very much closed. The only slight reason for optimism was that Venezuela−Colombia relations had improved, a bit. So I was sure the pressure from local people to re−open the border would at some point be successful, the only question was when. Despite all I'd heard on the news, once I sat down and did my own research, I realised that although I needed to *take care* just like I had done throughout my journey, it would be reasonable to carry on. The possibility of completing an entire circuit, whether just to Caracas or

God willing all the way back to Colombia, was within my grasp. And I went to bed as happy as a sand-boy.

The next morning, I set off for Boa Vista, the last Brazilian city before the border with Venezuela. I knew that I wouldn't make it all the way there because it was still eight hundred kilometres away, but after all those nights on boats, in lodges, and in hotels, I really fancied a night camping outside. So I decided to just ride until I got tired, and after 350km stopped at a petrol station, just outside an indigenous reserve, near Jundia. After filling up with petrol, I parked the bike next to the small restaurant and went inside to buy some empanadas and pastries for dinner. I also bought a huge tub of dulce de leche, just because. Then I sat down to eat, and started talking with the restaurant owner and some other customers, who were Brazilian truckers working the route into Venezuela. I told them that I was thinking of continuing up to Caracas, and they said I was insane. 'You'll get robbed, it's certain' said one 'It's impossible, there's no gas' said another. The restaurant owner, who was a bit xenophobic but was also trying to be helpful, said the stories he'd heard from people on the road were bad. 'The road from the border through Canaima park is full of bandits,' he said 'and your cash will be worth nothing after a few days', and although I knew he wasn't speaking from personal experience, it was still quite depressing to hear.

After ten minutes with the doomsayers, I couldn't take any more and went outside to sit in the sunshine. I took off my boots, emptied the rainwater, and tried not to let my nose get too close as I put them down to dry out. While I was enjoying a few spoonfuls of dulce de leche in the afternoon sun, I noticed two old Volkswagen beetles parked near a grassy area next to the petrol station. The grass was an ideal spot for camping, so I wondered if the cars might belong to some other travellers and went over to investigate. Then as I got closer, I noticed that both the beetles and another Volkswagen truck, were absolutely stacked with all kinds of stuff. Spare petrol cans, chairs, tents of course, and all manner of boxes and containers. When a young guy came out from behind one of the beetles, I asked him if they were camping there for the night and he said yes. So I told him that I'd be camping there too and asked if they'd mind if I parked the bike, and pitched my tent, next to theirs for security and company. He smiled broadly, said his name was Bruno, and that yes it would be fine to camp nearby, so I walked back over to the Apache to get my things.

As we pitched our tents and sorted out our kit before dinner, Bruno and I spoke about our different journeys. I told him some of the interesting things that had happened, like the breakdowns, the crashes, and the naked guy in the desert. And how the Apache had dragged me all over South America for 26,000km, with very few problems. Then Bruno told me how he had travelled with his mother and father, his sister and a friend all the way from the mid-east of Venezuela to Brazil. And how they were hoping to make it all the way to Ecuador. He told me how his Dad was originally from Ecuador and had emigrated to Venezuela decades ago for work, but now because of the economic situation, they were heading back. Bruno himself had already been living there for a long time, but had returned to Venezuela to help with the move.

As we were talking Bruno's Dad came over to say hello and I re-told some of the stories from my trip, while Bruno went to help pitch their second tent. He asked me about the boat from Porto Velho to Manaus, and I told him that it was fine but expensive. He said that the boat wouldn't be an option for all six of them plus the three cars, and that they'd need to find another solution. So I told him about route BR319, including the four hundred kilometre unpaved section that had been churned to pieces by trucks. They were going to have to face that infamous road in two 1970s beetles, and a Volkswagen truck. Later on I spoke more with Bruno about the difficult road ahead, and gave him the link for the overlander app, which they could use to find safer places to camp, and get information about road routes and obstructions.

Once the tents were pitched and we'd arranged all our things, the family invited me to join them for dinner, which I accepted, even though my feeble contribution was going to be peanuts, water, and dulce de leche. Then I took a shower in the excellent free washroom that is quite a common feature at petrol stations in South America, before sitting down to dinner. Bruno's mother kindly said that they loved dulce de leche, and that it was an excellent contribution for dessert. Before preparing a truly delicious meat dish that tasted like it had come straight out of a home oven. We washed it all down with a huge canteen of sweet coffee, then sat around chatting as the sun went down behind the horizon. The petrol station was the only building for miles, so we got to see a splendid sunset that turned the few white clouds in the sky, to a dark red. I definitely owe them a dinner when I see them again in Ecuador. The best thing about all of this though, was that the whole family were huge fans of 80s pop music, so throughout the tent pitching, the chatting, and dinner, I got to listen to Karma Chameleon, Let it Be, Girls Just Wanna Have Fun, and Hotel California. Literally four of my favourite songs, although I had none of them on my phone during the journey.

When I told Bruno and his Dad about my plans to ride to Caracas, they didn't call me insane. They were happy to see people visiting, and instead told me about all the amazing places that I could see in Venezuela. They did however offer me lots of advice about the route, and some of the challenges that I'd face along the way. 'Don't underestimate the fuel problem' they said, and told me that the only reason they'd made it to Brazil was because they'd brought along four giant cans, filled with petrol. There was almost no fuel anywhere in the south, and the first place where they knew there was petrol was Upata, around five hundred kilometres from the border. So I made a mental note of Upata as my second destination in Venezuela, after the border town of Santa Elena. 'Also the Canaima really is full of bandits' they said, but clarified that they hadn't had a problem themselves. They just hadn't felt secure driving through the area because there were lots of young guys on motorcycles checking out their cars, and the petrol, so advised me to be cautious. 'There are plenty of places to camp, and it's beautiful, just take care' they said, those words again, take care, cuidado.

The family had also brought along two dogs. One tiny and slightly aggressive poodle, and one friendly mongrel called Rocky, about the size of a Labrador, who loved playing fetch. They warned me not to play or he'd keep pestering me forever, but I didn't mind, and played fetch with him for an hour before bed. In the morning Rocky was waiting by the entrance to my tent, with his stick, so we played again for a while before breakfast. Bruno and his family set off early and by 7:30am they were on the road to Manaus, while I headed north to Boa Vista. Again the smooth Brazilian highways transported me there without incident, and I managed to find a great little hostel with an outdoor kitchen, and plenty of space to store the bike.

After a quiet evening in Boa Vista, and yet another generous breakfast, I set off a bit later than usual for Pacaraima, the last major town before the border. There I planned to fill the fuel tank one last time, and get some cash, before heading straight into the Canaima region of Venezuela the same day. I wasn't in a rush, because I only planned to go about ten kilometres past the border, to a town called Santa Elena de Uairen. So I had plenty of time to complete customs and arrive there by mid-afternoon. I'd calculated that my fuel tank would last around 640km until it completely ran out of fuel, including reserve. Which would be more than enough to get me to Upata or to find somewhere with petrol, even if I had to wait there a couple of days to queue for it. I had some Brazilian currency to use in Pacaraima, and a hundred dollars left from my emergency stash that I planned to exchange at the border into local currency. Because of the recent hyperinflation, Venezuela would be very low cost and I'd worked out that a hundred dollars would be plenty to get me to Caracas, where I could get more.

The road to Pacaraima wasn't quite as smooth as I was used to in the rest of Brazil, but it was still good.

There was even one short section that was absolutely immaculate and must have been laid within the last few weeks, so I made quick progress. I arrived around mid-morning and went directly to the petrol station, only to find a queue of over two hundred cars. It was the first time that I'd seen anything like it, but it wasn't surprising really, considering that this was the last town before the border with Venezuela where there was a petrol shortage. I pulled alongside the queue to speak with one guy in a huge 4x4 truck, just to confirm that the queue was indeed for the petrol station, and not some event that I hadn't heard about. And that's when I learned something truly astonishing.

In Venezuela, and here in Pacaraima, motorcycles do not need to join the fuel queue. They can go right to the front no matter how long the line, and fill up without waiting. As I sat there in stunned silence for a moment, the man laughed, and said I should get going as you never know when they'll run out. So I sheepishly rode past the two hundred cars right up to the pump, and parked the Apache on the opposite side of the dispenser. Sure enough, one of the two attendants on duty filled my tank, and I was on my way before the car opposite had even stopped filling. I started to believe that I might have been overthinking this, and it was perfectly possible that I may get to Caracas with very few problems.

Next I went over to Brazilian migration and was done in ten minutes, then I went to customs, but they were closed for lunch and I had to wait until it reopened at 3pm. Unfortunately, this meant that by the time I got to Venezuelan customs, it was closed, and I'd have to come back the next day. This wasn't a huge problem though, because Santa Elena de Uairen was only ten kilometres away, and I'd already planned to stay there one night. I'd just have to come back to the border early next morning to complete the formalities, and be on my way. So I continued on to Santa Elena and arrived around 5pm in the afternoon, here I was in Venezuela, the tenth and final country of my journey, and I felt fantastic. There was a respectable looking hotel on the high street, so I went to check–in. And it was at this point, that my plans started to fall apart.

The hotel cost fifty Brazilian Reales, about thirteen dollars. It was by far the cheapest in town and still well within my usual budget, but I'd drastically underestimated the costs for Venezuela. I read online that hotels would be the equivalent of just three to six dollars outside the capital Caracas, at the current exchange rate. But here in Santa Elena, a nice place just outside town wanted thirty and wouldn't negotiate, and I already knew from my research that there were no shared hostels. The hundred dollars' emergency fund that I thought would cover hotels, food, fuel and everything else all the way to Caracas, would not be enough, and I needed cash urgently. Not only that, but the hotel would not accept dollars, nor Venezuelan currency, and would only accept payment in Brazilian reales, but I'd spent all those in Pacaraima. I asked the hotel manager, just in case, if there was a working ATM in town but I already knew the answer. Then I asked him how far into Venezuela would I still need Brazilian currency, and he said that Upata, the town where I'd been told there was also some fuel, might accept dollars. Luckily the manager agreed to hold twenty dollars as security while I sorted myself out, and let me stay the night.

It was a big shock, but not the end of the world. I needed to go back to Pacaraima in any case to complete Customs, so I'd just need to withdraw a ton of Brazilian currency, exchange most into dollars at the border, and keep some for emergencies before I reached Upata. After finding that there wasn't even a working ATM in Santa Elena, I also decided to get enough dollars for my entire trip through Venezuela, just in case. Unfortunately, that meant that I'd be carrying a lot of cash, just as I was about to ride five hundred kilometres through the Canaima, one of the most dangerous parts of the country for travellers.

I set off early the next morning and was back in Pacaraima by 8am, but when I arrived at the bank, there was a problem, they wouldn't accept my visa card. Again it wasn't the end of the world because I knew there was another bank around the corner, but when I went there, the ATM was out of order. It was still only 8am so I had plenty of time, and decided to wait and talk to the bank staff just in case. The branch opened at 08:30 and I was about the sixth customer so it didn't take long, but the news was not good. The ATM would be out of action for a few days and they couldn't manage cash on the desk. Perhaps if I'd been in London I might have caused a fuss and complained until I got what I wanted. But this was not London, and as I emerged from the bubble that I'd been in while trying to get everything done smoothly, I looked around. Everyone was speaking Spanish, not Portuguese, and the customer before me was an unaccompanied blind man around 75 years old. The customer after me was a middle aged lady with two children being helped by a badged UN worker, who was also trying to help around twenty other people. There was also a very young looking Brazilian soldier topping up a services payment card, and some guys trying to do business banking while constantly talking with people outside. The guy standing next to me asked if the blind man had anyone with him, but he didn't. No one complained, no one argued, not here in the bank nor in the fuel queue, but it was clear that this town was feeling the strain of the crisis affecting their neighbour to the north.

It was also clear that I'd need to go all the way back to Boa Vista to get cash, but as I was already here at the border, I decided to complete the customs process anyway. That way I could make sure that there were no further issues, before starting the long trek back. I went over to Venezuelan customs, and although they did ask why my migration stamp was from the day before, they didn't pursue it. The process was a bit slow, but in the end I got the documents that I needed, including my Venezuelan Temporary Import Permit, and insurance. There were two slight complications though, the first was that they asked me if I'd be leaving Venezuela through this border post, and I lied, I said yes. Although I'd heard some rumours about the Colombian border reopening, on that day it was definitely still closed, so I had no option. The second complication was that I needed Venezuelan currency to pay for the insurance, because they wouldn't accept my visa card in the customs office. This was another sign that I needed to be careful about my assumptions in Venezuela, but the problem was easily solved. I just headed back down the road into town and dealt with one of the currency street-traders. While I was there I also exchanged some dollars into Brazilian Reales, then after completing customs, raced back to Santa Elena to pay the hotel.

I rode the two hundred kilometres back to Boa Vista very carefully, because I was now riding without Brazilian documents or insurance after completing customs in Venezuela. It was only one straight road though, and I hadn't seen any police checkpoints on the way there, so I decided to take the risk. The alternative would have been to go through the whole double customs process again, another night in a hotel here or in

Santa Elena, and running my emergency cash reserve down to nothing. It's seriously frustrating to go several hundred kilometres back on yourself in the middle of a motorcycle journey, but in the end I was relived to be back in the relative calm of Boa Vista. Plenty of ATMs, plenty of petrol stations, plenty of hostels, the only problem was that it was raining cats and dogs, again.

The next day I woke up late again, ate a huge breakfast again, and said hello and goodbye to Michael the hostel owner again. And it was beginning to feel a bit like deja vu as I left for my second attempt to complete the crossing into Venezuela. This time I made absolutely sure that I was prepared for what I was about to do, and withdrew enough Brazilian Reales to exchange into dollars for the whole route. I also kept some back in reserve just in case I needed to spend longer than planned in the Canaima, where they might only accept reales. I didn't bother with petrol as the tank was still three quarters full and I knew there would be plenty in Pacaraima, but I did plan to buy an extra fuel can to be absolutely certain I'd get to Upata. I also decided to make sure that the Apache was in 100% perfect working order. Because although I hadn't noticed any specific problems, it had been sounding a bit tired lately and I was now paranoid about what would, and wouldn't be possible north of the border. There was a decent looking service centre not far from the hostel, so I took the bike in for a check-up. One great thing about riding in South America is that more often than not, you get immediate service, there's no waiting around for a week just to get an appointment. I told the mechanic about the tired sound, and slight lack of power that I'd noticed on the road back to Boa Vista, and he started to poke around near the engine.

Three hours later, after virtually stripping the whole bike, getting four other mechanics on the job, and after enough time to let my boots dry in the sunshine, he said that it was the carburetor. I'm not sure why he didn't think of that a bit sooner, but in any case even including the new carburetor and all the labour, the final charge was very reasonable. So I didn't complain, and the Apache sounded superb, like a completely new bike. By now it was late in the afternoon and I didn't have enough time to make it all the way back to Santa Elena before dark, so I decided to spend one more night in the hostel. The next day I woke up late again, ate a huge breakfast again, and said hello and goodbye to Michael the hostel owner again. And it was beginning to feel a bit like deja vu as I left for my third attempt to complete the crossing into Venezuela. This time Michael gifted me a spare plastic petrol container because I'd forgotten to buy one the day before, and I set off, praying that I'd avoid any unwanted attention from the police. Without my temporary import and insurance documents, if I was stopped then I might be delayed longer in Brazil. And if that would have happened, then I wasn't sure that I had the will to try a fourth time. But I wasn't stopped, and made it all the way back to Pacaraima where I filled the tank, and the spare container, with petrol then crossed through the open border. I arrived back in Santa Elena, Venezuela, around midday.

12
Aqui no se habla mal de Chavez : VENEZUELA

Christopher Columbus' Garden of Eden, Venezuela is one of the most beautiful places on the planet and boasts Andes Mountains, Amazon Rainforest, Llanos Plains, Caribbean beaches, and the Orinoco Delta. It also happens to have the world's largest oil reserves, around 15% more than Saudi Arabia. Simon Bolivar, the aristocratic rebel who did most to drive Spain out of South America was born in Caracas, and the country was quick to declare independence, but they didn't make the full transition to a stable democracy until the 1950s. Then in 1998 another diehard independent, the socialist leader Hugo Chavez was elected President, and put the government in charge of the oil industry. He used the profits to pay for free healthcare, extensive house building, and to reduce inequality, but ultimately failed to bring on-board the rich. A collapse in the oil price, and economic errors plunged the country into crisis in 2015 and the opposition, backed by the US, saw their chance. The US started economic sanctions that according to economist Jeffrey Sachs, have contributed to the deaths of over 40,000 people, while the opposition started economic sabotage, and protest. The tensions are ongoing, and as I waited in the Customs hall at the border I saw a sign that read, *Aqui no se habla mal de Chavez* (Here we don't speak ill of Hugo Chavez). Fair enough, he's a deceased revolutionary hero. But then later I saw another sign that read, *Aqui no se habla mal de Chavez...ni Maduro* (Here we don't speak ill of Hugo Chavez...or current President, Maduro). It was either official, and the Government is terrible at propaganda, or some subversive in the customs department had a wicked sense of humour.

When I checked into the hotel in Santa Elena for the second time, it was a lot more relaxing than the first. I had plenty of reales to pay my bill and dollars to exchange later, I had plenty of petrol to get me to Upata, and I was confident that the Apache was in tip-top condition. I unpacked my things and rested for a while, before heading out to take a look around, and got a wonderful welcome back to the Caribbean region as soon as I stepped outside. A three-piece band was playing Latin jazz in the courtyard right opposite the hotel, violin, trombone, and drums. As border towns go Santa Elena was great, and as well as the band I found markets for meat and fruit nearby along with a panderia. The only slightly odd thing was that carrots cost double the price of mangos, so needless to say I bought a few of the latter.

As you might expect from a town in the middle of the do-not-travel zone, according to British Government travel advice, most buildings had metal security grilles on the doors, but no more than the cities in Brazil. After a couple of hours wandering around, and enjoying the opportunity to speak Spanish again, I had something to eat then headed back to the hotel. My room was huge so I also took the opportunity to lay out all my kit including the bag, my clothes, and the petrol, then take a picture. I'd been meaning to do this for ages to show the complete kit that was needed for a bike journey, but this was the first time I'd had a private room big enough. I'll include the picture at the end of this journal.

In the hotel lobby, which was the only place where the WIFI worked, I met a girl from El Tigre, a city in Anzoategui province, and we got talking. It turned out that she was here in Santa Elena with two friends, another young lady, and one tough looking guy wearing an impeccable black suit. They were here to buy cosmetics from Brazil, to sell back in their home town. Given that the man I'd spoken to in the queue at the bank in Pacaraima was in the same business, it felt like the industry was booming. I also asked her advice about a route through to the Caribbean coast, and she said why not stop by El Tigre. I didn't have any other plans so I said sure, why not, and we exchanged numbers. The next morning, I set off early on the five hundred kilometre ride through the Canaima National Park to Upata, where hopefully, I would find some more petrol.

The Canaima is listed by UNESCO as a World Heritage Site, and contains a region known as The

Grand Savannah. This was the place that I'd been warned about, that was full of bandits, but when I saw it I completely forgot about that, because it's stunning. The area is mostly flat as you might guess from the name, but dotted with table-top mountains called Tepuis, which means, House of the Gods. The plateaus on top of the tepuis are isolated from the surrounding area, often shrouded in clouds, and have completely different climates. They support unique ecosystems, with species that have evolved separately for thousands of years, and have still not been completely discovered, or understood. This incredible, and unusual region, was the inspiration for Arthur Conan Doyle's 1912 novel, The Lost World, about the discovery of dinosaurs, living deep in the Amazon basin.

The area is also home to the highest waterfall in the world, Angel Falls, that I first heard about years ago when some skydiving friends were planning a trip there to jump off. Angel Falls itself is incredibly remote, and accessible only by a plane and boat trip from Puerto Ordaz, so not the kind of place you could ride a motorcycle. But in the Canaima there was no shortage of other, more accessible waterfalls and I even managed to get a picture of the Apache standing right next to the top of one. As I raced along the wide sweeping roads that crossed the savannah, the time seemed to pass quickly, and before I knew it I'd travelled three hundred kilometres. I checked the fuel gauge, and it was about half full, so I took out the spare fuel can and refilled the tank. I arrived in Upata, unmolested by bandits, or dinosaurs, around 5pm, and checked-in to a massive hotel on the main square. The bike still had half a tank of fuel left because I'd brought so much, but the general lack of fuel was no joke. When people said there was no fuel in the Canaima, I thought they meant because of the shortages, but it turned out that there wasn't a single petrol station in the whole national park, at least as far as I could see. There were plenty of traders selling one litre bottles of who-knows-what in the villages along the way, so I could have played Russian Roulette with the engine in an emergency. But in the end I was glad that I'd brought the extra fuel.

Once I'd finished settling in to the hotel, I had to go and exchange some dollars, because they only accepted payment in local currency, and didn't take international cards. It wasn't a problem though, because the nearest informal bureau de change was the restaurant right next door. I went over to ask about the deal, before realising that I hadn't checked the rates online. With such high inflation this was serious, and I could have paid several times the going rate. But luckily on my way out of the hotel I saw the room prices displayed in dollars as well as Bolivars, despite them not actually accepting dollars, which gave me a ballpark figure. Later on I did check online and found that the restaurant owner had given me quite a reasonable rate, within 10% of what was being quoted on the exchange websites.

The cost of the hotel was five dollars for a large double room with private bathroom and Wi-Fi. Right in the middle of the three to six dollar range that I'd seen on the internet. Clearly the hotels back in Santa Elena were making a killing from being right on the border where the traders met, but it was still good to know that I would certainly have enough cash for the journey. Another group making a killing were the hotel security guards, who were running a protection racket on the parking. But I didn't pay, and luckily the Apache did not end up stripped for parts in some garage in northern Brazil, as the guards were heavily implying. The next morning there was a scheduled electricity outage from

07:30am to 09:30am, to manage demand because of the shortages. The timing makes sense because it's daylight, people are commuting, and it's before the real work of the day starts, but it was super annoying for me, because I was trying to do some work online before I set off. In any case, my trusty book came in handy again and I just read in the lobby until it came back on. Then I set off around 10am, and my first objective was to find fuel.

The two petrol stations in town were both closed which seemed like a bad sign. But then I found one open on the highway, and instead of sheepishly cruising past the line of cars, I confidently raced right to the front of the line. The entrance was being guarded by military police who were managing the traffic with a rope across the entrance. I couldn't seem to catch their attention to ask, so I just rode around to the exit where the rope was lowered for several trucks leaving, and rode in that way straight up to a pump. It was all very well managed, and a lady with a clipboard came over to talk with me. Her usual job would be to take the registration of the cars to enforce fuel rationing, but she didn't do that with me, presumably because I had a foreign plate. Then she told me that motorcycles were only allowed in after 11am, and I would have to come back in an hour. The time wasn't a problem, but in the middle of a shortage I just really wanted to get the fuel in case it ran out. So I pretended not to understand. She explained again and I made a face like I had no idea what was going on and luckily she took pity on me, or perhaps it was because I was blocking the cars, but in any case she let me fill up. I smiled thankfully, then seriously pushed my luck by pulling out the extra fuel can. 'NO WAY!' she said, and even if I really hadn't understood Spanish, I'd still have gotten the message. Then she explained that cans were illegal now because of the rationing. So I only filled up the fuel tank, but it was more than enough to cover the 250km to the city of El Tigre where I was heading.

When the attendant had finished filling the tank, I pulled out my wallet and asked how much? The lady with the clipboard said, 'You can pay him whatever you wish'. This time I really didn't understand so she pointed to the gauge on the pump, which read the equivalent of less than three pence. I paid the minimum that my conscience would allow, and the attendant smiled and waved me on my way. Incredible, here I was cruising on smooth hardened asphalt roads, with no tolls, and skipping the fuels lines, and on top of all that, the fuel was virtually free. Truly a biker's paradise. Well mostly, I have to say that the road to El Tigre was boring as hell. Although I did get a nice picture of a tree. As I left the petrol station I waited for a truck to overtake me, then tail-gated him through as the military guard lowered the rope. I probably didn't need to do that, but it seemed prudent as he didn't look in a very good mood.

The next day was my birthday, and I arrived in El Tigre full of hope and optimism as I texted the beautiful girl that I'd met in Santa Elena, about meeting up for a coffee. She replied that she'd confirm later, because she had some things to do with her family first, so I went to the mall next door for McDonald's instead. After dinner I did some shopping in the well-stocked supermarket, again feeling utterly ridiculous that I'd believed the things I heard on the BBC, then headed back to the hotel. I called my parents so they could wish me happy birthday, and to let them know how it was all going, then checked the news. I did get a birthday present after all, because President Nicolas Maduro had just announced the re-opening of the border with Colombia. A year to the day after my experience in Lisbon, Portugal, God was shining a light on me again, and I went to bed with a huge smile on my face. Although that could also be partly explained by the fact that my next destination was the beach, at Puerto La Cruz.

The road to the coast was much better, and much faster, than the one to El Tigre. But I was still surprised when, just after passing through another toll-booth, without needing to pay, I noticed a group of Venezuelan bikers. They were riding awesome machines including a Ducati and some Yamaha R1s, and had pulled over for a rest. I was going the other way, but turned around further down the road where the central barrier ended, and went back to say hello. The bikers had all come from Puerto La Cruz, and were part of a Venezuelan motorcycle club. It was fantastic to talk with bike enthusiasts again, and they were gracious enough to let me take a photo of the tiny Apache alongside their bikes. Despite the fact that it had less than a fifth of the power. After I arrived in Puerto La Cruz, I quickly found a hotel near the port, parked up the bike, and went to check-in. Everything seemed fine until I went to pay for two nights, and the lady behind the counter asked me if I was sure, then told me that they didn't have any internet, or water. Initially I thought that she meant drinking water, so I didn't think it was a problem, but then realised that she meant the whole water supply. I wanted to explore the coast near here though, so definitely needed a base for a couple of nights, and the hotel down the street wanted three times the price. So after confirming that she expected both the internet and water to be back on in a few hours, I took the room, put my things down, and went out for a long walk.

Puerto La Cruz is one of those places where the inequality hits you like a brick. While there are gated marinas with elegant canals to park million-pound yachts on one side of town, there are half built apartment blocks that people have made into their homes, on the other. The blocks were presumably started during the tourism boom, but put on hold when it ended, and although they did appear to have connected services, they didn't have windows. It's a shame because the beach is fantastic, and the place is clean. But the tourism industry in Venezuela has taken a real hit, and Puerto La Cruz had the feeling of somewhere waiting for the next boom

When I got back to the hotel there was still no water service, and it wouldn't come back until the next day, but we did have a small amount. The hotel had a rainwater storage tank on the roof, so we rationed with buckets, one per room, to shower and flush the toilet. It wasn't quite as bad as the shortage I'd experienced in Ecuador, where the temperature was forty degrees and the air was full of dust because it was so dry, but it was still uncomfortable. There was plenty of drinking water in the shops and the prices weren't insane, so from a traveller's perspective it really wasn't a huge problem. But those who couldn't afford bottled water needed to share and filter from each other's storage tanks. Later on I went out for dinner and found a Grill restaurant down on the beachfront. They served an excellent Filet Mignon, cooked rare with fries and a salad, for just five dollars, I might not have running water, but I was certainly eating well. You can understand why the more fortunate folks chose this place to build their mansions, and keep their yachts. The mainland beaches are excellent of course, but more than that, the town is just a few hours' cruise from the Isla Margarita, a large island just off the coast with some of the best beaches in the Caribbean. It's actually not difficult to get there either, and there's a regular ferry, but when I went to buy a ticket I was told that I'd have to wait three days just to purchase it. And another company that was selling tickets on that day, wasn't allowed to sell to foreigners. I decided instead to see more of the beaches along the mainland coast, which were still excellent, and spent an afternoon on one of them just relaxing, and reading my book.

My next planned stop after Puerto La Cruz was the capital Caracas, but I didn't fancy doing the whole 350km trip in one go. So I just kept my eyes open for interesting looking places along the coast to stay one or two nights. After around 150km I stopped to take a rest and looked at the map. I was less than five hundred metres from a side-road that led to a small town called Tacarigua de la Laguna. It was right next to a huge lake and nature reserve, hence the name, and it was perfect, so that's where I went. The entrance to the reserve is right there in the town, but a lot of tourism comes to the area from Caracas by boat, so it's not as developed, or touristy, as you might expect. There was quite a large school, so on the way into town I mostly saw kids in their neat uniforms hopping along trying to get home to avoid the afternoon heat. I made a bee-line straight for the beach, and parked the Apache while I took a walk along the sand, it was incredible. One of the best beaches I'd seen in South America, and not a person there. Well except for one older gentleman, his two granddaughters, and two great-grandchildren, playing under a sunshade. As far I could see from riding around town for a while there were very few hotels, so I went over to the family on the beach, to ask if they knew a place.

Not only did they know all about the town, but said that if I wasn't in a rush they'd help me to find a place to stay, and get some dinner, because they were about to head home and lived just around the corner. That I should randomly run into such wonderful people on the beach was a godsend, and I chatted to the grandfather while his family gathered their things. His name was Clodio, he was 73 years old and was a musician, he was also mostly blind.

Clodio was a larger than life character, who in his youth had served in the Venezuelan navy. He then worked as a truck driver for many years, and as an Official Composer of Music in the government. He told me all this as we walked along the quiet streets of Tacarigua, me slowly pushing the Apache, and him helped by his 14-year-old great-grandson. On every single street we passed, some random person would shout 'En serio!' which was his catchphrase. It's just something people say, but a strict translation would be 'seriously?' and I'd heard it a lot throughout South America, although not quite like this. Old folks, children, tattooed groups of young men, mothers with babies, everyone knew by-heart the lyrics to some of the songs he had written, and the streets literally filled with music as we passed. I was completely exhausted after a day's riding and pushing the Apache across town in the midday heat, but it was fun. We arrived at his house and I parked the bike in his front garden behind the gate, then went inside to have some sweet coffee. Clodio had had a tough life, and was not a rich man, but he made me feel extremely welcome in his home, and I sat on a stool by the kitchen as the family went about their business, feeding the little ones, and cleaning up. No-one including myself was in a huge rush, so we just relaxed at home as he showed me some of his old CDs, some books, and some photos from his youth. Then as the sun started to set, he suddenly lit up and said 'Let's go to the Lake! You can record me performing and put it on the internet when you're famous'.

There was no gym in Tacarigua, which was fine, because as well as pushing the Apache uphill for an hour I now had to carry a huge yellow drum down to the lakeside, so I certainly got my exercise that day. The same shouts of 'En Serio!' and lyrics from the songs followed us as we went, and we setup the drum in a corner next to the jetty where the fishermen set off. One of the fishermen brought over a stool for Clodio, and I set the drum down in front of him, then sat on the floor and held my camera as steady as possible. We chatted with the fishermen for a few minutes, and then he got to work. He confidently set down thirteen minutes of music and chat, and that was that, done, one take, no messing around, what a professional. As he went through his repertoire, the fishermen on the jetty started to join in, and as other fishermen passed by on their way to and from the fishing waters, they joined in too. It was a fantastic way to spend the afternoon, and I was pleased that his great-grandson got to see him perform so confidently and be appreciated by others. I got some more exercise as I carried the drum back along the street to shouts of 'En Serio!' and more of the lyrics that I'd just heard for real.

Although the plan had been to introduce me to someone who ran an hospedaje in the town, one of Clodio's old friends Jose came over to help fix a desk-fan, and offered to put me up for the night. He lived alone in a two-bedroom house, and said it would be no trouble for me to stay in one of the rooms, so I accepted. Jose knew how to fix a fan because he'd been an engineer and came to Tacarigua with an engineering company many years before, then stayed when they relocated elsewhere because he liked it so much. We talked, and talked, and late afternoon had turned into evening when another visitor arrived. Clodio was a religious man, and enjoyed speaking with a spiritual counsellor from a Christian organisation that preached in the town. He invited the counsellor in, and we sat in a circle and listened to advice and teachings from the bible, on dealing with the difficulties of life and in particular, loss. The family had suffered significant loss, and the talk was clearly beneficial to everyone, including myself, although I couldn't follow everything that was said. At the end of the talk, Clodio said something that I will never forget, he said that our meeting on the beach was a sign from God.

Now I've never thought of myself as a religious man, I've never been to church, and I don't pray. Except perhaps a few times when I've been going way too fast into a tight corner, and instinctively hoped someone would step in. But as he said the words, I didn't doubt them to be true. Because it was almost a year to the day that I met a guy with the same birthday as me, on the day of my birthday, in a hotel in Lisbon and I'd been expecting a sign. If you're not into signs that's fine, and you can interpret this as simply my own mind coming to a satisfying conclusion. And that's probably what actually happened, but in any case, now I was expecting another assignment, and I got one.

Clodio asked me if I planned to go to Caracas, and when I said yes, he asked me to deliver a message to his friend Richard who he said could help me out with anything that I needed in the city. Easy enough you might think, and so did I until he told me it had been over thirty years since he'd met Richard, and didn't have an address or phone number. 'No problem!' he said and asked his great-grandson to write down some directions which boiled down to: Go to the Candelaria area of Caracas. Find Parque Carabobo metro station. Go to the park opposite, and find any old guy playing cards, or reading the Ultimas Noticias newspaper. Ask them for Richard M., and if he's not there then he's having dinner, so go to the Flor de Espana restaurant and he'll be there. He even stamped the note with his personal seal, so Richard M. would know it was him. Although this wasn't necessary because he'd also shown me lots of photos from his youth, including one of Richard, and I'd taken a copy on my phone. What could I do, I promised that I'd do my best, and put the note in my pocket.

Clodio had my next day all planned out. After I finished breakfast at Jose's house, I should check out the beach because it was amazing in the morning, then come straight over to his house for lunch after which we'd visit the lake with one of the fisherman. And that's exactly what we did, I cooked some oats and raisins for myself and Jose, that we ate with a huge plate of cashew nuts, then I went to the beach. It was as beautiful as Clodio had said and the morning light was stunning. I swam for around thirty minutes before heading back, then later in the morning I went over for lunch. We walked back down to the same place that I'd recorded him performing the day before, and arranged with one of the fishermen to take us on a tour of the lake, for a reasonable fee. Clodio got right into the spirit of things and even wore his old Navy uniform for the trip. Entertaining us with his repertoire of songs as we set off, by manpower alone, to cruise in the shallows of the lake. The weather was ideal again and we saw thousands of exotic birds while the fisherman told us about every inlet, and showed us where all the different animals lived. The branches of floating clusters of trees were crawling with tiny crabs, and others not so tiny, and we saw a flock of bright red birds like cardinals, but I can't remember the name.

Just like on the streets of Tacarigua, as we glided across the lake other fishermen we passed would shout 'En Serio!' and offer a few lyrics from a song, which Clodio would pick up with gusto. Then later that evening we went for dinner together with all the family, at the back of a small shop owned by one of his friends. It was a splendid day and later as I was settling down to bed, I still had the tune of my favourite song, *Pan con Queso,* ringing in my ears. The song was infectious, and apparently a bit rude, although I couldn't understand all the words, you'll have to go to Tacarigua if you want to hear it. And his other songs definitely included less than flattering things about the Policia, so I didn't ask about that. The next morning, I got up early and set off for Caracas, with the instructions that he'd given me in my jacket pocket.

Another easy and uneventful ride along the wide highways of coastal Venezuela brought me to Caracas, the capital, and one of the most dangerous cities in the world. My fuel was getting low again so I stopped at the first petrol station to fill up, and it wasn't until I'd left that I realised there hadn't been a queue. Quite a different story to the South of the country. I knew that I wanted to stay somewhere fairly close to the University, because usually this kind of area is relatively safe and low cost. So I cruised through the uber-luxury area of Altamira and the embassy district, until I found Plaza Venezuela which was near the Central University. Far from the chaos, tension, and destruction that I was half expecting from watching too much BBC News. Caracas had a laid back feel, and people were going about their business as normal. The shops and cafes were plentiful and full of customers, and I parked the Apache on the street without a lock, before sitting down for lunch.

The bike was still there, safe and sound, when I finished lunch a couple of hours later. And as I was loading my bag onto the back, I asked a guy standing nearby if he could recommend a hotel, which he did. He was like almost every other person that I'd met on my journey, warm, friendly, considerate, and unfazed by my terrible foreigner's Spanish. I didn't actually use the hotel he recommended though, because as I was riding there I passed another hotel on a main road with underground parking. It also turned out to be better, and cheaper, than the ones I'd seen on the internet, so I was more than happy with that. There was one problem though, no internet, and although Caracas had escaped the problems with water and petrol that I'd seen in other places, it seemed that patchy internet was an issue everywhere. To be fair though, this wasn't only the case in Venezuela. About half the places I'd been on my journey had some kind of issues with internet, whether it was just unusably slow, or actually down for a while. And the internet in the hotel came back after a couple of hours. Once I'd put my things away in the room, I went outside to take a look around and do some shopping down near Plaza Venezuela.

The things I'd heard about Caracas still hadn't quite left my mind yet, and so I found myself feeling like an amateur journalist as I over—analysed everything that I saw. *How many people were in the streets? Who had escaped to Colombia? What were people eating, was there fruit, was there meat? How were people coping without toilet paper? When would I see a murder?* But of course, everything was normal, and it was just a city full of people going about their business just like every other city that I'd been to on my journey. I'm not saying there are no problems here, I'm just saying that I was here, for two days. I walked all over the city without ever feeling uncomfortable and the Apache sat on the street for hours unlocked with no problems. I didn't hear one police siren, and there were no gangs, nothing. The supermarkets were full, the restaurants were full, the street—side cafes were full, and this was definitely not a city on the brink.

Anyway once I'd gotten over the shock of the mundane, I bought some mangos and bananas from a street vendor, and a new book in Spanish from the second—hand book market because I was about to finish Treasure Island. Then I went to buy a pastry in the Panderia, and while I was standing in the queue I got chatting to the guy in front of me, and told him about my journey. He said it sounded exciting, but didn't understand how I was going to get to Colombia. Because he heard that although the border was open for pedestrians now, it was closed to all vehicles including motorcycles.

When I crossed over from Brazil, I knew that the Colombian border was closed. But when I heard on my birthday a few days later that the Simon Bolivar bridge at the frontier post had re—opened, I thought that it was the present I'd been waiting for. True, a huge iron gate had been installed across the road to prevent larger vehicles from crossing but the Apache was tiny, and could be wheeled through any pedestrian passageway. All that I'd need to do was convince the border patrol that the journey was worth something, and they could make a special case. There was no physical barrier to crossing, only a social one, and I'd persuaded people to make exceptions for the Apache all over the continent. Besides, motorcycles were simply not treated the same here as larger vehicles and I'd ridden through hundreds of police checkpoints without checks, ridden straight into petrol stations during a shortage, skipped fuel lines, and used a special free lane at toll booths. But now someone was telling me, very specifically, that they heard it was strictly foot traffic only, and I started to have doubts. When I got back to the hotel, the internet service had returned so I went online to re-check. The border was definitely open to foot traffic, and general vehicles were definitely blocked from using the road. But nothing was said about motorcycles that could be wheeled through the pedestrian bridge. There was still a glimmer of hope, but I no longer believed and it was a bitter pill to swallow. The sense of triumph that I'd felt since hearing that my Circuit might be happening after all, disappeared in an instant. All of a sudden I realised that the mental gymnastics had been at work for a long time. This was not just another police checkpoint, or an open border. The Colombia-Venezuela frontier at San Antonio was the flashpoint of an international conflict, where I'd seen people rioting just weeks before.

I'd come a long way and already achieved more than I ever thought possible. I'd travelled further around this continent than any motorcyclist I'd ever heard of and even if I got a flight home from Caracas, it had been the journey of a lifetime. But the Circuit had become something special to me, something not done before, something new that I would remember for the rest of my life. And if I didn't complete it, if I was beaten almost at the finish line, then that is what I'd remember. In any case there was nothing more that could be done about it that evening, so I packed away my things, read the last few pages of Treasure Island, then went to sleep.

The next morning, I woke up early, and after a light breakfast, started writing this journal. As I began writing I stopped being disheartened, and remembered that I'd talked my way into and out of so many difficult situations on the journey, that I would find a solution. There really was a pedestrian walkway, the Apache really was tiny, and my journey really was something unique that even hardened border guards would hopefully want me to complete. And anyway, after all that'd happened, I wasn't about to get turned back after six months within a few days of the end. I would complete the circuit come what may. After writing for a couple of hours, I put down my notes and took out my map, because today I was going to Parque Carabobo to find Richard M. and to give him the message from Clodio.

The weather was kind to me again, and it was a glorious, sunny day in Caracas. Parque Carabobo station was about four kilometres away, so I decided to take a long walk, and see some of the city on the way. I walked back down through Plaza Venezuela, then carried on through the main university campus which was like a quiet oasis away from the traffic. Then I walked around the Botanical gardens and on through a few tired looking streets, before coming to a museum and Musical Theatre that was holding a small outdoor concert. I found a fantastic little restaurant with colourful reliefs on the walls and ate a huge plate of steak and chips for lunch, washed down with something that tasted exactly like Irn Bru. I mention this because the bottle marketed itself as Venezuela's National Drink, just like Irn Bru does in

Scotland, and while I was living in Medellin I found almost exactly the same drink, that marketed itself as the National Drink of Colombia. So I suspect there's something fishy going on there.

After lunch I walked the last kilometre or so down Avenue Mexico to Parque Carabobo station, and took out the note from Clodio. After re-reading the note, I walked across to the Plaza, and there were indeed lots of older guys playing cards. So I stood by the side of the park for a moment, trying to choose the right one to ask. Someone not too engrossed in a game, someone who looked like they'd been there a few years, maybe someone reading the newspaper. Then I noticed two older guys sitting together on a low wall, and talking in a way that seemed like they were putting the world to rights. No newspaper, but otherwise spot-on. I walked slowly up to them with the note in my hand, and when I started speaking in my terrible foreigner's Spanish, they looked bemused.

I told them the story of the note, and one of them said 'What's the address?' but of course I wasn't sure. 'Well, don't you have his phone number?' the other guy said, but of course I did not. And I explained how my friend had last seen Richard over thirty years ago, but had lost touch, and that he didn't have a telephone, so the only thing I had was the note. As I was speaking, I realised how ridiculous it was, what I was doing, walking up to a random guy in a park to ask about a random guy in a photo. But when I showed them the note, one of the guys said 'No problem!' and assured me that if Richard was here, we would find him. They started asking people nearby, but with no luck. Then we walked a bit more around the park, and asked more people, while they told me more about the area, but still no luck. They thought about who among their friends had been here the longest, and who was most likely to have known a guy who came here thirty years ago but again, no one had heard of Richard M. Finally, they said there was a guy who ran the card games in the park, as well as a lot of other things, and if anyone knew, it would be him. So we walked over to a very intense looking game of cards, being watched by about thirty people, and they spoke to one serious looking guy near the table.

He came over and looked me up and down and said 'What was the name?' and when I told him, he walked away. I could literally see the ripple of people, as the question permeated through the whole park, people walking from game to game asking about someone called Richard M. Then after around ten minutes, the guy came back, and said 'there is definitely no Richard M. here. I've been here 20 years, and never heard of him, nobody's heard of him'. And at this point, I was super happy to have had the note with me, so that this very serious looking guy knew I wasn't some prankster. I thanked him for trying to help, and he went back to his game of cards.

Clodio had told me that if I didn't find Richard in the park, then he would definitely be in the restaurant, the *Flor de Espana*, and the two older guys told me how to get there. I found the restaurant, eventually, but it took a while because it was set back from the road, and had a sign that been designed like camouflage. Inside I found that it wasn't so much a restaurant, as a bookies, and was full of televisions showing the horse racing. It was also full of nervous looking men, all with their eyes glued to the screens. I spoke to the barman, who directed me to the cashier, and so I showed him the note. He said he'd never heard of Richard M., but then walked over to an ancient looking man sitting by a table in front of one of the televisions. They spoke for a minute, then he came back and said 'that guys been coming here for twenty years, there's definitely no Richard M.'. But he also gave me one last tip, that there was a music shop around the corner that might have heard of him, if he had anything to do with music like Clodio. I found the shop, and showed the owner the recording of Clodio playing drums by the lagoon, but he'd never heard of Richard M. either. So that was that.

Thirty years is a long time, and people move on. Two friends had drifted apart and I felt incredibly sad that I wasn't able to reconnect them. I tried the number of his granddaughter to let him know how it went, but there was no answer so I couldn't even tell him. Then I remembered the girl told me she was having some problems with her phone, so I hoped that she'd call me once it was fixed. On the way back to my hotel, I stopped by the musical theatre and asked the lady on reception, Mary, to do me a favour. I said that I knew an excellent musician from Tacarigua, and that he was looking for a guy called Richard M., then sent her the recording. I gave her the number of his granddaughter, and asked if she could let the girl know if anything ever came up. Then I took a long walk through a few more neighbourhoods around the centre, before heading back to the hotel.

The next morning, I set off early as usual, on my way to Merida in the west of Venezuela. Again I knew that I wouldn't make it all the way, so just decided to ride until I got tired and find somewhere along the way. As I swept down the highway out of the city I was amazed by the number of big bikes that I was seeing. Kawasakis, Ducatis, Yamaha R1s like those I'd seen on the way to Puerto La Cruz, I would guess over a hundred, and I was missing the power of my Kawasaki 650 back home. But I was making good progress, just cruising along at my usual 90kmph and gradually eating up the miles. I stopped for a quick lunch, then continued on, covering almost three hundred kilometres before I passed a town called San Carlos. Then about twenty minutes outside the town, I came across a police checkpoint.

I'd been though hundreds of police checkpoints on my journey, probably thirty in Venezuela alone and nine times out of ten I just sailed right through. Occasionally an officer would signal me to pull over for a document check, but they'd do that when I was still fifty metres away and the officers at this checkpoint didn't do that, so I sped up again as I went past. Then suddenly, and without warning, one of the policemen shouted at me to stop. He stretched out his arm and grabbed hold of my jacket almost pulling me off the bike. But the momentum was too much, and I'd gone ten metres past the checkpoint by the time I pulled over to the side and lifted my hands up off the handlebars. As I turned around the policeman was walking over, gun drawn, with a dark look on his face.

He was young, very young, I would guess not more than 19 or 20 years old and as he let off steam about me not stopping he started waving the gun about in my direction. Then he started looking me up and down, and looking all over the bike. He didn't say anything for an uncomfortably long time so I had to speak, I said, 'Document check?' and reached for my jacket pocket. The young officer shrugged in agreement, and took my license and registration documents as I handed them to him. His partner who was clearly the more senior of the two, was still dealing with another motorist on the other side of the road. He looked at my documents for a long time but seemed distracted, then he said 'step off the bike and open the bag.' I did as I was told and started pulling everything out, but he got impatient and nudged me aside to start taking things out himself. He was throwing most of it down on the floor but looking very carefully at small items like electronics. He also completely ignored my heavy tent and sleeping bag, which took up half the space in the bag. Perhaps I was being paranoid, and maybe he had some specific instructions about electronics, but to me it felt like I was about to be extorted, like he was looking for something valuable, and that our conversation would start when he found it. Fortunately, or unfortunately for me, he wasn't going to find it because I didn't carry a computer, or large camera. The only thing I had of value was a small GoPro, but he missed that in the mess. My phone, which is also my camera, was in my pocket, and my cash was stashed on my person and on the bike. What he did find was the machete that I used to clear ground when camping, so this would be the start of our conversation.

He asked me why I was carrying a machete, and said that it was illegal. He said that we had a problem that might take some time to resolve, and asked me for my Venezuelan Driving License. I told him that the machete was for camping, clearing ground, and that I knew it was legal to carry. As for the Venezuelan license I said that I didn't have one, but knew it wasn't needed and even confirmed at the border that for less than a month, I could use my British license. He looked me up and down again, holding my documents in his hand then said, bold as anything 'Where's your wallet?' I couldn't believe it, he was standing there with all the identity and insurance documents he needed except one that I already said I didn't have, but still had the nerve to say that. I reached into my other jacket pocket and pulled out a wallet stuffed with low value Venezuelan currency, and a single twenty-dollar note. Despite travelling almost 30,000km across South America and having absolutely no problem with corrupt police or robbers, I was still paranoid. And although I was carrying a large amount of dollars on my person and on the bike, I kept only the minimum in my wallet, for exactly this reason.

In any case, he missed the single twenty-dollar note, looked disgustedly at all the other worthless notes in the wallet, and said in an angrier tone 'empty your pockets'. I did as I was told and put my phone, headphones, debit card, and a few other bits and pieces on the bike seat. Then looked over at his colleague who had just finished checking the documents of a passing motorist. I was hoping that my look would communicate there was a problem because two bad officers would be no worse than one, but there was a chance the other guy was OK. The other officer, who was a bit older than the first guy and seemed to be his superior, came over to see what was the fuss. But before the younger officer had a chance to speak, I said hello, and explained the situation. I said that I didn't need a Venezuelan license because I was travelling on my British one, which I'd confirmed was OK at the border. He thought about it for a moment, then looked at all my stuff on the ground. And at this point, the younger officer looked again into my wallet, and noticed the twenty-dollar note. He mumbled something about checking documents and walked off into the building behind him.

As he walked away I got talking with the older officer who said the machete was fine, but I really did need a Venezuelan license. He even pulled over another bemused motorist and took his license to show it to me, but I insisted that the border guards had said it was fine. We continued talking for a while about the area and about my journey, and made a connection, just in time for the other guy to come back with my stuff. He handed me back the wallet minus one twenty-dollar note, and I said in as confident a voice as possible, 'there's a twenty-dollar note missing, perhaps it fell out, please could you check.' He looked at me with a shocked expression on his face, then looked at his colleague, then back at me. His face was as black as night as he took back all the documents, and said he needed to do more checks. Then he returned five minutes later and gave me everything back, plus one twenty-dollar note. Now I wasn't exactly sure how to interpret what happened next, either we were stepping up the shakedown, or the returned money had been the end of it. In which case they both genuinely believed that I should have a Venezuelan license, because although the first cop's manners improved a lot, they still took me to the station. And the really worrying part was that I'd join Good Cop in a car, while Bad Cop who I believed had just tried to rob me, took my bike. What could I do, this was two guys in uniform with pistols and one of them had already drawn his, so I wasn't going to cause a problem. I handed over the keys and said goodbye to my bike, my bag containing all my stuff, and most of the dollars that I'd withdrawn to cover the journey. The one saving grace was that I'd kept hold of my phone and passport. It was a frightening situation, and when I realised that they didn't even have a police car as the older guy flagged down another passing motorist, I thought the worst. South America is notorious for criminal gangs setting up fake police road blocks, and these guys hadn't even bothered with a sign. The motorist looked at me with obvious pity as we got into the car, and I watched my bike being ridden away by someone else. I started taking a sneaky video to show the real police if I escaped with my phone, until five minutes later, the Apache disappeared.

'Where is he going?' I asked the cop in the car

'Don't worry about it, he went another way' he replied, without explaining why on earth if we were going to a local police station, he would need to take a different route with my bike. We arrived at a rundown building on a quiet street, and as we got out of the car the driver said to me 'Good luck my friend' and I gave him a wry smile. Then just as we were walking into the building, to my great relief, the Apache came round the corner, still carrying my bag. Maybe I've been lucky I thought, maybe I really am dealing with real cops, and maybe I'm just going to spend a few days in jail for driving without a license that I didn't even know I needed.

We walked inside the building and Bad Cop went into a back room while Good Cop sat down on a stool next to a small round table, around which sat three other officers. Then the most senior cop made a phone call to ask about the license rules and after a couple of minutes she put down the phone, stood up, handed my documents back and said 'Yes, you can ride on your British license while travelling through Venezuela, sorry for the inconvenience'. I thought about asking why that phone call couldn't have been made while I was still at the checkpoint, and reporting bad cop for messing with my cash, but instead took the documents and went on my way. The police stop had cost me two hours, but it was still quite early, so I pushed on all the way to Barinas, 520km from Caracas at the edge of the western mountains and just 300km from the border with Colombia. There I found a fantastic roadside motel with swimming pool, single story cabins with parking for the bike, and a Burger King across the street. It also happened to be the place where one of the best female soccer teams in Venezuela was staying, so we spent the evening chatting about the Women's World Cup that was going on in France.

The next morning, I woke up late, ate some breakfast by the pool, then set off for Merida. It promised to be a splendid day's riding judging by the twisting mountain road that I could see on the map, and it didn't disappoint. After a short burst along the highway from Barinas, the road started to climb and there was almost no traffic. It was awesome to be leaning into the corners of a winding mountain road again and although the weather was changing all the time, it seemed totally appropriate for the ride. The sky cleared just where there were some spectacular mountain and valley views, then closed in again when I was focusing on the fast sections. The area is beautiful, and all along the way there are villages that seemed to be much less affected by the economic difficulties than other parts of the country. The riding was so good that I ended up pushing all the way through to Merida, but in hindsight I regret that. My basic hotel on a quiet street in the city was fine, but I'd passed some incredible places with hotels on mountainsides, or in valleys full of cows, and even a castle. Also the city itself didn't live up to my expectations.

Firstly, all the petrol stations were closed, and I'd run out of fuel. I'd assumed things would get better as I approached the border with Colombia but it was actually getting worse, apparently because locals buy up all the Government subsidised fuel and sell it to Colombians. Secondly the weather was terrible, and although the surrounding mountains would be nice on a sunny day, they just looked dull. Thirdly, there was hardly anyone there, although to be fair it was a Sunday during the summer break, in a University City, but still. On the plus side, I could now start using the Colombian pesos that I had left over from living in Medellin.

The next morning the weather was even worse, and I got soaked as I put my bag onto the back of the bike, and set off. I still had no idea where I was going to get fuel, but felt safe in the knowledge that if there was some, at least I'd be able to skip the queue. I stopped at a corner restaurant, and had some eggs and toast for breakfast. I paid in Colombian pesos and got Venezuelan Bolivars back in change which was lucky because I'd run out, and needed some for petrol. I asked the owner where there was a petrol station and he said that there was only one place in town and I better hurry, because they'd had a delivery that morning. What he didn't tell me, was that it was the only place in town where, motorcycles, could get petrol.

They had a completely different system here in the west than in other parts of Venezuela and not only could motorcycles not skip the fuel queues, they couldn't even use some pumps. I turned onto the street where the petrol station was, and came across the largest group of bikes I've ever seen. Hundreds of them. About fifty filled the petrol station forecourt itself, another hundred were lining up along the street, and another two hundred or so were in side streets waiting to join the main queue. I parked up the Apache near a doorway alongside the main queue and just watched in awe, and took a few photographs. Then I got talking to some bikers near the back of the queue, and they said that actually it would only take a few hours to service everybody, but I needed a Venezuelan ID. There was a guard standing around looking at his phone, so I explained my situation and asked him what I should do. He shrugged his shoulders and said that he had no idea 'just join the queue', he said unhelpfully. But I couldn't do that because I didn't have a Venezuelan ID card and now I could see everyone showing these cards to the Military Policeman on duty before they were allowed to join the main queue. It's not usually a great idea to bother a soldier in the middle of his duties, but I had no choice, and walked up to the front of the line and tried to explain as nicely as I could, that I didn't have the document.

At first he just looked at me for a second, then ushered me away without saying anything, before going back to his job. He was taking the ID numbers of all the bikes, then communicating with another few armed officers who were checking at the front of the line, near the petrol pumps. I was thinking that I'd been ignored again, and wondering what on earth I should do, when a friendly biker came up and said don't worry, I could use his ID. I didn't have time to question the logic of this, given that the whole point of the queue was to ration the fuel and make sure everyone used their ID only once, before the soldier guy came back and said 'come with me'. I raced over to the Apache, then rode over to where he had gone to talk with another officer, who was clearly in charge of the whole scene. He didn't smile or say anything, he just directed me, to my relief and also serious concern, to the front of the queue. Now you might think brilliant, you got to skip the queue again, why the concern? Well the concern was because I'd read in the news that only a week before in this very city, a man had been shot dead at a fuel pump. The argument broke out over who got served first, and here I was pushing in front of three hundred frustrated bikers, on a rainy Monday morning. I was a tourist hoping to get to a pretty lake a bit quicker, and they were working people with jobs to go to, but what could I do. I pushed the Apache into the petrol station and lined up behind only two other people at the pumps.

As I sat nervously waiting to be served, I noticed that the guy waiting at the next pump was riding a Suzuki 650. It was quite similar to my Kawasaki back in the UK, and we got talking about bikes. I was super grateful to have a friend to talk to, and it didn't hurt that he was also pretty big, and a no-nonsense type of character. He actually stayed on after he'd finished getting his petrol to help me talk with another man about replacing a tyre, so he was really nice. Once I had some petrol I was on my way, and set off on the highway to Puerto Concha, a small port town on Lake Maracaibo.

The road to Puerto Concha was not as fun as the winding mountain road from Barinas, but it was a decent, relatively pothole free highway, with just one problem. It had a series of tunnels which, perhaps because of the economic situation, or perhaps because someone just forgot to turn the lights on, were completely pitch black. In a big car with halogen headlamps this might not have been a huge problem, but on the Apache with headlights that were less bright than my phones screen, it was a very big problem indeed. I'd been through similar tunnels on the journey, so I already knew that it would be an issue, and stopped before the entrance to clean the headlight. I also cleaned my scratched up visor, and in any case also put on my super clear safety glasses that had been fantastic for seeing the views in the mountains. I started up the bike and slowly rode into the tunnel, but about twenty metres inside, the darkness closed in and I saw nothing. I couldn't see the road, I couldn't see the walls, and the tunnel was curved so I couldn't even see the end. Just blackness, with a dull circle of half–light in front of me where my headlight struggled to penetrate all the way to the ground. I continued on for another few hundred metres, until I noticed lights in my rear view mirror, it was a truck and there was no room in the tunnel for safe overtaking. That is, without blocking the other lane that went round what seemed like a blind corner.

As the truck came closer I started to speed up, partly because I was nervous that the driver just wouldn't notice how slow I was going and crash straight into me. But also partly because the lights from the truck were beginning to brighten the tunnel. As I went faster I got closer to the side of the lane, and the walls, when the tunnel curved, and started hitting occasional pot–holes, it was not a comfortable few minutes. Then when the truck was right behind me it's headlights fully lit up the road and I accelerated again to something like normal speed. And after a few hundred metres more, we exited the tunnel. I had to do the same thing eight more times, through eight more tunnels, before I finally found the road that led to Puerto Concha, only to find it blocked by a local protest. It was a small group though, good natured, and in fact they let me pass by on the pavement, so it didn't cost me much time. I'm not sure how effective those protests are but I've seen them throughout South America and they seem to be tolerated by the police, for a short time at least. I hope the grievances did get sorted out. By the time I arrived in Puerto Concha to look for a hostel it was still only lunchtime, but I was exhausted.

The port at Puerto Concha is quite substantial for a tiny village, and it's used by a local factory as well as hundreds of small fishing boats working the farthest reaches of the Lake. I parked the bike directly on the dockside, and looked around not really knowing what to expect. I knew that I wanted to hire a boat there, but wasn't sure if it was somewhere a visitor could easily find a place to stay. As it turned out there was a hostel right there on the dock, but there was a problem, it had no electricity. That meant no air conditioning, and the temperature was around 40 degrees.

There were no other realistic options so I unloaded my bag and went in to talk with the manager, who also turned out to be someone who could arrange a boat, and something to eat before I set off. Well I say arrange, what I mean is that she was able to find me a guy, who could arrange a boat. So I spent the next twenty minutes negotiating with him. I was trying to get a better boat+accommodation+food deal, when he told me that it was possible to pitch a tent out on the lakeside. He could take me out in the evening, then come and collect me in the morning, it sounded perfect. At this point, one of the ladies who worked in the factory invited me over to a birthday party that was happening at the dockside. So it was only after stuffing myself with cake, then eating a huge barbecue with the hostel owner, that I gathered my things ready to leave.

Around 5pm a fisherman turned up at the dock with his two young nephews in a boat whose best years were clearly behind it. I realised that I'd actually been through two middlemen to arrange this trip, and wished that I'd just gone straight over to the fishermen on the dock to ask. We set off immediately, and after breaking down a few times in the reeds around the port we entered into a long channel surrounded on both sides by thick jungle. We saw a ton of wildlife, monkeys, sloths, eagles, everything, and I was super excited about what I'd see while staying overnight in this place. Then once we got out into the open water of the lake, we motored for just ten more minutes or so, before stopping at a house on stilts. At first I thought we were making a pit-stop but when I saw the armed policeman come out to meet us, I thought perhaps it was to register before setting off out into the lake proper.

But no, after a short conversation the fisherman told me to step off the boat here, and he'd come and collect me in the morning. I'd been massively ripped-off in terms of what I paid for a twenty-minute boat ride, and there would be no jungle adventure, but it did also look like quite an interesting place to stay. I unloaded my things and chatted with one of the policemen for a while, before setting up the tent. There were two policemen, and as well as a pistol each they were sharing a machine gun that was sitting on the table where they'd been charging their mobile phones. At first I thought great, no need to worry about being robbed in my tent at night with two armed guards. But then I started thinking about why two pistols wasn't enough, and what exactly were they expecting to deal with during the night? Anyway I put that to the back of my mind, and went to look around what was a unique place to camp. It was like my own private cabin on the water, complete with armed guards of course, and the wide horizon views were incredible. When I wanted to take a swim in the lake, I just jumped straight in.

I'd brought my new book, so I took a chair from inside the cabin and put it out on the deck, then started to read the first few pages of Jules Verne's *Twenty Thousand Leagues Under the Sea*. It was the ideal setting, because although I was only on a lake and not the sea, the water stretched out all the way to the horizon. And in fact, Lake Maracaibo does indeed meet the sea eventually a long way to the North. It was easy to imagine the giant squid and submarines from Verne's book gliding through the dark abyss surrounding the cabin, especially when a small pod of dolphins swam through. The book was in Spanish, so I'd only struggled through about three pages when one of the policemen came out onto the deck, and we got talking again.

It turned out that they guarded this part of the lake 24hrs a day for a two-week tour, then switched with another pair. The cabin had food and electricity, and they slept in hammocks on the deck. I was congratulating him on whatever luck or magic he'd used to get such a fantastic assignment, when he said that there are two downsides. One, he said, is the boredom of sitting in one place for a very long time. The other downside, was insects, and they would come in huge swarms from the jungle during the night. It just depended on the direction of the wind, and if the wind was blowing in from the lake, then we'd have a peaceful night. But if the wind was blowing from the jungle, then we'd be bitten to death if we left our nets. At that moment a slight breeze was blowing in from across the lake so it was just right, but it could change at any moment he said. Then he told me that the reason for the police guard was that criminals used the lake as a route for smuggling, piracy, and illegal fishing. And the reason that they needed a machine gun, was because the criminal gangs that ran those operations had machine guns too.

Lake Maracaibo is famous not only for being a picturesque place, but also for impressive lightning displays that happen on about 140 nights per year over the mouth of the Catatumbo river. I was in exactly the right place to see them, and in the evening around 8pm I went out on to the deck, sat down, and waited. And waited, until around 10pm when as I was looking down at my ankles disappearing into the pitch black water, the surface of the lake turned white. It was the reflection of a huge sheet of lightning that had lit up the night sky, and there followed what I can only describe as a kind of dry storm. The sky was full of lightning, but there was no rain, and no wind, it was beautiful. The next morning, I told the policemen, who had gone to sleep early, about the display and they said that it probably wasn't one of the best nights because the weather conditions weren't quite right, so God only knows what it's like at its best. After a light breakfast and a swim in the lake, the fisherman and his nephew returned and I took the boat back to Puerto Concha, then set off for the border with Colombia.

I was about to face the most serious challenge of the journey, but the possible outcomes were really quite straightforward. Either I would successfully cross the border with my bike and this evening I'd be in Cucuta, Colombia, sipping hot chocolate and eating brevas, with the Apache safely locked away in the hotel car-park. Or I would not. And if not, then I'd need to ride nine hundred kilometres back to Caracas just to give the Apache away for free. Then I'd need to pay someone to arrange a permanent import, so that I could get documents to leave Venezuela without the bike. Frustrating, time consuming, but also not the end of the world. Another option would have been to ship the bike back to the UK, but that would have cost three times what it cost to buy. And yet another option would have been to sell the bike to another traveller going back the other way who would then leave before the temporary import permit expired. But in June 2019 in Venezuela, there were no other travellers.

In any case, these practicalities were not the main thing on my mind. Because this journey had already become something that I would never forget. The beautiful and the frightening things that had happened had been seared into my memory, and the journey would become part of who I am. I hadn't made it this far by taking the most sensible options, which at many points along the way, would have been to turn back. I'd made it this far for the same reason that I'd come to South America in the first place. I was here to explore, and to discover, and I would overcome any difficulty that presented itself. Not because I had some urgent mission to complete or because there was a damsel-in-distress to save, but just because.

Before you travel it's always sensible the check the British Government's colour-coded travel advisory website to understand some of the risks that might be involved. Most of the world is coloured Green, but that doesn't mean that it's safe. It just means to take the usual travel precautions and to check the specific advice on the website. Then there is Yellow, which means that the

Government advises against all travel to those areas unless it's absolutely essential. It also means that embassy staff may not be keen, or able, to go there and help you if you're stupid enough to go. Then there is Red, which means you're on your own. I'd been in the Red area covering the Venezuela–Colombia border since I left Merida on my way to Lake Maracaibo a few days before. And wouldn't get back to a Yellow area until I left Cucuta in Colombia the next day. But from there it's Green all the way through central Colombia, to Medellin.

The road that I took from Lake Maracaibo back to the highway at Santa Barbara del Zulia was not on google maps. So I got lost, a few times, and wasted about an hour. But eventually I made it back to what was a very decent, well maintained asphalt highway, that looked like it might take me all the way down to the border crossing at San Antonio. It didn't of course, I've never been that lucky, and after another forty-five minutes I found myself winding through tiny mountain roads and traditional villages dodging tractors and cows. I was trying to reach the border post with time to cross over before it closed but it was difficult, because this area was absolutely gorgeous. I'd ridden across a fairly hot and dusty region in the lowlands around Santa Barbara, but since then I'd been tracking the border with Colombia, high up in Andes Mountains. Here it was luxuriously green and verdant, if a little cold, and whereas I'd been expecting a difficult ride through poor areas in crisis, I found myself riding through something that looked more like Switzerland. With impressive, and well maintained churches, agricultural estates, and clean prosperous towns.

Suddenly I remembered the bizarre, duelling-concerts, that Colombia and Venezuela had had here a few months before. The British businessman Richard Branson paid for a concert near Cucuta in Colombia to raise money for poor Venezuelans. While the Government of Venezuela did the same on the other side of the border, to raise money for poor Colombians. Neither attracted much support from music lovers and Branson's one was embroiled in a corruption row. But I wondered how the rich Venezuelans in this area, and the disadvantaged Colombians over the border, felt about it all.

The ride to the border had turned out to be one of the best morning rides of the tour, and I arrived at the town of San Antonio around lunchtime. I was completely refreshed, and ready to charm my way onto the Simon Bolivar bridge, then all I had to do was push the Apache across to it's homeland, Colombia. As you might expect though, San Antonio was chaos, and it came as quite a shock to the system after the tranquillity of the Venezuelan mountains. I was riding through crowds of people streaming over the border to see friends and relatives, and to do business, and it was slightly unnerving. But the chaos was also a positive sign because surely in all the commotion, it wouldn't be a big deal to let me wheel a tiny motorcycle across. I parked the Apache on a side-street from where I could see the border guards, and went to talk with them. The first guy I spoke with was polite, but as soon as I mentioned the motorcycle he said, 'No way'. I pestered him a bit until he went to speak with the man in charge, and once I knew who that was, I went to pester that guy a bit as well. We talked about my journey and how far I'd come, and how I just needed to move a few more metres to complete my circuit of 32,000km. I gave it everything I had for ten minutes. Initially smiling and laughing with the guard as he enjoyed the story, but then half pleading as he started to get annoyed. But he was adamant, there was absolutely no way that this bike, or any vehicle, was crossing the bridge.

As I walked back over to the Apache I was surrounded by dodgy looking people telling me they could sort out all my problems. It was intense, and the place was so crowded that the guys pestering me were physically right up close, while twenty people stood around the bike. I was trying to talk with the guards thirty metres away, watch my bike and stuff, and understand the border arrangements all at the same time, and it wasn't comfortable. So I left my bike and bag where they were and went to sit on a small verge on the opposite side of the street. From there I could see the bike, the guards, and the crossing, as well as the fascinating flow of people going about their cross-border business, and I had space to think.It was crystal clear now that the Apache would not be crossing the bridge. At the same time, I knew that pedestrians could cross over so at least I myself could leave, and get my official stamps to enter Colombia, but there was a problem. When I entered Venezuela, as in every other country, they'd put a stamp in my passport that mentioned the motorcycle. If I tried to walk through without it, I'd have to come up with some reason for not having the bike with me. And in any case, what would I do with the bike, leave it right there at the border? While I was sitting going through the options another even dodgier looking guy came over to talk, and while I wouldn't have trusted him as far as I could throw him, he did say something interesting. He said that he could simply ride the bike over the border in another place, then give it back to me on the other side. Kind of like a shipping service, but for international conflict zones. Not particularly wanting to donate my bike to a local Chop Shop I politely turned him down, but then stole his idea.

I'd heard about alternative routes across the border, or *truchas* as they're called in Spanish, from reading about drug smuggling and people trafficking. But they'd really come to prominence when the border closed because people started using them for ordinary things like seeing relatives or trade. It's illegal to do this, but while the border bridge itself is tightly controlled by the army, the surrounding areas are not and criminal gangs have operations that allow for people and goods to flow freely across. These operations can exist because of the social influence that the smugglers have in the communities on the border. And they're not really designed to let foreigners get their motorcycles back to Colombia after a road-trip, but at least they existed. It's a risky business even for a local with connections but for a foreigner, especially a British foreigner, it's far more complicated.

A few months before, Britain had recognised a non-elected person as the President of Venezuela ignoring the fact that they already had an elected one. The Venezuelan Government had in turn accused British and American nationals of travelling around the country to organise anti-government opposition, and train people for civil unrest. Although I hadn't had any problems until this point, it did occur to me that if I was caught trying to smuggle a motorcycle across the border my being British might not be a gold star in my favour. Then there was the issue of kidnapping. Using a trucha would mean voluntarily approaching someone who probably worked for the same organisation that did the kidnapping, about doing something illegal. It wouldn't take a genius to calculate, firstly that I might be worth more as a kidnap victim than a fee paying customer and secondly, that I might not want to explain to the police what I was doing there. Despite the obvious risks involved, I decided to do it anyway. Because I calculated that all of those risks depended on just one thing, finding the right guy. If I could find someone who was reliable, a professional who took the task seriously, who knew what they were doing and wouldn't cheat me, then it could work out.

Initially I wasn't quite sure what I was looking for, and there were hundreds of people standing around offering all kinds of services. There were the young gangs of tattooed men who were probably offering grocery delivery, but looked like they were waiting to assassinate someone. And there were smiling middle aged ladies with waist-packs full of cash, who were probably running the whole border crossing. One option would have been to straight up ask one the border guards, and I thought about it when I clearly identified a crooked one. I'd stashed my motorcycle helmet at the guard station as I was talking to them, and left it there when I went to sit down. Then when I went back one of the guards said, without humour, that it was his. I laughed, thinking that it was a joke and put my hand on the helmet. But he didn't laugh, and showed no sign of letting it go. It was only after a tense minute or so, and when another more senior guard walked over, that he gave it up.

Then just as I was considering going back to the dodgy looking guys who had harassed me earlier, just to see what they knew. I noticed a man talking with the border guard in charge. He didn't look like an official but at the same time seemed to be tolerated by what was a very senior person, doing a serious job. He was scruffily dressed with the same kind of waist pack that the mysterious ladies kept their cash inside, and he was laughing and joking with the guards. He hung around for about ten minutes and no-one seemed bothered, then he started talking to a wealthy looking couple who were going through immigration. I thought he might be the right man for the job, so went over to have a chat.

From the moment we started talking, I knew that I'd made a good decision. Despite what I was asking him to do, he remained professional and good humoured and he said plainly that yes, he could indeed help me to get my bike to Colombia. 'How much money do you have for this?' he asked 'I have twenty dollars' I lied, with a smile, which luckily he appreciated so we were on the same wavelength. 'It will cost 150 dollars but first, let's get your immigration done so we know if it's possible.' he said, which I took as a good sign. No money up front, some time and service given for no payment, and confident demeanour. I was either dealing with a professional, or a policeman.

You might think that a credible excuse for the border guard, as to why I was leaving Venezuela with my backpack but not my bike may be part of the service. But apparently not, and the guy was nowhere to be seen as I reached the end of the migration queue. I handed over my passport and said 'Good afternoon' in as neutral a tone as possible, wondering if that *Red Notice* for Kirk Wilson that I'd been questioned about in Ecuador was still in force. The border official didn't answer, and instead just scanned my passport through a machine. Great, I thought, he's going to stamp it without even looking up, but then he started flicking through the passport and came to the page with both my entry stamp, and the reference to the bike. He looked up and said 'you entered with a motorcycle?' and instead of answering, I tried to look as confused as possible and said in English 'I'm sorry, I don't understand?' an oldie, but a goodie. He turned to a colleague and they spoke for a few minutes. Then he called over a supervisor and they spoke for a minute before the supervisor said to me 'Where is your motorcycle?' and again I mumbled something about not understanding. Despite my ridiculous act, they weren't in the mood to investigate further and stamped the passport and handed it back to me. As soon as I started walking away my guy, who I'll call Oscar, reappeared and said 'What did they say about the bike?' And I thought, we could have discussed this earlier. But I just told him that I pretended not to understand, and he laughed. I now had my exit stamp and could have walked straight over the bridge into Colombia, but I needed to sort out the business with the Apache.

Oscar was physically tiny, a wiry man of about sixty years old who'd kept his good humour despite the experience written on his face. We walked back to my bike and he said that we needed to find another guy who would actually ride the bike to Colombia. Fair enough I thought, he's being transparent with me and I confirmed with him that this was all coming out of the same budget. He took my backpack, which was about the same size and weight as himself, and hoofed it up without any effort onto his back, then hopped onto the rear seat. We rode to four different places and spoke with four different people before the wife of one man said she thought her husband would do it, and we should wait. Then Oscar and I had a quick conversation about price, and agreed on one hundred dollars in total with him picking up any unforeseen costs. The husband returned after a while on a Suzuki 650 motorcycle, another good sign, he was a biker, and they started negotiating over who would get the lion's share of my money. I think Oscar won because I'm sure I heard him agree a price of thirty dollars, and I wished I'd known about the other guy before. Then I handed over my motorcycle, my keys, and my ownership documents to a man who I'd just met, on the basis of his being an acquaintance of another man I'd just met. But God willing, now everything was set and I'd be in Colombia with the Apache within hours. And in any case, I'd certainly done everything that I possibly could to make that happen. But then things started to get weird.

I was expecting to just walk back to the border, cross over the bridge to Colombia, get my entry stamps, and wait in a cafe on the Colombian side for the bike. But Oscar said that would not be possible, because there was extra security on the bridge that would be asking questions about the bike and might turn me away, or worse. In order to make certain of success, I myself also needed to be smuggled out of Venezuela and once in Colombia, we could walk back to the border post on the other side to complete immigration. I couldn't believe what I was hearing, he'd said nothing about this when we discussed the deal at the border and now just at the point that I was at my most vulnerable, he was saying I'd have to walk with him into the jungle. What on earth would I say if we got picked up by one of the hundreds of armed police and military personnel who were guarding the forest? 'I'm awfully sorry, I thought this was the border post.' might not go down very well. And what exactly would they think was going on, a British guy trying to smuggle himself out of the country, why? The risk was just insane and I explained all this to Oscar. 'Don't worry' he said 'you're with me and if we get caught I know what to do…oh and anyway we won't get caught' were literally, in Spanish, the not-very-reassuring words that he used. It was an impossible situation but there were also reasons to be positive. I still believed that he really did know what he was doing and that I was dealing with a professional. He could have just told me to ride into a garage somewhere in San Antonio, and pulled a gun. He could have asked me to pay upfront, and I probably would have, and anyway he would also be taking a risk by using the crossing with me. So eventually I agreed, and we started walking down a dusty alley in San Antonio until we found a side street that led to the river.

This time I was carrying the backpack, and Oscar was walking ten metres in front of me clearly trying to look as if he was both with me, and not with me, depending on who might ask. We walked down the rocky slope that led to the water, and found twenty other people doing exactly the same thing. Oscar explained that the operation is run by a group that had people stationed throughout the forest, and he'd have to pay a fee later for using the service. They would use whistles to communicate the location of border agents, and give you cryptic messages to help you find the right route. So for example, a man with his leg across the path who wouldn't move it when asked, was not just someone in a bad mood, he was letting you know to take the forked path just before where he was sitting. And the reason that he didn't just tell you that, is because there are also undercover agents who pretend to cross the border in order to expose the network. We pushed on through the forest, which was no easy thing because we were quickly told to move off the main path and into the thick undergrowth. Then we started jumping over small streams and ducking under fallen branches, my backpack getting caught on just about everything it touched. Oscar wasn't waiting around. Whereas in San Antonio he'd been attentive and followed me about everywhere except the border official's office, now he was sprinting ahead and didn't seem to notice when I fell behind. Then incredibly, just as we came out of a thick copse of trees, we walked right into a military patrol.

Oscar walked straight up to them and started talking and I walked straight past, just like he told me to, with my cap down over my forehead fooling nobody. My heart was racing, but nobody called to me or asked me to stop and a few minutes later he caught up with me on the road. He looked relieved, and I imagine so did I. We exchanged a nod and a smile and continued on in relative silence, then after another thirty minutes of hiking we stopped. He turned around with a big smile and said 'We're in Colombia' and I just looked at him like he was insane. But of course I was the one who was insane, and I'd let my determination to complete the circuit lead me, yet again, into a dangerous situation. I'd been lucky to walk away from a night time crash in Bolivia, and now I'd been lucky to avoid a Venezuelan prison or kidnap.

We walked back through a small town called La Parada to the border post, skipped the queue, and a friendly official completed the paperwork. We were done in ten minutes, then walked to a cafe for a beer and to wait for the bike. We waited, and we waited, and we waited. Then after two hours Oscar started to get nervous, and we went to look for the bike. I met just about every shopkeeper in La Parada over the next couple of hours as we tried to work out what happened to the Apache, and the guy riding it, before we got a phone call. The bike was here in La Parada, but there was a problem. The rider had been stopped on the Colombian side by the police and because he clearly wasn't *Kirk Wilson* per the ownership document, it had been confiscated. I expected the worst, and tried to imagine how on earth we would explain the situation to the police, but when we got to the station they were only interested in proving the bike was mine and not stolen. I covered the fine which was about twenty dollars, then paid Oscar his hundred dollars. The bike was damaged and part of the front faring was hanging on by a piece of rope, but in light of the circumstances I didn't say anything. I just thanked him and wished him well, then got back on the Apache and set off for Cucuta city.

After all the excitement of the day, I was exhausted as I rode west to Cucuta watching yet another wonderful sunset. And I had a feeling of immense relief and gratitude, that I'd made it so far on my journey. No more borders to cross, no more Red Zones, just a six hundred kilometre ride through the Andes Mountains back to where I started in Medellin. I booked into a four-star hotel in Cucuta to be certain of a good night's sleep, then went out for a snack. I got my hot chocolate, but they didn't have Brevas.

13
Deja vu all over again: COLOMBIA (Second leg)

The next day I left Cucuta early, and enjoyed another fantastic day's riding through the Andes Mountains of eastern Colombia. I got absolutely soaked as usual, but I didn't care. It was a tremendous feeling to be back, knowing that I would complete everything I'd set out to achieve, in just one or two days more. I rode until I reached Giron, and technically that's where I completed the circuit because I'd ridden out this far six months before. I found the same hotel in the same street, and booked the same room, and it was beginning to feel a bit like deja vu all over again as I went to the same supermarket to buy some fruit. Whereas six months before I'd been filled with ambition and excitement, now I was walking the same streets with a sense of achievement that I've only felt a few other times in my life. I'd completed a twenty-thousand-mile circuit of the continent and I would remember it until the day I died, no-one could take that away from me. But if I was feeling a bit proud of myself, I was quickly brought back down to earth by a message from Bruno. He was the guy that I'd met camping in northern Brazil, who was migrating with his family around the Amazon from

Venezuela to Ecuador. If you remember I'd explained to Bruno that if his family couldn't take the boat, then they'd have to take BR319 also known as, *The Worst Road in the World*. The road where people go to try out their 4x4 Monster Trucks, and where the mud gets so churned up that it's metres deep in places. The road that I'd skipped, in favour of a leisurely boat trip up the Amazon. Well their Volkswagen Beetles had clearly taken some punishment and he was covered in mud in every picture, but they'd made it, with a bit of help. All along the way complete strangers had offered to lend a hand whether by towing with 4x4s, or just getting out and pushing, and it reminded me of the kindness that I'd received along my own journey.

The next day it began to feel even more like deja vu as I retraced my steps back to Medellin, and I was thankful that I'd not had to do more backtracking on the route. The mountain roads were somehow even more beautiful than last time probably because the air was crystal clear, and I arrived around 4pm in the afternoon. I'd called Andrea a few days before to let her know that I'd be back, and booked a hostel five minutes' walk from her place in Belen. But if you're hoping for a romantic reunion story, I'm afraid I'm going to disappoint you. We did meet and it was lovely to see her again, but it was clear that we were just friends now. I told her about my journey, and we went out for drinks with my old flatmates, then I walked her back to her place and we said goodbye. The next day I headed back over to Exposiciones, Motorcycle City in Medellin, to sell the Apache.

After twenty thousand miles, I rode the bike back to the exact same place where I'd bought it, and actually the exact same spot where I'd first sat on the seat, in the middle of the TVS showroom. The same salesman was there working in the store and he recognised me so must have thought I'd come back about some other problem. But despite the fact that on the first day the gear lever had fallen off, I still gave him what must have been one of the best customer satisfaction stories he'd ever heard. I told him that I wanted to sell the bike and he recommended a guy who would buy Apaches for 3,900,000 Colombian pesos, around 1100 USD, minus any damage. The only problem was that he was an hour away and I'd have to go and find him, so as I was already in Exposiciones I decided to check a few dealers nearby, and one of them offered me 3.8mil. The dealer had seen the surface damage so it seemed like a good offer and I handed over the bike there and then. I'd bought it originally for 4.9mil plus registration costs so if I did finally get the price offered, the difference would have been just 1.7mil or £413. Of course it wasn't so simple, and the dealer said that they didn't have the cash on-site so I'd have to come back to complete the sale in two days. Then the next day they called me to start the real negotiation.

First they said I'd need to pay to repair the surface damage, despite the fact that the guy had made me the offer, after, seeing the bike. Then they said they'd found a more serious fault, a twisted chassis, that would be expensive to fix, and made me a new offer of 2.9mil or about £700. I had a mechanic friend in Medellin so I asked the dealer to send a photo and after seeing the pictures we agreed there was a fault. But it wasn't a twisted chassis, it was a twisted steering column, presumably from the crash in Bolivia, and the issue was so slight that I hadn't noticed it in months of riding. So I offered to sell for 3.7mil and he countered with 3.6 which I accepted. Then my 3.6 turned into 3.2 when I collected the cash as they reeled off a long list of taxes and official fees that hadn't been mentioned before. But even so, the Total Cost of Ownership including fuel, maintenance, repairs, and the buy/sell price difference, had been £1430, less than the cost of shipping a BMW from Europe.

Total Cost of Ownership	
Purchase Price:	£1340
Sold Price:	£780
Difference:	**£560**
Total Fuel:	984 litres
Total Fuel Cost:	**£720**
Maintenance/Repairs:	**£150**
TOTAL COST:	**£1430**

Despite the fact that it wasn't a Harley or a Ducati, or even a classic like a Norton, I felt a real sense of loss when I walked out of the dealership. The Apache had barely left my side for the last six months and the red and black paintwork is part of what I think about now, when I think about the deserts, jungles and mountains that I crossed. I went for lunch in the same cafe in Exposiciones where I'd noticed all the motorcycles racing along six months before, and I watched them again, going like bats-out-of-hell, over pot holes, up kerbs, and between cars. Some of those bikes had probably done similar mileage to the Apache, or would within a few months, and I smiled at the memory of all the incredible things that I'd experienced. Now as I look back, I imagine sitting there in the cafe again and seeing the Apache riding by, happily working away making deliveries, or taking someone to the office. I imagine the new owner has no idea that his bike has been to almost every part of the continent, and that makes me smile too.

My flight back to London went via Panama so I stayed there for a few days diving in Bocas del Toro, then finally arrived home in Luton, minus most of the cash I'd gotten for the Apache, on 10th July. The first thing that I did when I got home was to dust off the Kawasaki and head out for a ride. Far from satisfying my need for adventure, the journey had made me want more.

Appendix A:
Kit List

Waterproof backpack, Waterproof jacket and trousers, Waterproof boots (high), Sandals (thick rubber soles), Bungees (2 in use, 1 spare), Repellent, Books, Toiletries, Pens (3), Sun cream (factor 80), Pegs and wire (hanging clothes and sealing bags), bag padlock (unused), Bike lock (unused, then stolen), Earplugs (for riding and sleeping), Helmet (with internal sunshade), Gloves (summer/winter), Socks (3), Underwear (3), Inflatable bed (standard single), Tent (Kelty two-man, second-hand), Food for the road (oats, bread, powdered milk, dried fruits/nuts), Denim jacket (durable), Phone keyboard (unused), Bank card reader + bank cards, Condoms, Soft cloth (for polishing screens, sunglasses and helmet sun-visor), Swiss utility knife, Chargers and wires for phone, Headphones (2) + splitter, Medicine (Pain/diarrhoea), USB sticks (journal backup), Needle and thread, SD Convertor (GoPro), Water 1 litre, Chain lubricant, Dirty toothbrush (for chain), Masking tape, Toilet roll, Rag for cleaning outer visor, Towel, Folding hangar for formal shirt, Video camera, Shoelace (as string, and spare), Wallet/cash, Travel/access cards, Sunglasses, Camping Machete (clearing ground), Thermal hat (mountains), Binoculars, Inflatable pillow, T-shirts (4), Formal shirt, Gasoline can (in shortage region), Durable denim jeans, Llama embroidered day bag, Swimming shorts and goggles, Cap with neck cover, Sleeping bag, Umbrella, Casual shorts, Huawei P8 Lite 2017, Mapping app (offline by GPS only), Spanish dictionary, VOIP/text/comms apps, Notepad app for journal, Music/FM Radio, Cloud storage backup.

Appendix B:
Route

COLOMBIA: Rio Negro, Puerto Berrio, Giron, Barichara, Villa de Leyva, Bogota, Girardot, Filandia, Solento, Palmaseca. ECUADOR: Lluman, Coca, Shushufindi, Mindo, Mashpi, Zumbahua, Quilotoa, Puerto Lopez, Guayaquil, Cuenca, Arenillas. PERU: Mancora, Chiclayo, Barranca, Lima, Paracas, Islas Ballestas, Ayacucho, San Francisco, Kiteni, Santa Teresa, Machu Picchu, Cusco, Patria, Pilcopata, Urcos, Puno. BOLIVIA: Copacabana, Isla Del Sol (Lake Titicaca), La Paz, Oruro, Salar de Uyuni, Laguna Pastos Grandes, Laguna Capina. CHILE: Ollague, San Pedro de Atacama, El Tatio, Antofagasta, Caldera, Bahia Inglesia, Vicuna, Elqui Valley, Valparaiso, Santiago.

ARGENTINA: Mendoza, San Luis, Villa de Merlo, Cordoba, Rosario, Buenos Aires, Gualeguaychu. URUGUAY: Tacuarembo, Durazno, Montevideo, Punta del Este, Punta del Diablo. BRAZIL: Porto Alegre, Serra do Rio do Rastro, Curitiba, Ilha do Mel, Sao Paulo, Londrina, Foz de Iguazu. PARAGUAY: Ciudad del Este, Asuncion, Filadelfia, Neuland Colony, Refugio Carretero Canada el Carmen. BOLIVIA (Second Leg): Villa Montes, Boyuibe, Santa Cruz de la Sierra, San Jose de Chiquitos, San Ignacio de Velasco, San Matias.

BRAZIL (Second Leg): Pontes-e-Lacerda, Vilhena, Caucaulandia, Porto Velho, Manaus, Jundia, Boa Vista. VENEZUELA: Santa Elena de Uairen, Canaima, Upata, El Tigre, Puerto La Cruz, Playa Colorada, Tacarigua de la Laguna, Caracas, San Carlos, Barinas, Merida, Puerto Concha (Lake Maracaibo), San Antonio.

COLOMBIA (Second Leg): La Parada, Cucuta, Giron, Medellin.

Printed in Poland
by Amazon Fulfillment
Poland Sp. z o.o., Wrocław